The Encyclopedia
of Italian Cooking

The Encyclopedia of Italian Cooking

EDITED BY PINO AGOSTINI

PRODUCED BY VICTOR BENEDETTO

LAUREL
GLEN

Key to the photos at the beginning of each section:
page 1: Venice, Veneto
page 6: Rome, Latium: Campo dei fiori
page 7: Mattinata, Puglia
pages 18-19: Carezza Lake, Trentino-Alto Adige
pages 112-113: Sommacampagna, Veneto
pages 206-207: Trasimeno Lake, Tuscany
pages 310-311: Positano, Campania

This book has been edited by Pino Agostini
with the contribution of
Sara Agostini *and* Silvana Signorato.

Produced by Victor Benedetto

English translation by Peter Eustace, C.S.A. snc, Verona

Supervision by Denise Landis
Photographs of the recipes by Fotocronache, Firenze
Other photographs Deltaprint, Verona (cover)
Luca Steffenoni, Verona (ingredients), Pino Agostini, Verona (maps)

Drawings by Luca Montanti, Verona

Graphic design by
EBS - Editoriale Bortolazzi Stei
San Giovanni Lupatoto (Verona)

Copyright © 1998 *Arsenale Editrice srl*
S. Polo 1789 - 30125 Venezia
and *Camex International, Inc.*
535 Fifth Avenue - New York, N.Y. 10017

Fisrt edition: September 1998

First published in the United States in 1998 by
Laurel Glen Publishing
5880 Oberlin Drive, Suite 400
San Diego, CA 92121-9653
1-800-284-3580

Printed by
EBS - Editoriale Bortolazzi Stei
37057, San Giovanni Lupatoto (Verona), Italy

The Encyclopedia of Italian cooking / edited by Pino Agostini;
produced by Victor Benedetto.
p. 416 cm. 20,5 x 28
Includes index.
ISBN 1-57145-610-4
1. Cookery, Italian. I. Agostini, Pino. II. Benedetto, Victor.
TX723.E53 1998
641.5945--dc21
98-25051
CIP

1 2 3 4 5 98 99 00 01 02

Contents

Introduction

TYPES OF PASTA

Pasta is the fundamental ingredient in Italian cuisine, from the north to the south of the country, following hors d'oeuvres (if served). First courses are almost always pasta of some kind: pasta can be served dry with sauces, in broth and even in vegetable soups (but not fish soups, which are usually main courses rather than starters); pasta is made on an industrial scale but also at home (as explained on pages 10-11). Pasta is eaten all over Italy and in a great many other countries. There are innumerable varieties, and names change from region to region. This list covers the most common types and names. Pasta can be baked or cooked in a broth, whether bought in a store or made at home. Bear in mind that pasta is very versatile and different types can be used for the same recipe (macaroni, tortiglioni, and penne can all be used to prepare the same first course).

TYPES OF PASTA USED IN OUR RECIPES

1. Bigoli
2. Bavette or trenette
3. Ditalini
4. Ditali
5. Tortellini or agnolini
6. Ravioli
7. Tortelli or agnolotti
8. Bauletti
9. Farfalle (Bow-tie pasta)
10. Fusilli
11. Cannelloni
12. Rigatoni
13. Macaroni
14. Sedani
15. Fischioni or pipe
16. Mezzepenne (Half penne)
17. Penne
18. Spaghetti
19. Linguine
20. Ziti
21. Bucatini
22. Pizzoccheri
23. Pappardelle or lasagnette
24. Tagliatelle or fettuccine
25. Tagliolini
26. Lasagne

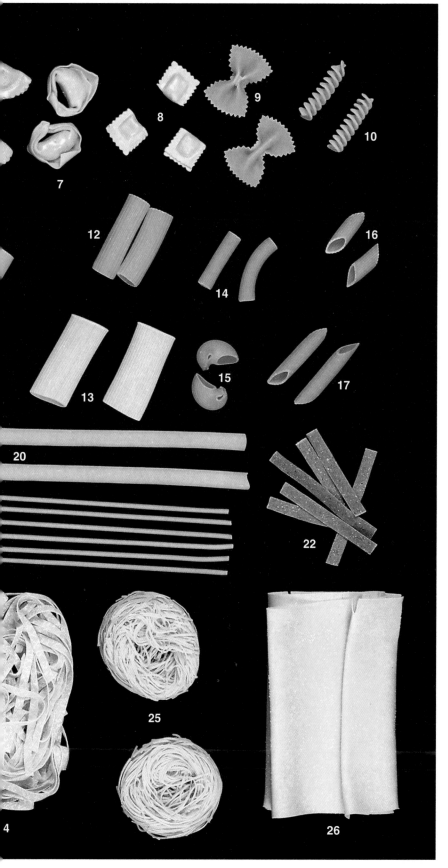

HOW TO COOK PASTA

Ingredients:
3 cups of water and ½ teaspoon coarse salt for every ¼ pound of pasta

1. Bring the water to a boil.

2. When the water comes to a boil, add the salt and the pasta. The water will stop boiling for a moment or two but quickly comes back to a boil.

3. The most important and difficult thing is to drain the pasta at exactly the right moment. Cooking time depends on the kind of pasta and may even vary between commercial products (the cooking time is always indicated on the package). Pasta should be cooked to a firm bite and not over-cooked: first, because it is easier to digest like this and, second, because the flavor is heightened by having to chew it a little more. Homemade pasta cooks rather quickly: taste it as it cooks to decide the right moment to drain.

OTHER TYPES OF PASTA USED IN ITALIAN COOKING

1.   Capellini (Angel Hair)
2.   Conchiglie (Shell pasta)
3.   Mafalde (Curly pasta)
4.   Manicotti
5.   Tortiglioni (Elbow macaroni)
6.   Acini di pepe

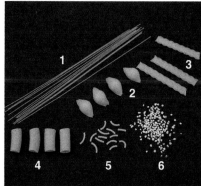

HOW TO MAKE PASTA AT HOME

Making pasta at home was once a common tradition but today's busy lifestyle means that families prepare homemade pasta only on important festive occasions. Yet pasta will always be made at home because it is something special and memorable. Moreover, it is quicker and easier to prepare homemade pasta than may appear at first sight. Even if your first attempt isn't quite perfect, the second will certainly be a rewarding experience. In any case, it takes no more than 1 hour to prepare pasta at home: 15 minutes to knead the dough, 30 minutes to leaven, and 15 minutes to roll it out. As easy as that!

Ingredients:

1 egg for every ¾ cup of flour and a pinch of salt

1. Heap the flour with a hollow in the top on a work table (a wooden work-top is best because it is "rougher" than modern plastics—one of the secrets for obtaining excellent results). Break the egg into the hollow and add a pinch of salt. Mix the egg with a fork, making sure it doesn't ooze out of the flour. Knead the dough, scooping the flour a little at a time from the outside into the egg and working with your fingers. Knead the dough for at least 10 minutes, turning and folding continually, pressing it against the palms of your hands until it is smooth and elastic.

2. Roll the dough up into a ball and let it rise for 30 minutes in a draft-free place; cover with a cloth dusted in flour.

3. Dust the work-top with flour and use a rolling pin to roll out a little pasta at a time (keep the rest covered) to a thickness of about 1/10 inch or less (make sure the pasta is the same thickness all

over). Wait a few minutes so that the pasta can dry a little (but not too much).

4. Roll up the sheets of pasta and use a sharp knife to cut slices to the desired width (1/10 inch for tagliolini, 4/10 inch for tagliatelle, 1½ inch for pappardelle and so forth). Unroll the strips and shake onto a cloth to separate the strips of pasta and avoid sticking them together. You can cook the pasta immediately, or leave it to dry out completely and store in the kitchen cupboard. You can also leave it to dry a little and then keep in the freezer.

You can also roll out and cut up the pasta using a pasta-making machine. In this case, pass the dough through the machine several times, beginning with the wide rollers and progressively changing to the smaller ones; replace the smooth rollers with the grooved ones and cut the pasta into strips.

It is also possible to color pasta or give it different flavors: for red pasta, mix 1 pound of flour with 2 eggs, salt and 4 tablespoons tomato purée; for green pasta, mix the same portions of egg and flour with 7 ounces cooked and puréed spinach; black pasta is made by adding the ink of 3-4 cuttlefish.

11

HOW TO MAKE TORTELLINI AT HOME

Tortellini take their name from the Italian verb "torcere," to twist, because they are twisted twice when being made. They are also called "cappelletti" because they resemble small hats.

Ingredients:

1 egg for every ¾ cup of flour and a little water; meat or vegetable filling (see the recipes on pages 131 and 135-136).

1. Prepare the pasta as indicated on page 10. Roll out the dough to about 1/10 inch thick and then cut out squares about 3 inches per side with a roller cutter.

2. Place a little of the filling in the middle.

3. Fold the squares into a triangle with your fingers, pressing on the edges to seal.

4. Join the corners of the triangle around your index finger and then fold the tip upward.

Square and round ravioli are prepared in a slightly different way. Roll out 2 pieces of pasta: the filling is then arranged in separate little heaps and the second piece of pasta is placed on top. Press down with your fingers around the filling to seal the two pieces of pasta together; then use a roller cutter to make the ravioli squares or a mold to cut out round ravioli (see the illustrations, right).

CUTS OF BEEF

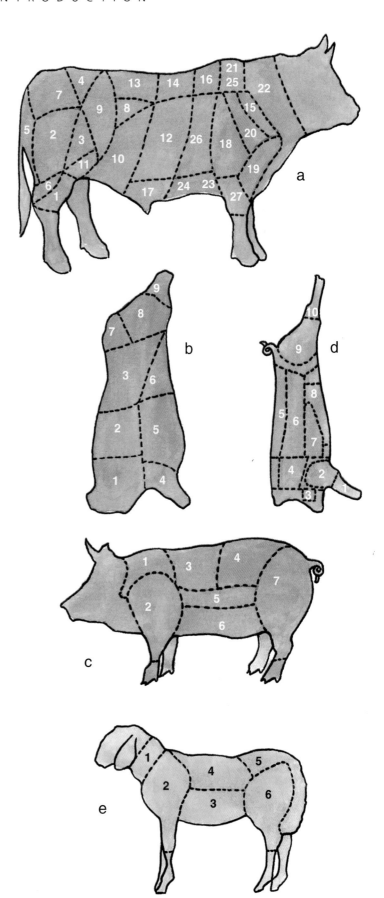

a) Italian cuts:

Quarto posteriore:

1. geretto posteriore
2. rosa
3. noce
4. codone
5. girello o magatello
6. pesce o piccione
7. fetta di mezzo
8. filetto
9. scamone
10. scalfo
11. spinacino
12. bianco costato di pancia
13. controfiletto o roastbeef
14. costate

Quarto anteriore:

15. fusello
16. coste della croce
17. pancia
18. fesone di spalla
19. brione
20. cappello del prete
21. reale
22. collo
23. punta di petto
24. fiocco
25. bianco costato di reale
26. bianco costato della croce
27. geretto anteriore

b) American cuts:

1. chuck
2. rib
3. loin, tenderloin
4. shank
5. brisket, plate
6. flank, suet
7. rump
8. round
9. soup bone

CUTS OF PORK

c) Italian cuts:

1. collo
2. spalla
3. carré
4. filetto
5. puntine
6. pancetta
7. cosciotto

d) American cuts:

1. pork hock
2. picnic shoulder
3. jowl butt
4. shoulder butt
5. fat back
6. pork loins
7. spareribs
8. bacon
9. ham
10. foot

CUTS OF LAMB

e) Italian cuts:

1. collo
2. spalla
3. petto
4. schiena
5. sella
6. gamba

f) American cuts:

1. neck
2. shoulder
3. breast
4. rack
5. saddle
6. leg

SOME ITALIAN CHEESES

Asiago
This is a semi-fat cheese typical of the Asiago High Plateau (Veneto) and is made from cow's milk. The cheese is cylindrical in shape and about 12-16 inches in diameter. It is a firm cheese with a straw yellow color with small to medium holes. When young (up to five months) it has a delicate flavor; when cured (after a year) it becomes piquant and can also be used as a grating cheese.

Caciocavallo
A typical cheese of southern Italy made from cow's milk. It is shaped like a wine flask, narrowing toward the top. It is a firm, stringy cheese with a white or pale straw yellow color. When young (up to three months) it has a rather sweet taste; when cured (after six months) it becomes stronger and piquant in flavor. It is sometimes smoked (a process carried out during curing).

Caciotta
A cheese made from cow's milk, sheep's milk, or a mixture of both, especially in central Italy. There are a great many varieties. It is generally round and not very large. It is firm, white to straw yellow in color, sometimes with small holes. The flavor varies from sweet to piquant depending on the variety and degree of curing.

Crescenza
A semi-fat cheese typical of Lombardy and made from cow's milk. It is square or rectangular, generally small, and has no rind. Soft and smooth and white in color. Best eaten fresh because it is perishable.

Fontina
A fat cheese typical of Val d'Aosta made from cow's milk. It is cylindrical and about 18-22 inches in diameter, with a reddish or brown rind. It is soft and smooth, with a more or less intense straw yellow color. It has an aromatic flavor, especially if made in the summer (when dairy cattle are taken to the higher mountain pastures). It is widely used in cooking.

Gorgonzola
A fat cheese made from cow's milk. It is cylindrical in shape and measures 10-12 inches in diameter. The green veins are produced by molds that develop inside the cheese as it is ripened. In recent times, a variety is prepared with a central hole where *Penicillium glaucum* forms spontaneously, the bacteria responsible for the particular coloring of gorgonzola cheese. Precisely because of the presence of *Penicillium*, flavor is rather piquant.

Mascarpone
A very fat cheese originating in Lombardy but by now made all over Italy. It is made by coagulating cream with citric acid. It is a young, very soft, easily spread white cheese. The flavor is very delicate and neutral. For this reason, it is often used as the basic ingredient for sweet creams or savory condiments.

Mozzarella
A soft cheese originating from central and southern Italy by now made all over the country. It is made from cow's or buffalo milk. It has a spherical or elongated shape. It is very soft, compact, and white. It has a delicate flavor (mozzarella made with buffalo milk has a stronger flavor). Best eaten very fresh or used to prepare a wide variety of dishes (including pizza).

Parmigiano Reggiano
A semi-fat cheese made from cow's milk, originally from Emilia-Romagna, but eaten all over Italy. It is cylindrical and about 12-14 inches in diameter. It is a hard, grainy cheese with tiny holes that are often invisible to the naked eye; it is light straw yellow in color. It is a cured cheese with a rather salty and intense flavor, but not piquant. It can be served with a cheeseboard but is often used grated with pasta and soups.

Pecorino romano
A semi-fat cheese from central Italy (but also made in Sardinia) made from sheep's milk. It is medium sized and cylindrical. It is firm, very compact, and white. It is a cured cheese with a very salty, piquant flavor, and is grated with pasta dishes.

Provola
A cheese from central-southern Italy made with buffalo milk and also cow's milk. It is not very large and spherical. It is stringy and compact and white or pale straw yellow. When young, it has a sweet and delicate flavor similar to mozzarella; when ripened, it becomes more savory.

Provolone
A cheese made from cow's milk, similar to caciocavallo. It has a rounded, cylindrical shape up to 14-16 inches high. It is firm and compact, with slight holes and white or light straw yellow in color. It has a sweet flavor that becomes piquant when cured. May also be smoked (a special process performed during curing).

Ricotta
A young cheese made from cow's milk or, more rarely, from sheep's milk. It is made by "re-cooking" the whey left over from making other cheeses. It is generally round and not very large. It is compact, rather soft, and white in color. It has a very delicate, neutral flavor and is often used to make dessert or savory dishes.

Scamorza
A cheese typical of central and southern Italy made from buffalo or cow's milk. It is made in various shapes and sizes, all more or less oval and elongated. It is firm and compact, with a white or slightly straw yellow color. It is sweet in flavor and often smoked.

HOW TO MAKE HOMEMADE BREAD

Homemade bread is a staple in Italian homes, accompanying every meal, and used as an ingredient in many recipes. Each region has its own typical bread, characterized by its shape and flavoring. Some breads, such as Tuscan country bread, have the distinctive flavor of an unsalted dough. Other breads are seasoned with seeds (fennel, poppy, sesame, and others) herbs, olives, onions, bacon, sausage, and nuts.

The following recipe for rolls is easily adapted to make loaves of varying shapes and sizes. Adjust the baking time as needed; baked rolls should be crusty with a moist interior, larger breads will be well-browned and sound hollow when thumped on the bottom.

BREAD ROLLS
makes 6 rolls

2 teaspoons active dry yeast
1/2 teaspoon sugar
1 cup milk
1 pound all-purpose flour
1 teaspoon salt
3 tablespoons olive oil

1. Dissolve the yeast and sugar in lukewarm milk and let it rest for 10 minutes. In a mixing bowl stir together the flour and salt, then add the olive oil and yeast mixture.

2. Mix by hand until the mixture forms a firm dough. (Alternatively, combine all ingredients in a food processor and blend until the mixture forms a ball). Place the dough in a bowl, cover it with a towel and let it rise in a warm place for at least 2 hours (maximum 3 hours).

3. Preheat the oven to 400°F. To make rolls, shape them to taste. A typical method of shaping is to roll the dough to 1/3 inch thick, cut it into 4-inch squares and sprinkle with olive oil and aromatic herbs. Roll up each dressed square into a sausage shape and place seam-side down on a baking sheet. Bake until golden, about 30 minutes.

The Alpine Region:

1. Valle d'Aosta
2. Piedmont
3. Liguria
4. Lombardy
5. Trentino-Alto Adige
6. Veneto
7. Friuli-Venezia Giulia

The Po Plains

2. Piedmont
4. Lombardy
6. Veneto
7. Friuli-Venezia Giulia
8. Emilia-Romagna

Central Italy:

9. Tuscany
10. Umbria
11. Marches
12. Latium
13. Abruzzo
14. Molise

The Mediterranean Area:

15. Campania
16. Puglia
17. Basilicata
18. Calabria
19. Sicily
20. Sardinia

Alpine Regions

Antipasto con il salame

APPETIZER WITH SALAMI (Various regions)

Preparation: 20 minutes

Ingredients for 4 people:

2 dry baguettes
10½ ounces salami cut into thin
slices
2 cucumbers
4 tablespoons butter
1 tablespoon mustard
salt
a few leaves of lettuce for dressing

1. Cut one loaf in half lengthwise and remove the soft bread, taking care not to break the crust.
2. Cut the loaf into thin slices.
3. Remove the skin from the salami.
4. Cut the cucumbers into slices.
5. Place the butter, mustard, a drop of water, and a pinch of salt in a bowl. Work these together with a spoon until they form a paste.
6. Spread this on each slice of bread.
7. Place a slice of bread, a slice of salami, and a slice of cucumber on the two loaf halves until they are filled completely. Garnish the serving dish with a few leaves of lettuce.

Antipasto di fontina

APPETIZER WITH FONTINA CHEESE (Valle d'Aosta)

Preparation: 15 minutes;
*   20 minutes resting*
Cooking time: 30 minutes

Ingredients for 6 people:

3 bread rolls
5 tablespoons butter
salt
pepper
12 thin slices of fontina cheese
2 eggs
2 cups of milk

1. Cut each bread roll into four slices.
2. Work 4½ tablespoons of butter with a wooden spoon to soften it and season with salt and pepper.
3. Spread the butter on the slices of bread.
4. Grease an oven-proof dish with remaining butter and arrange the slices of bread.
5. Arrange the slices of fontina cheese over the bread.
6. Beat the eggs with salt and pepper.
7. Pour the egg mixture and the milk over the slices of bread and leave the bread to soften for about 20 minutes.
8. Bake in the oven at 350° F for 30 minutes. Serve piping hot.

Antipasto trentino
APPETIZER FROM TRENTINO (Trentino-Alto Adige)

Preparation: 15 minutes

Ingredients for 6 people:

1 horseradish root
a pinch of sugar
salt
a cup of heavy cream
18 slices of speck* (or ½ lb. speck in a single piece)

1. Grate the horseradish.
2. Mix the grated horseradish with sugar and salt.
3. Whip the cream into soft peaks and fold it into the horseradish.
4. Serve three slices of *speck* (or 1/6 of the single piece) and a spoonful of horseradish per person. The *speck* and the horseradish should be eaten together.

If any horseradish is left over, it can be kept in the refrigerator for some considerable time in a glass jar, completely covered with olive oil.

* Speck is a smoked ham that is available in Italian or German delicatessens.

Crostini saporiti
SAVORY CROSTINI (Valle d'Aosta)

Preparation: about 5 minutes
Cooking time: about 5 minutes

Ingredients for 4 people:

8 slices of brown bread
a clove of garlic
¼ pound smoked pancetta in thin slices
8 thin slices of fontina cheese

1. Heat the oven to 300°F.
2. Rub the slices of bread with the garlic.
3. Arrange a slice of smoked *pancetta* and fontina cheese on each slice of bread.
4. Arrange the crostini in an oven dish and bake. When the cheese has melted, serve piping hot (two per person).

Bagna caöda
HOT GARLIC AND ANCHOVY DIP (Piedmont)

Preparation: 10 minutes
Cooking time: about 15 minutes

Ingredients for 4 people:

2 ounce can flat fillets of anchovies
4 cloves of garlic (soak them for 2
hours in 1 cup of milk to make
them easier to digest)
4 tablespoons butter
1⅓ cup extra-virgin olive oil
boiled or raw vegetables as pre-
ferred (bell peppers, celery, carrots,
fennel, onions, beets...)

1. Rinse and drain the anchovies.
2. Cut the cloves of garlic in half; chop finely.
3. Melt the butter and oil over low heat and then add the chopped garlic and cook for 15 minutes, stirring continually (if the anchovies and garlic do not blend fully, cook a little longer).
4. Wash the vegetables and cut into strips.
5. Serve the sauce piping hot (it is a good idea to serve it in table ovenware to keep it hot). Place the vegetables in bowls so that diners can serve themselves, each choosing the vegetables they prefer and dipping them in the sauce.

Farinata
FLOUR TART GENOVESE-STYLE (Liguria)

Preparation: 15 minutes; 2 hours
resting
Cooking time: 30 minutes

Ingredients for 6 people:

1 pound chickpea flour
4 cups water
pinch of salt
½ cup of olive oil
pepper

1. Slowly dissolve the chickpea flour in the water, being careful to avoid forming lumps.
2. Add salt and set aside for at least 2 hours.
3. Then heat the oven to 400°F.
4. Skim off the head formed on the surface of the chickpea sauce.
5. Grease an oven-proof dish with oil and then add the mixture. Mix well with a wooden spoon so that the oil and sauce blend well.
6. Bake until the surface browns (about 30 minutes–the cooking time depends on the consistency of the mixture and the size of the dish, best if about ½-inch deep).
7. Serve cut into pieces, seasoned with freshly ground pepper.

This dish makes an excellent snack at any time of day.

◀ *Bagna caöda*

Focaccia ligure
FOCACCIA BREAD (Liguria)

Preparation: 20 minutes; 2½ hours for leavening
Cooking time: about 40 minutes

Ingredients for 6 people:

½ ounce beer yeast
3 cups all-purpose flour
salt
½ cup olive oil
pepper
a sprig of rosemary

1. Dissolve the beer yeast in a little lukewarm water.
2. Prepare a heap of flour and place a pinch of salt and the yeast in the hollow at the top. Mix with a little water and knead for about 10 minutes. Let rise for at least 2½ hours.
3. Heat the oven to 400°F.
4. When the dough has leavened, grease an oven-proof dish with a little oil and spread out the dough.
5. Make little dimples on the top of the dough with your fingers, then add salt and pepper and brush with oil.
6. Rinse the sprig of rosemary, strip the leaves from the stalk, and distribute over the focaccia.
7. Bake for about 40 minutes. Serve hot.

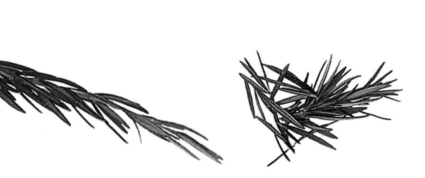

Fonduta valdostana
WARM CHEESE FONDUE (Valle d'Aosta)

Preparation: 10 minutes; 2 hours of resting
Cooking time: about 30 minutes

Ingredients for 4 people:

14 ounces fontina cheese
1 cup milk
4 egg yolks
4 tablespoons butter
8 slices of bread (preferably brown)
pepper

1. Dice the fontina cheese, cover with ½ cup of milk, and marinate for at least 2 hours.
2. Having marinated the fontina cheese, mix the egg yolks with the remaining milk.
3. Heat the fontina cheese, 2 tablespoons butter, milk, and egg yolks in a double-boiler. Mix continually with a wooden spoon. It should become creamy but not stringy; if the fondue is too thin, add a little starch.
4. Dice the bread. Melt the remaining butter in a pan and fry the bread (if you prefer, the bread can be toasted rather than fried).
5. Arrange the bread on plates, pour the boiling cheese on top, and season with pepper. Serve immediately, while the cheese is still creamy.

Insalata di nervetti
TIDBIT SALAD (Lombardy)

Preparation: 30 minutes
Cooking time: about 2 hours

Ingredients for 4 people:

3 pork knuckles (about 3 pounds)
1 stalk of celery
1 carrot, peeled
1½ onions
salt
a sprig of parsley
olive oil
vinegar
pepper

1. Clean the knuckles and singe them over a flame.
2. Place the knuckles in a pot with the celery, the carrot, and one onion; cover with cold water and add ½ teaspoon salt. Cook with the lid off. When the water begins to boil, skim it and boil for 2 hours.
3. When the meat has cooked, drain and allow to cool; then bone the knuckles and cut the meat into strips.
4. Wash the parsley and chop with the remaining half onion.
5. Mix the meat with the chopped parsley and onion. Season with plenty of oil, vinegar, salt, and pepper. Serve cold.

Tartine al pâté di olive nere
BLACK OLIVE PÂTÉ SAVORIES (Piedmont)

Preparation: 15 minutes; 3 hours resting in the refrigerator
Cooking time: 5 minutes to toast the bread

Ingredients for 4 people:

7 ounces black olives
half a lemon
3 tablespoons olive oil
4 tablespoons butter
2½ tablespoons breadcrumbs
salt
pepper
8 slices of white bread
lemon for garnishing

1. Pit the olives and chop finely.
2. Squeeze the lemon and strain the juice.
3. Mix the olives, the lemon juice, and olive oil.
4. Cut the butter into cubes and work with a wooden spoon, then add to the olives.
5. Mix this with the breadcrumbs and add salt and pepper to taste. Mix well with a wooden spoon and leave in the refrigerator for about 3 hours.
6. Toast the bread, cut each slice into four triangles, and spread with the olive pâté. Serve on a table dish garnished with slices of lemon.

Torta pasqualina
EASTER CAKE (Liguria)

Preparation: 1 hour, 30 minutes
Cooking time: 1 hour

Ingredients for 6 people:

2¼ cups flour
salt
olive oil
2¼ pounds spinach, chard, or beet tops
10½ ounces ricotta cheese
½ cup heavy cream
¾ cup grated Parmesan cheese
3 eggs
pepper
butter

1. Prepare a heaping cup of flour on the table top. Make a hollow at the top and add a pinch of salt and a tablespoon of olive oil. Mix with cold water until a smooth, soft dough is made.
2. Divide the dough into four pieces, cover with a moist cloth, and set aside for about 30 minutes.
3. Boil greens for about 10-20 minutes until tender. When they are ready, drain well.
4. Mix the ricotta cheese, the cream, three tablespoons of Parmesan, two tablespoons flour, and a pinch of salt in a bowl. Then add the greens and mix well.
5. Grease a medium-size deep oven-proof dish. Roll out one of the four pieces of dough very thinly, so that it fits in the dish with its edges overhanging.
6. Roll out the next piece of dough and position it over the first.
7. Pour the beet mixture over the two pieces of dough.
8. Make three holes in the mixture and break an egg into each hole.
9. Sprinkle with Parmesan cheese, salt, pepper, and a few pats of butter.
10. On the work-top, roll out the third piece of dough so that it is just large enough to cover the pie; place it over the dish and brush with a little oil.
11. Heat the oven to 350 °F.
12. Prepare the fourth piece of dough as for the third and place it loosely over the pie so that it remains somewhat separate from the rest of the pie. Blow between the two layers to achieve the best result.
13. Push down the edges of the dough hanging over the sides of the dish to enclose the pie.
14. Brush the surface with oil and then prick with a fork.
15. Bake for about one hour.

◄ *Torta pasqualina*

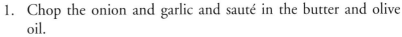

Agnolotti

LARGE RAVIOLI PIEDMONT-STYLE (Piedmont)

Preparation: 3 hours
Cooking time: 25 minutes

Ingredients for 4 people:

for the pasta:
10½ ounces (about 2⅝ cups) flour
3 eggs
salt

for the sauce filling:
1 onion
1 clove of garlic
2 tablespoons butter
2 tablespoons olive oil
½ pound ground beef
7 ounces canned crushed tomatoes
2 ladles (about 1 cup) of stock
salt
¼ pound fresh spinach
½ cup grated Parmesan cheese
for the filling
2 eggs
a little nutmeg
pepper
3 tablespoons Parmesan cheese for
sprinkling

1. Chop the onion and garlic and sauté in the butter and olive oil.
2. Gently fry the meat with the chopped onion and garlic.
3. Add the crushed tomatoes and stock, salt to taste and cook over low heat.
4. Carefully clean the spinach. Bring a pot of water to a boil and then add salt and the spinach. Cook for 5 minutes, then chop.
5. Also chop up the meat as soon as cooked. Drain the meat mixture, reserving the juices.
6. Mix the meat, spinach, Parmesan cheese, eggs, a little nutmeg, and a pinch of salt and pepper.
7. Prepare the pasta as explained on page 10.
8. Roll out the pasta into two very thin pieces.
9. Place little balls of the meat and spinach mixture about 2 inches apart on the base.
10. Cover with the second piece of dough and press down with your fingers around the filling so that the two parts stick together. Cut out the agnolotti using a mold, a toothed wheel, or a knife.
11. Bring plenty of water to a boil for the pasta. When it comes to a boil, add salt and the agnolotti. Cook for 12 minutes.
12. In the meantime, heat the cooking juice of the meat.
13. When the pasta is cooked, flavor with the heated sauce. Serve the agnolotti piping hot, sprinkled with three tablespoons of grated Parmesan cheese.

◄ *Agnolotti*

Casönsèi

LARGE RAVIOLI MILANESE STYLE (Lombardy)

Preparation: 1 hour 30 minutes
Cooking time: 15 minutes

Ingredients for 4 people:

for the pasta:
10½ ounces (about 2⅝ cups) flour
3 eggs
1 tablespoon olive oil
salt

for the filling:
1 clove of garlic
1 tablespoon chopped parsley
2 tablespoons butter
¼ pound ground beef
1 egg
⅓ cup breadcrumbs
3 tablespoons grated Parmesan
cheese
salt
pepper

for the sauce:
6 sage leaves
7 tablespoons butter
4 tablespoons grated
Parmesan cheese

1. Knead the flour with the eggs, oil, and a pinch of salt. Knead the dough well and then set aside for a while.
2. Cut the clove of garlic in half. Sauté the garlic and parsley in the butter.
3. Add the ground beef and cook for a further 10 minutes. When cooked, drain and set aside to cool.
4. Prepare a thin piece of pasta. Then cut out rectangles 3x6 inches in size.
5. Prepare the filling by mixing the ground beef, egg, breadcrumbs, Parmesan cheese, salt, and pepper. Mix well.
6. Place a tablespoon of filling on each rectangle of pasta, then fold in half along the long sides, and press down with your fingers around the edges to seal. Fold them into a half-moon shape (you can do this only if the pasta is soft and not too dry).
7. Bring a pot of water to a boil and then add salt and the casönsèi. They cook in 5 minutes.
8. Heat the sage leaves with the butter in a saucepan.
9. When the casönsèi are cooked, drain and season with the melted butter and grated Parmesan cheese. Serve immediately.

Ditali al ragù di maiale

PASTA TUBES WITH PORK SAUCE (Various regions)

Preparation: 10 minutes
Cooking time: 45 minutes

Ingredients for 4 people:

1 onion
1 clove of garlic
½ pound pork loin
2 tablespoons butter
2 tablespoons olive oil
7 ounces canned crushed tomatoes
½ cup of stock
salt
pepper
14 ounces grooved pasta tubes
3 tablespoons grated Parmesan cheese

1. Chop the onion.
2. Cut the clove of garlic in half.
3. Dice the pork.
4. Sauté the onion and the clove of garlic in butter and olive oil. When the onion browns, add the meat and fry gently for a few minutes.
5. Add the tomatoes and the stock, salt and pepper; cook for about 45 minutes.
6. Boil water in a pot for the pasta. When it comes to a boil, salt and add the pasta.
7. When the pasta is cooked, drain and flavor with the pork sauce. Serve piping hot with Parmesan cheese.

Farfalle con prosciutto cotto e cipolla

BOW-TIE PASTA WITH HAM AND ONIONS (Various regions)

Preparation: 10 minutes
Cooking time: about 35 minutes

Ingredients for 4 people:

2 onions
4 ounces boiled ham (3 slices)
2 tablespoons butter
5 sage leaves
4 tablespoons olive oil
salt
14 ounces Farfalle (bow-tie) pasta
3 tablespoons grated Parmesan cheese

1. Boil plenty of water for the pasta.
2. Chop the onion finely.
3. Dice the ham.
4. Cook the ham in a saucepan with the butter for about 5 minutes.
5. In a pan large enough to hold all the pasta afterward, heat the sage leaves in the oil.
6. After a few minutes, remove the sage and pour the oil over the onions, add a little water and salt, and cook for about 20 minutes.
7. In the meantime, when the water has come to a boil, add salt and the pasta.
8. When the pasta is cooked to a firm bite, drain and add to the pan with the onions. Add the ham. Mix well and cook for a couple of minutes, stirring continually with a wooden spoon. Serve piping hot, sprinkled with grated Parmesan cheese.

Maccheroni con cavolfiore e salsiccia
MACARONI WITH CAULIFLOWER AND SAUSAGE (Various regions)

Preparation: 15 minutes
Cooking time: 40 minutes

Ingredients for 4 people:

1 cauliflower (about 1 pound)
salt
1 onion
5 tablespoons olive oil
1 sprig of rosemary
¼ pound Italian sausage
1 pound macaroni
3 tablespoons grated Parmesan cheese
pepper

1. Clean the cauliflower and cut into pieces.
2. Boil the cauliflower in salted water (used later to cook the pasta) for about 10 minutes.
3. Slice the onion, chop the rosemary, and dice the sausage.
4. Sauté the onion in the oil and, when golden, add 2 tablespoons water, rosemary, and the sausage. Cook for 15 minutes.
5. When the cauliflower is cooked, drain with a skimmer. Add the cauliflower to the sausage and heat for a few minutes.
6. Bring the water used to cook the cauliflower back to a boil and then add the pasta.
7. When the pasta is cooked, drain, season with the caulifower and sausage sauce, sprinkle with Parmesan cheese and a pinch of pepper. Serve immediately.

Maccheroni saporiti
MACARONI with tomatoes and anchovies (Liguria)

Preparation: 5 minutes
Cooking time: 30 minutes

Ingredients for 4 people:

½ onion
5 tablespoons vegetable oil
3 anchovies
9 ounces canned peeled tomatoes
9 ounces canned peas, or 1 10-oz package frozen peas
1 tablespoon chopped parsley
salt
1 pound macaroni
3 tablespoons pecorino cheese

1. Finely chop the onion and sauté in the oil with anchovies.
2. Add the tomatoes to the onion.
3. After 5 minutes, add the peas, parsley, and a pinch of salt. Cook for 25 minutes, stirring occasionally.
4. While sauce is cooking, bring pasta water to a boil. Add salt and pasta, and cook to taste.
5. Drain the pasta when cooked and flavor with the sauce. Serve immediately, sprinkled with grated pecorino cheese.

◄ *Maccheroni saporiti*

Mezzepenne al mascarpone
HALF PENNE WITH MASCARPONE CHEESE* (Lombardy)

Cooking time: 25 minutes

Ingredients for 4 people:

salt
1 pound grooved mezzepenne*
¼ pound butter
7 ounces mascarpone
3 tablespoons grated Parmesan
cheese

1. Bring a pot of water to a boil for the pasta.
2. When it comes to a boil, add salt and the pasta.
3. Mix the butter and mascarpone together well with a wooden spoon until blended.
4. When the pasta is cooked, drain and mix with the mascarpone and butter mixture; sprinkle with Parmesan cheese. Mix well and serve piping hot.

*Can also be prepared with regular penne.

Paglia & fieno ai funghi
WHITE AND GREEN TAGLIOLINI WITH MUSHROOMS (Various regions)

Preparation: 5 minutes
Cooking time: 30 minutes

Ingredients for 4 people:

6 ounces mushrooms (porcini are best but champignons [white button mushrooms] can also be used)
1 clove of garlic
2 tablespoons butter
5 tablespoons olive oil
1 tablespoon chopped parsley
2 ounces fontina cheese
½ cup heavy cream
salt
¾ pound "paglia e fieno" pasta (half egg tagliolini and half green spinach tagliolini)
pepper

1. Boil the water for the pasta.
2. Clean and slice the mushrooms.
3. Chop the garlic and sauté in a saucepan with butter and oil. After a few minutes, add the mushrooms and parsley and cook for about 20 minutes.
4. Dice the fontina cheese and heat with the cream in a pot large enough to hold all the pasta later.
5. In the meantime, when a water comes to a boil, add salt and the pasta. When the pasta is ready, drain and add to the cream; then add the mushrooms, mix well, and heat for a couple of minutes. Sprinkle with pepper, and serve immediately.

Mezzepenne pasticciate
BAKED HALF PENNE* (Various regions)

Preparation: 1 hour 30 minutes
Cooking time: 20 minutes

Ingredients for 4-6 people:

1 onion
7 tablespoons olive oil
3 ounces beef & 3 ounces pork,
    ground together
1 cup dry white wine
9 ounces fresh white mushrooms
5 tablespoons butter
1 tablespoon chopped parsley
salt
pepper
1 pound grooved half penne*
3 tablespoons Parmesan cheese

for the white sauce:
4 tablespoons butter
½ cup flour
2 cups cold milk
½ teaspoon salt

1. Chop the onion and sauté in the oil. Add the ground meat and fry gently for a few minutes; then add the cup of white wine and cook for about 1 hour on low heat.
2. Bring water to a boil for the pasta.
3. Clean and slice the mushrooms. Cook them in a casserole with 2 tablespoons butter and 2 tablespoons oil, parsley, salt and pepper, for about 20 minutes.
4. In the meantime, when the water comes to a boil, add salt and the pasta. The pasta must be cooked to a firm bite. When ready, drain, mix with 2 tablespoons butter, and cover the pot with the lid.
5. Prepare the white sauce as follows: heat the butter in a small saucepan over low heat; then add the flour and mix with a wooden spoon off the heat to avoid forming lumps. When thoroughly mixed, return the saucepan to the heat and stir for 1 minute without browning the flour; then add the milk and continue stirring without bringing to a boil. If the sauce is too thick, add more milk; add salt and, if desired, flavor with pepper and nutmeg to taste. Cook slowly for another 10 minutes. If lumps form during cooking, strain the sauce.
6. Now mix the penne with the meat sauce, mushrooms, and grated Parmesan cheese. Mix well.
7. Pour the white sauce over the penne and mix.
8. Heat the oven to 400°F.
9. Grease an oven-proof dish with the remaining tablespoon of butter, and fill with the mezzepenne and sauce. Bake in the hot oven for 20 minutes. Serve piping hot.

*Can also be prepared with regular penne.

Pappardelle alla boscaiola
WOODSMAN'S EGG NOODLES (Various regions)

Preparation: 1 hour 30 minutes
Cooking time: 20 minutes

Ingredients for 4 people:

1 ounce white mushrooms
7 ounces Italian sausage
1 onion
1 stalk of celery
1 carrot, peeled
1 sprig of parsley
3 tablespoons butter
1 cup dry white wine
3½ ounces canned peeled tomatoes
salt
pepper
12 ounces pappardelle
¼ cup heavy cream
3 tablespoons Parmesan cheese

1. Clean and slice the mushrooms.
2. Dice the sausage.
3. Chop the onion, celery, carrot, and parsley.
4. Cook the chopped vegetables in the butter over low heat for 5 minutes, stirring frequently.
5. Add the mushrooms and sausage to the vegetables and fry gently for a few minutes, then add the wine.
6. Blend the tomatoes and then cook them with the mushrooms and sausage over low heat for one hour, adding water if the sauce becomes too thick. Add salt and pepper.
7. Bring water to a boil for the pasta, then add salt and the pappardelle.
8. Just before the sauce is ready, add the cream and cook for a few more minutes.
9. When the pasta is ready, drain and flavor with the sauce. Serve the pappardelle piping hot, sprinkled with grated Parmesan cheese.

Pasta integrale allo speck*
WHOLE-GRAIN PASTA WITH *SPECK** (Trentino-Alto Adige)

Preparation: 10 minutes
Cooking time: 30 minutes

Ingredients for 4 people:

5 ounces *speck* (three slices)
1 sprig of parsley
1 clove of garlic
5 tablespoons olive oil
4 anchovy fillets (in olive oil)
salt
1 pound whole-grain pasta as preferred
3 tablespoons Parmesan cheese

1. Boil the water for the pasta.
2. Cut the *speck* into thin strips.
3. Chop the parsley.
4. Sauté the clove of garlic in the oil. Remove the garlic after a couple of minutes and add the anchovy fillets, crushing them with a fork as they cook.
5. Add the *speck* and parsley and cook for 5 minutes.
6. In the meantime, add salt to the boiling water and then the pasta.
7. When the pasta is cooked, drain and season with the sauce, heating for a few more minutes. Sprinkle with grated Parmesan cheese and serve immediately.

*Speck is a smoked ham that is available in Italian and German delicatessens.

◄ *Pappardelle alla boscaiola*

Pasticcio di pane e funghi
BREAD AND MUSHROOM PIE (Lombardy)

*Preparation: 35 minutes; 30 minutes
    resting*
Cooking time: 15 minutes

Ingredients for 4 people:

3⅓ pounds white mushrooms
2 cloves of garlic, chopped
8 tablespoons butter
½ cup olive oil
2½ tablespoons chopped parsley
salt
pepper
4 eggs
3 ounces grated Parmesan cheese
firm bread
2 cups stock

1. Clean and slice the mushrooms.
2. Sauté the garlic in 7 tablespoons butter and the oil. Add the mushrooms, parsley, a pinch of salt, pepper and cook for about 20 minutes.
3. Beat the eggs with the grated Parmesan cheese and add the mushrooms when cooked.
4. Grease an oven-proof dish with the remaining butter and arrange alternating layers of firm bread and mushrooms until full; finish with a layer of bread.
5. Pour the stock over top and set aside for 30 minutes.
6. Heat the oven to 400°F and, when hot, bake the pasticcio for 15 minutes.

Penne con prosciutto cotto e formaggio
PENNE WITH HAM AND CHEESE (Various regions)

Preparation: 5 minutes
Cooking time: 25 minutes

Ingredients for 4 people:

¼ pound boiled ham (6 slices)
6 tablespoons butter
salt
1 pound grooved penne
3 ounces Emmenthal cheese
3 tablespoons grated Parmesan cheese

1. Boil the water for the pasta.
2. Dice the ham and fry gently in 3 tablespoons butter for a few minutes
3. When the water comes to a boil, add salt and the pasta.
4. Finely dice the Emmenthal cheese.
5. When the pasta is ready, drain and flavor with the remaining butter, ham, Emmenthal, and grated Parmesan cheese. Mix well and serve immediately.

Pipe al sugo di salame

PIPE PASTA WITH SALAMI SAUCE (Various regions)

Preparation: 10 minutes
Cooking time: 30 minutes

Ingredients for 4 people:

1 onion
sprig of parsley
4½ ounces salami, cut into ¼ inch
thick slices
4 tablespoons olive oil
3 ounces canned crushed tomatoes
salt
1 pound pipe pasta*
3 tablespoons Parmesan cheese

1. Boil the water for the pasta.
2. Chop the onion, parsley; dice the salami.
3. Sauté the onion in the oil; when browned, add the parsley and salami and cook for a few minutes.
4. Add the tomato to the salami and cook for about 30 minutes.
5. When the water comes to a boil, add salt and the pasta. When the pasta is ready, drain and flavor with the sauce. Serve hot sprinkled with grated Parmesan cheese.

* Use any hollow pasta.

Pipe al sugo di salsiccia

PIPE PASTA WITH SAUSAGE SAUCE (Various regions)

Preparation: 10 minutes
Cooking time: 30 minutes

Ingredients for 4 people:

½ onion
½ pound Italian sausage
5 tablespoons olive oil
7 ounces canned peeled tomatoes
salt
1 pound pipe pasta*
3 tablespoons grated Parmesan
cheese

1. Boil the water for the pasta.
2. Chop the onion and dice the sausage.
3. Sauté the onion in the oil; when golden, add the tomatoes and sausage and cook for 25 minutes.
4. When the water comes to a boil, add salt and the pasta.
5. When the pasta is ready, strain and mix with the sauce. Serve hot sprinkled with grated Parmesan cheese.

* Use any hollow pasta.

Pizzoccheri

HOMEMADE BROWN PASTA WITH POTATOES AND CABBAGE (Lombardy)

Preparation: 30 minutes
Cooking time: 40 minutes

Ingredients for 4 people:

for the pasta:
10½ ounces (about 2⅝ cups)
buckwheat flour
3½ ounces (about ¾ cup) white
flour
water
salt

for the sauce:
3 potatoes
½ pound green cabbage or spinach
(you can also use 1 pound of
spinach or cabbage alone
without the cabbage leaves)
½ pound cabbage leaves
7 ounces Valtellina or fontina cheese
10 tablespoons butter
6 sage leaves

1. Knead the buckwheat and white flour with water and a pinch of salt. Roll out not too thinly. Cut out strips about ½ inch wide by 2-3 inches long.
2. Peel and dice the potatoes.
3. Wash the spinach and cabbage and cut the leaves into 2-3 pieces.
4. Boil the potatoes, spinach, and cabbage in salted water.
5. After the water returns to a boil, cook 15 minutes, then add the pizzoccheri.
6. In the meantime, dice the cheese and melt in a saucepan with butter and sage.
7. When the pizzoccheri are ready, drain them together with the vegetables.
8. Season immediately with the melted cheese and butter (remove the sage leaves). Mix well and serve piping hot.

Sedani alla tirolese

SEDANI PASTA ALTO-ADIGE STYLE (Alto Adige)

Preparation: 5 minutes
Cooking time: 30 minutes

Ingredients for 4 people:

5 medium sausages
1 onion
4 tablespoons butter
1 tablespoon chopped parsley
½ cup dry white wine
salt
1 pound sedani pasta
3 tablespoons grated Parmesan
cheese

1. Boil the water for the pasta.
2. Cut the sausages into thin slices.
3. Chop the onion and cook in the butter with two tablespoons of water so that it doesn't fry. After 10 minutes, add the würstel, parsley, and wine. Cook for about 10 minutes.
4. When the water has boiled, add salt and the pasta.
5. When the pasta is ready, add the sauce and Parmesan cheese, mix well and serve immediately.

◀ *Pizzoccheri*

Strangolapreti

STRANGOLAPRETI* PASTA (Trentino)

Preparation: 10 hours resting, 1 hour preparation
Cooking time: about 25 minutes

Ingredients for 6 people:

1 pound firm bread
1 cup milk
1 pound cabbage or spinach
salt
2 eggs
4½ cups flour
10 tablespoons butter
10-12 sage leaves
4 tablespoons Parmesan cheese

1. Dice the bread and place in a large bowl; add the milk. Cover and set aside for about 10 hours.
2. Boil the cabbage or spinach in lighlty salted water, then drain and squeeze lightly and set aside to cool.
3. Add the cabbage, eggs, flour, and salt to the bread. Mix well to a uniform consistency.
4. Blend the mixture and work into a kind of dough (if it is too soft, add breadcrumbs). Divide into pieces and roll out on a floured work-top to form cylinders about ½ inch in diameter, which are then cut into pieces.
5. Boil plenty of salted water. When it comes to a boil, add the pieces of "dough" one at a time. When they rise to the surface, boil for a further 5 minutes. In the meantime, melt the butter in a saucepan with the sage leaves.
6. Drain the strangolapreti with a slotted spoon and serve piping hot with the melted butter and grated Parmesan cheese.

*It seems that the name (priest's tidbit) derives from their proverbial flavor.

Tagliatelle con porri e besciamella

TAGLIATELLE WITH LEEKS IN WHITE SAUCE (Various regions)

Preparation: 40 minutes
Cooking time: 45 minutes

Ingredients for 4 people:

½ cup chopped green parts of leeks
sprig of parsley
¼ pound smoked *pancetta*
2 tablespoons butter
olive oil
salt
12 ounces tagliatelle
3 tablespoons grated Parmesan cheese

for the white sauce:
2 tablespoons butter
¼ cup flour
1 cup cold milk
salt

1. Boil the water for the pasta.
2. Chop the parsley.
3. Finely dice the *pancetta.*
4. Sauté the chopped leeks and parsley in butter and 3 tablespoons oil; add the *pancetta* after about 5 minutes and cook for another 10 minutes.
5. Prepare the white sauce as explained in recipe on page 35.
6. In the meantime, when the water has boiled, add salt and the pasta.
7. When the pasta is ready, drain and mix with the white sauce and the leek and *pancetta* sauce. Serve piping hot sprinkled with the grated Parmesan cheese.

Trenette pasticciate

Trenette pasta (Liguria)

Preparation: 30 minutes
Cooking time: 25 minutes

Ingredients for 4 people:

1 tablespoon chopped onion
3 tablespoons olive oil
7 ounces canned crushed tomatoes
1 pound trenette
3-4 tablespoons "pesto" sauce
(see recipe on page 45)

1. Boil the water for the pasta.
2. Sauté the onion in the oil.
3. Add the crushed tomatoes to the onion and cook for 25 minutes.
4. When the water comes to a boil, add salt and the pasta.
5. When the pasta is ready, drain and flavor with the "pesto" and tomato sauce. Mix well and serve piping hot.

Trenette al pesto alla Genovese

TRENETTE PASTA WITH GENOESE BASIL SAUCE "PESTO" (Liguria)

Preparation: 30 minutes
Cooking time: 25 minutes to boil the
water and cook the pasta

Ingredients for 4 people:

1 pound trenette

for the Genoese basil sauce:
1 cup fresh basil (about 2 ounces)
1 garlic clove
salt
1 cup olive oil
2 tablespoons pine nuts
1 tablespoon grated Parmesan
cheese
2 tablespoons grated pecorino
cheese

1. Wash the basil leaves and dry on a cloth.
2. Boil the water for the pasta.
3. Cut the clove of garlic in half.
4. Chop the basil with a pinch of salt and the garlic. Ideally, it should be worked with a pestle and mortar but a blender works as well. Add the oil a little at a time, the pine nuts, the Parmesan and pecorino cheese, blending continually to form a uniform sauce.
5. In the meantime, when the water has boiled, add salt and the pasta.
6. When the pasta is ready, flavor with the "pesto" sauce.

This sauce can be kept for some time once prepared but in this case do not add the grated cheese or the pine nuts because they will ferment. Keep in a glass jar covered with oil; add the chopped pine nuts and grated cheeses when preparing the dish again.

◄ *Trenette al pesto alla Genovese*

Minestra di riso con le verze

RICE SOUP WITH CABBAGE (Lombardy)

Preparation: 5 minutes
Cooking time: 35 minutes

Ingredients for 4 people:

½ cabbage
½ pound ripe fresh tomatoes
4 tablespoons butter
1 clove of garlic
5 cups stock
1¼ cups rice
salt
3 tablespoons grated Parmesan cheese
pepper

1. Wash the cabbage and cut into strips.
2. Cut the tomatoes into pieces and cook in 2 tablespoons butter with the clove of garlic for 10 minutes.
3. Heat the stock and when it comes to a boil add the cabbage and the tomato. Cook for 10 minutes.
4. Add the rice and a pinch of salt and cook for another 15 minutes, stirring occasionally.
5. When the rice is cooked, remove from the heat, add the grated Parmesan cheese, remaining butter, and a pinch of pepper. Serve piping hot.

Minestrone lombardo

MINESTRONE (Lombardy)

Preparation: 30 minutes
Cooking time: 1 hour 20 minutes

Ingredients for 4 people:

3½ ounces fresh or canned beets
½ pound potatoes
1 carrot
½ pound zucchini
1 leek
1 onion
1 clove of garlic
1 sprig of parsley
½ pound borlotti, bolita, or pinto beans (if dry, soften in advance for 12 hours in water)
1 stalk of celery
salt
⅔ cup rice
4 tablespoons olive oil
pepper
3 tablespoons grated Parmesan cheese

1. Cut the beets into narrow strips.
2. Peel and dice the potatoes and carrot.
3. Cut the zucchini and the inner, tender part of the leek into slices.
4. Chop the onion, garlic, and parsley.
5. Wash and drain the beans.
6. Remove the stringy fibers of the celery and cut into pieces.
7. Place all the vegetables in a large pot with 6 cups of water and add salt. Cook for 1 hour once it comes to a boil.
8. Add the rice and cook for about another 15 minutes.
9. When the rice is cooked, serve the soup piping hot, seasoning with a little olive oil, a pinch of pepper, and the grated Parmesan cheese.

Minestrone ligure
MINESTRONE (Liguria)

Preparation: 30 minutes
Cooking time: 1 hour 20 minutes

Ingredients for 4 people:

1 eggplant
salt
2 zucchini
1 carrot, peeled
1 stalk of celery
½ cabbage
2 potatoes
¼ pound green beans
¼ pound loose borlotti, bolita or
pinto beans (if dry, soften in advance for 12 hours in water)
2 tomatoes
pepper
½ pound ditalini
3 tablespoons pesto alla genovese
(Genoese basil sauce, see the recipe on page 45)
4 tablespoons olive oil
3 tablespoons grated Parmesan cheese

1. Dice the eggplant and sprinkle with salt to extract the bitter juice.
2. Slice the zucchini, carrot, and celery.
3. Wash the cabbage leaves and cut into strips.
4. Peel and dice the potatoes.
5. Top and tail the green beans and then cut into 1-inch pieces.
6. Wash and drain the beans.
7. Skin and seed the tomatoes and cut into pieces.
8. Place the vegetables in a large pot with 6 cups of water. Add salt and pepper and cook for 1 hour once it comes to a boil.
9. Add the pasta.
10. When the pasta is ready, take the soup off the heat and mix with the uncooked pesto sauce and olive oil. Serve piping hot, sprinkled with grated Parmesan cheese.

Minestra d'orzo
BARLEY SOUP (Trentino)

Preparation: 10 minutes
Cooking time: 1 hour 15 minutes

Ingredients for 4 people:

7 ounces pearl barley
1 onion
1 clove of garlic
2½ ounces smoked *pancetta*
2 tablespoons olive oil
salt
2 potatoes
1 carrot, peeled
1 stalk of celery
1 tablespoon chopped parsley
pepper
heavy cream (optional)

1. Wash the barley in plenty of water.
2. Chop the onion and garlic.
3. Dice the *pancetta*.
4. Gently fry the *pancetta* and the chopped onion and garlic in oil for a few minutes in the pot used to make the soup.
5. Then add 4 cups water and the barley. Salt and cook for 1 hour once it comes to a boil, stirring occasionally.
6. In the meantime, peel and dice the potatoes; chop the carrot and dice the celery. After 30 minutes cooking the barley, add all the chopped vegetables and cook for the remaining 30 minutes.
7. When ready, remove from the heat, sprinkle with chopped parsley and a pinch of pepper. Serve piping hot.

If you wish, before serving the soup, you may stir in a couple of tablespoons of heavy cream.

Canederli

BREAD BALLS (Alto Adige)

Preparation: 1 hour resting plus 30 minutes preparing
Cooking time: 20 minutes

Ingredients for 6 people:

10½ ounces stale bread (about 5 buns)
3 ounce thick slice of *speck**
3 ounce thick slice of smoked *pancetta*
2 ounces salami
1 tablespoon chopped scallions
2 tablespoons chopped parsley
salt
1 cup milk
3 eggs
⅔ cup flour
4 cups stock

1. Finely dice the bread.
2. Finely dice the *speck, pancetta,* and salami and mix with the bread in a large bowl.
3. Add the chopped scallions and parsley, salt, and mix well with the mixed dry ingredients.
4. Add the milk and eggs, mix, and set aside (it will still seem rather dry) for at least 1 hour to flavor thoroughly.
5. Add the flour to this mixture, moisten your hands, and then prepare balls about 3 inches in diameter. If they are too soft, add a little more flour; if too hard, add a little more milk.
6. Bring the stock to a boil and then add the canederli. When they float to the surface, boil for another 10 minutes, then drain with a slotted spoon.
7. Place 2 canederli in each serving bowl, and top with about ½ cup hot stock.

They are many variants to this recipe. You can make smaller canederli, cook them in salted water and season with melted butter and Parmesan cheese or tomato sauce.

*Speck is a smoked ham available in Italian and German delicatessens.

◀ *Canederli*

Pasta e ceci
DITALINI PASTA AND CHICK PEAS (Friuli-Venezia Giulia)

Cooking time: 2 hours 15 minutes

Ingredients for 6 people:

10½ ounce can chick peas (if dry, soften in advance for 12 hours in water)
salt
1 sprig of rosemary
1 clove of garlic
2 ounce thick slice of smoked *pancetta*
4 tablespoons olive oil
10½ ounces ditalini pasta
1 tablespoon chopped parsley
pepper
3 tablespoons grated Parmesan cheese

1. Cook the chick peas in 6 cups salted water (without ever removing the lid) for 2 hours.
2. Strip the rosemary leaves from the sprig and chop finely with the clove of garlic.
3. Dice the *pancetta* and fry gently in a pot with the oil and chopped garlic and rosemary.
4. When the chick peas are ready, add the *pancetta*, garlic, and rosemary sauce. Salt if necessary.
5. Add the pasta and cook for about another 12 minutes.
6. When the pasta is ready, serve the soup piping hot, seasoning with chopped parsley, a pinch of pepper, and a sprinkle of grated Parmesan cheese.

Pasta e fagioli
TAGLIATELLE PASTA AND BEANS (Veneto)

Preparation: 5 minutes
Cooking time: 2 hours

Ingredients for 4 people:

5 cups stock
1 onion
1 clove of garlic
1 cup oil
10½ ounces fresh borlotti, bolita, or pinto beans (if dry, soften in advance for 12 hours in water)
salt
7 ounces egg tagliatelle
3 tablespoons grated Parmesan cheese
pepper

1. Bring the stock to a boil.
2. Chop the onion and garlic and sauté in the oil in the pot where the soup will be cooked.
3. Add the beans and the hot stock to the chopped onion and garlic, add salt, and cook for about 1 hour 30 minutes on low heat with the lid on.
4. When the soup is ready, use a slotted spoon to remove half the beans, blend, and return to the soup (this makes it thicker). If it is then too thick, add boiling water.
5. Break up the tagliatelle and cook in the boiling soup.
6. When the tagliatelle are ready, remove from the heat, add the Parmesan cheese, a pinch of pepper, and serve.

Riso al latte

RICE WITH MILK (Piedmont)

Cooking time: 20 minutes

Ingredients for 4 people:

4 cups whole milk
1½ cups rice
salt
4 tablespoons butter
3 tablespoons grated Parmesan cheese

1. Heat half the milk in a pot.
2. When the milk comes to a boil, add the rice. Add salt and cook with the lid off, stirring frequently, for about 15 minutes.
3. In the meantime, heat the rest of the milk in another pot and add it to the rice a little at a time as it is absorbed.
4. When the rice is ready, remove from the heat and add the butter and grated Parmesan cheese, mix well, and serve hot.

Riso alla valtellinese

VALTELLINA RICE (Lombardy)

Preparation: 10 minutes; 2 hours if the beans are dry
Cooking time: 20 minutes

Ingredients for 4 people:

7 ounces cannellini beans (if dry, soften in advance for 12 hours in water)
salt
1½ cups rice
9 ounces cabbage
3 sage leaves
4 tablespoons butter
3 tablespoons grated Parmesan cheese

1. Place the beans in cold water and add salt. Bring the water to a boil and cook for 2 hours.
2. Remove the tougher outer leaves and heart of the cabbage. Cut into slices.
3. Heat a pot with plenty of salted water and when it comes to a boil add the rice and cabbage and cook for 20 minutes.
4. Two minutes before the rice is ready, add the boiled beans.
5. Heat the sage leaves in the butter in another saucepan.
6. Drain the rice and flavor with butter and grated cheese. Serve hot.

Riso al prezzemolo
RICE WITH PARSLEY (Lombardy)

Cooking time: 20 minutes

Ingredients for 4 people:

4 cups vegetable stock
1½ pounds rice
2 tablespoons chopped parsley
3 tablespoons grated Parmesan cheese

1. Heat the stock and add the rice when it comes to a boil. Cook for 15 minutes.
2. When the rice is ready, remove from the heat and add the parsley and grated Parmesan cheese. Mix well and serve hot.

Riso e fagioli
RICE AND BEANS (Friuli-Venezia Giulia)

Preparation: 10 minutes
Cooking time: 2 hours

Ingredients for 4 people:

1 onion
1 stalk of celery
1 pound potatoes
7 ounces beans (if dry, soften in advance for 12 hours in water)
6 cups stock
salt
1½ pounds rice
2 tablespoons olive oil
3 tablespoons grated Parmesan cheese

1. Chop the onion and celery.
2. Peel and dice the potatoes.
3. Place the vegetables and beans in a pot with the stock and boil for 1 hour 30 minutes.
4. Add salt if needed, add the rice, and cook for a further 20 minutes.
5. When the rice is ready, flavor with olive oil and grated Parmesan cheese.

Risotto ai funghi
MUSHROOM RISOTTO (Various regions)

*Preparation: 1 hour if dried mush-
rooms are used*
Cooking time: 15 minutes

Ingredients for 4 people:

1½ ounces dry porcini mushrooms
or ½ pound fresh mushrooms
3 cups meat stock
1 small onion, chopped
4 tablespoons butter
1¾ cups arborio rice
1 cup dry white wine
salt
1 tablespoon chopped parsley
3 tablespoons grated Parmesan
cheese

1. Clean and slice the fresh mushrooms. If dried mushrooms are used, soak in lukewarm water and milk for an hour, changing the liquid after the first 30 minutes.
2. Boil the stock.
3. Finely slice the onion and sauté with 3 tablespoons butter over a low heat.
4. Add the mushrooms and sauté for 1 minute.
5. Add the rice, the dry white wine, and salt; mix well.
6. After 2-3 minutes, add a ladle of hot stock and stir well.
7. Add stock to the rice a little at a time as it is absorbed.
8. After 15 minutes, the risotto should be ready. Turn off the heat, add the rest of the butter, parsley, and grated cheese.

Risotto al Barolo
RISOTTO WITH BAROLO WINE   (Piedmont)

Preparation: 5 minutes
Cooking time: 15 minutes

Ingredients for 4 people:

3 cups stock
½ chopped onion
6 tablespoons butter
1¾ cups arborio rice
salt
1 cup Barolo (strong red wine)
3 tablespoons grated Parmesan
cheese

1. Heat the stock.
2. Sauté the onion in a casserole with half the butter.
3. Add the rice and salt; mix.
4. A few minutes after beginning to cook the rice, start adding a little stock at a time, stirring continually and waiting until the liquid is absorbed. Half-way through cooking, add the wine, stir well, and allow it to be absorbed.
5. Continue adding stock, one ladle at a time, until it is all absorbed. It should take about 15 minutes.
6. When the rice is ready, remove from the heat and season with the remaining butter and Parmesan cheese, mix well, and serve hot.

◀ *Risotto al Barolo*

55

Risotto bianco alla Piemontese

WHITE RISOTTO PIEDMONT-STYLE (Piedmont)

Preparation: 5 minutes
Cooking time: 15 minutes

Ingredients for 4 people:

5 cups stock
½ onion
3 tablespoons butter
1¾ cups arborio rice
½ cup dry Piedmont white wine
salt
3 tablespoons grated Parmesan
cheese

1. Boil the stock.
2. Finely slice the onion and sauté in half the butter.
3. Add the rice to the onion and mix for 2-3 minutes. Add the wine and evaporate; then add the hot stock a little at a time. Add salt if needed and cook for 15 minutes.
4. Take the risotto off the heat. Add the remaining butter and grated Parmesan cheese and mix well. Serve hot.

Zuppa di cipolle e patate

ONION AND POTATO SOUP (Veneto)

Preparation: 10 minutes
Cooking time: 1 hour 30 minutes

Ingredients for 4 people:

¾ pounds onions
2 tablespoons olive oil
1 clove of garlic
2 tablespoons butter
½ cup milk
3 cups stock
¾ pounds potatoes
salt
1 tablespoon chopped parsley
3 tablespoons grated Parmesan
cheese

1. Finely slice the onions and cook in a casserole with the oil, clove of garlic, butter, and milk for 30 minutes.
2. Heat the stock separately.
3. Peel and dice the potatoes.
4. After the first 30 minutes cooking time, remove the garlic, add the potatoes to the onions, and add the salt.
5. Pour the stock over the potatoes and onions and cook for another hour. The soup should be thick and creamy.
6. When ready, add the chopped parsley. Serve the soup piping hot, sprinkled with grated Parmesan cheese.

Bolliti misti con salsa verde

MIXED BOILED MEATS WITH GREEN SAUCE (Piedmont)

Preparation: 10 minutes for the green sauce
Cooking time: 3 hours

Ingredients for 6 people:

1 carrot, peeled
1 stalk of celery
1 onion
kosher salt
14 ounces beef (shoulder)
half a chicken
10½ ounces veal knuckle
1 pound tongue
table salt
olive oil

for the green sauce:
¼ cup chopped parsley
1 tablespoon salted or pickled capers
1 clove of garlic
2 salted anchovies
olive oil
2 tablespoons breadcrumbs
vinegar
salt

1. Clean the carrot and the stalk of celery, remove the outer leaves of the onion, and cut all into 2-3 pieces. Place in a pot with plenty of water and bring to a boil.
2. Boil another pot of water to cook the tongue.
3. When the water of the first pot begins to boil, add the kosher salt and the beef and cook for 2 hours. Forty minutes before the beef is cooked, add the chicken and, after 10 minutes, the veal knuckle.
4. When the water in the second pot comes to a boil, add salt and the tongue. Boil for one hour and a half.
5. In the meantime, prepare the green sauce as follows: chop together the parsley, the capers, the clove of garlic, the anchovies (wash well if you use salted anchovies), and oil. Moisten the breadcrumbs with vinegar and squeeze; add this to the other ingredients and mix well, add salt, and then cover with olive oil.
6. When the tongue is cooked, drain and remove the skin (which detaches easily if well cooked).
7. When the meats are cooked, drain and cut into slices (it is best to allow them to cool a little); arrange on a serving dish and season with salt and olive oil. Serve with green sauce.

The ideal way to boil 2½ pounds of meat is to cook it in 3 quarts of water, 1 tablespoon kosher salt, and ½ pound mixed vegetables to season the stock.

◀ *Bolliti misti con salsa verde*

Agnello alla Ligure
LAMB LIGURIAN-STYLE (Liguria)

Preparation: 10 minutes
Cooking time: 1 hour 10 minutes

Ingredients for 4 people:

1½ pound boneless lamb
2 artichokes
1 onion
4 tablespoons butter
1½ tablespoons chopped parsley
1 sprig of rosemary
salt
pepper
1 cup dry white wine
12 ounces fresh or canned peeled tomatoes
1 pound new potatoes

1. Cut the lamb into several pieces.
2. Wash the artichokes under running water, pare the tougher outer leaves, and cut off the tips. Cut the artichokes into quarters.
3. Finely chop the onion and brown in the butter together with the parsley.
4. Add the lamb, the sprig of rosemary, salt, and pepper, and fry gently on medium heat.
5. After a few minutes, add the wine and evaporate over high heat, then continue cooking the lamb on medium heat.
6. Add the artichokes and the tomatoes and cook for about 30 minutes without the lid.
7. In the meantime, peel the potatoes.
8. Heat the oven to 350°F.
9. Add the potatoes to the lamb and vegetables, and roast in the oven for 40 minutes. Serve hot.

Bocconcini di vitello con purè di patate
VEAL STEW WITH MASHED POTATOES (Various regions)

Preparation: 10 minutes for the meat
*   and 10 minutes for the potatoes*
Cooking time: 1 hour

Ingredients for 4 people:

1¼ pounds veal (neck, belly, back, shin, roast...)
2 onions
2 tablespoons butter
3 tablespoons olive oil
1 cup dry white wine
½ cup canned crushed tomatoes
¼ cup flour
1 tablespoon chopped parsley
salt
pepper

for the mashed potatoes:
1 pound potatoes
1 cup milk
4 tablespoons butter
salt

1. Boil the potatoes with their skins (about 40 minutes).
2. In the meantime, cut the meat into 1-inch cubes.
3. Slice the onions and sauté with butter and oil over medium heat; when they are brown, add the meat and fry gently for a few minutes.
4. Sprinkle the wine over the meat, mix well, and evaporate over high heat. Reduce heat to low.
5. Dilute the tomatoes with a cup and a half of water and add to the meat.
6. Sprinkle the flour and the chopped parsley over the meat, add salt and pepper, mix well, and cook for an hour over low heat.
7. In the meantime, prepare the mashed potatoes as illustrated on page 181.
8. When cooked, serve the meat on a table dish garnished with the mashed potatoes.

Carrè di maiale ai sapori
SEASONED RACK OF PORK (Alto Adige)

Preparation: 2 hours 30 minutes
Cooking time: 1 hour 30 minutes

Ingredients for 6 people:

3 leaves of sage
3 sprigs of rosemary
5 pounds center-cut pork roast
salt
pepper
2 tablespoons butter
3 tablespoons olive oil
1 jigger brandy
½ cup dry white wine

1. Chop the sage and the leaves of a small sprig of rosemary and arrange over the rack of pork.
2. Tie up the rack of meat with kitchen string, inserting two sprigs of rosemary and three leaves of sage inside.
3. Sprinkle with salt and pepper. Leave to season for about two hours.
4. Heat the butter and oil in a pan. Add the rack of pork and gently fry until it is browned all over.
5. Heat the oven to 350°F.
6. Pour the brandy over the meat while still browning and allow to evaporate. Then baste with wine.
7. Place the rack of meat and the cooking sauce in a roasting pan and cook for about one and a half hours. Baste with the sauce occasionally, and add half a cup of water at a time.
8. Turn off the oven and leave the dish in the oven for a further 10 minutes. Cut into slices, arrange on a serving plate, and season with the cooking sauce. Best served with boiled potatoes or cabbage.

The potatoes or cabbage can be cooked in the sauce in the oven together with the rack of pork.

Carrè di maiale con i crauti
RACK OF PORK WITH CABBAGE (Alto Adige)

Preparation: 5 minutes
Cooking time: 1 hour 30 minutes

Ingredients for 6 people:

3 onions
5 tablespoons butter
5 pounds center-cut pork roast
3 cups stock
¼ pound smoked *pancetta* cut into thick slices
1 apple
2¼ pounds cabbage
salt
dill seeds

1. Slice the onions and sauté in the butter with the rack of pork.
2. When the meat is browned (be careful not to burn the onions), add the stock and cook for about 20 minutes.
3. In the meantime, cut the *pancetta* into cubes and gently fry in its own fat.
4. Peel and dice the apple.
5. Heat the oven to 350°F. Add the *pancetta*, the cabbage, the apple, the salt, and the dill seeds to the meat and cook for an hour. When cooked, turn off the oven and leave the dish for a further 10 minutes. Then cut meat into slices and serve together with the cabbage.

Cotolette valdostane
VEAL CUTLETS (Valle d'Aosta)

Preparation: 15 minutes
Cooking time: 15 minutes

Ingredients for 4 people:

4 very thick slices of veal
(about 1½ pounds)
3½ ounces fontina cheese
4 slices of boiled ham
1 egg
salt
pepper
flour
breadcrumbs
5 tablespoons butter

1. Cut the slices of veal in half leaving one edge intact (like an open book).
2. Cut the fontina cheese into four slices.
3. Place a slice of cheese and a slice of ham on each slice of veal and close again.
4. Beat the egg with a pinch of salt and pepper.
5. Turn the cutlets in the flour, then in the beaten egg, and then in the breadcrumbs.
6. Heat the butter and cook the cutlets for about 15 minutes. They should become golden.

◀ *Cotolette di vitello alla valdostana*

Costata di manzo alla boscaiola
WOODSMAN'S T-BONE STEAK (Lombardy)

Preparation: 10 minutes
Cooking time: 35 minutes

Ingredients for 4 people:

10½ ounces porcini or other exotic
mushrooms
½ onion
1 clove of garlic
3 tablespoons olive oil
2 tablespoons butter
3½ ounces canned crushed
tomatoes
salt, pepper
4 t-bone steaks
½ cup stock

1. Clean the mushrooms and cut into thin slices.
2. Finely chop the onion and the clove of garlic and brown in the oil and butter in pan large enough to contain the meat.
3. Add the crushed tomatoes and mushrooms; add salt and pepper, and cook for 20 minutes.
4. Add the meat and stock and cook for ten minutes or until meat is done.

Coniglio con i peperoni
RABBIT WITH BELL PEPPERS (Piedmont)

Preparation: 15 minutes
Cooking time: 1 hour 10 minutes

Ingredients for 4 people:

1 young rabbit (about 2.6 pounds)
a little flour
4 tablespoons olive oil
2 cloves of garlic
½ cup white vinegar
1 tablespoon chopped parsley
salt
pepper
1½ cups stock
3 red and yellow bell peppers

1. Clean the rabbit, cut into pieces, wash and dry.
2. Dust these pieces in flour.
3. Heat a pan with oil and one clove of garlic. When the oil is hot, remove the clove of garlic and gently fry the pieces of rabbit.
4. Sprinkle with vinegar and evaporate over high heat.
5. Chop the other clove of garlic, mix with the parsley, and add to the rabbit.
6. Add salt and pepper and half the stock and replace the lid. Cook on low heat for 30 minutes, stirring occasionally.
7. In the meantime, clean the peppers (remove all the seeds and white fibers inside). Wash, dry, and cut into strips.
8. Add these to the rabbit after the first 30 minutes' cooking time; cook for a further 30 minutes turning the pieces of rabbit occasionally. If necessary, add the remaining stock from time to time.

Fasoi e luganeghe
BEANS AND SAUSAGES (Veneto)

Cooking time: 35 minutes

Ingredients for 4 people:

8 fresh pork sausages
½ cup dry white wine
1 onion
1 pinch of rosemary
1 clove of garlic
3 tablespoons olive oil
14 ounces boiled cannellini beans
1 tablespoon chopped parsley
salt
pepper

1. Poke the sausages all over with a fork, cut into 4-5 pieces, and cook in a pan with their own fat. After 5 minutes, add a third of the wine. Remove from heat before they are completely cooked.
2. Slice the onion, chop the leaves of rosemary, and crush the clove of garlic. Fry all these in the oil. Add the beans after a few minutes.
3. Add the sausage sauce and parsley, salt and pepper. Continue cooking on low heat for 10 minutes.
4. Add the remaining wine and the sausages and cook for an additional 10 minutes. Serve hot.

Fesa di tacchino allo speck*
TURKEY STEAKS WITH *SPECK* (Trentino)

Preparation: 10 minutes
Cooking time: 35 minutes

Ingredients for 4 people:

salt
pepper
21 ounces breast of turkey
3½ ounces *speck* (the slices should
not be too thick)
1 clove of garlic
3 tablespoons olive oil
2 tablespoons butter
½ cup dry white wine
(meat stock)

1. Salt and pepper the breast of turkey.
2. Wrap the slices of *speck* around the turkey and tie up with kitchen string.
3. Cut the clove of garlic in half. Sauté in butter and oil.
4. Remove the clove of garlic and gently fry the breast of turkey in the oil and in the butter for a few minutes.
5. Add the white wine and cook for 30 minutes, turning the turkey occasionally; add meat stock if needed.
6. When cooked, untie and cut into slices. Serve with piping hot sauce.

*Speck is a kind of smoked ham available at Italian and German delicatessens.

Fettine di fegato di vitello impanate
BREADED SLICES OF VEAL LIVER (Lombardy)

Preparation: 10 minutes
Cooking time: 10 minutes

Ingredients for 4 people:

1 egg
salt
pepper
a little flour
some breadcrumbs
1 pound veal liver, cut into thin
slices
5 tablespoons olive oil
1 lemon

1. Beat the egg with salt and pepper.
2. Place the flour in one plate and the breadcrumbs in another.
3. Dip the slices of liver in the flour, then in the egg, and then in the breadcrumbs.
4. Heat the oil in a pan and cook the liver slices until they are browned.
5. Squeeze the lemon and pour the juice over the hot liver slices before serving.

Fettine di manzo con le cipolle
BEEF AND ONIONS (Various regions)

Preparation: 5 minutes
Cooking time: 30 minutes

Ingredients for 4 people:

3 onions
4 tablespoons olive oil
5 tablespoons butter
1 cup stock
4 slices of beef
salt
pepper

1. Slice the onions very thinly and cook for about 10 minutes in the oil with half of the butter; add the stock little by little.
2. Cook the slices of beef for a minute or two in the remaining butter and then add the remaining stock. Bring the sauce to a boil for a few minutes; add the meat sauce continuously. Salt and pepper. Serve hot.

Frico
COOKED CHEESE (Friuli-Venezia Giulia)

Preparation: 10 minutes
Cooking time: 10 minutes

Ingredients for 4 people:

7 ounces soft fresh cheese, such as fresh mozzarella
7 ounces "stravecchio" cheese, such as Montasio, Parmesan, or Asiago
1 onion
5 tablespoons butter
salt
pepper

1. Cut the cheese into slices.
2. Chop the onion and cook on low heat in the butter for a few minutes.
3. Add the cheese, salt and pepper, and brown over higher heat, stirring continually with a wooden spoon until everything is crisp.
4. Cook on the other side and serve immediately.

A "stravecchio" cheese is an aged grating cheese.

◀ *Frico*

Frittata con la salsiccia

SAUSAGE OMELETTE (Various regions)

Preparation: 15 minutes
Cooking time: no more than 10 minutes

Ingredients for 4 people:

6 eggs
salt
pepper
2 tablespoons milk
2 tablespoons grated Parmesan cheese
3½ ounces sausages (or salami)
2 tablespoons olive oil

1. Beat the eggs for 5 minutes with a pinch of salt and pepper, milk, and Parmesan cheese (you can use an electric mixer).
2. Cut the sausage or salami into small pieces and gently fry in their own fat for 5-10 minutes.
3. Mix the eggs and sausages.
4. Grease a non-stick pan with oil, bring to heat, and add the eggs and sausage. Cook for a few minutes on low heat.
5. When cooked on one side, slide on to a plate or lid and then flip over onto the other side in the pan. When cooked on this side, serve hot.

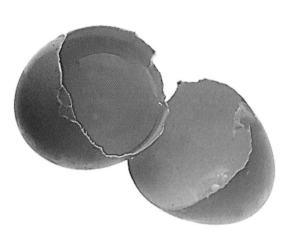

Gulasch tirolese

TYROLEAN GOULASH (Alto Adige)

Preparation: 5 minutes
Cooking time: 1 hour

Ingredients for 4 people:

1-1½ pounds rump of beef
1 onion
½ cup olive oil
7 ounces canned peeled tomatoes
1 clove of garlic
salt
paprika
1½ cups stock

1. Dice the meat 1¼-inch cubes.
2. Finely slice the onion and sauté in the oil. When browned, add the meat, the peeled tomatoes, the clove of garlic, salt, and flavor with paprika.
3. Add the stock and mix well. Cover with the lid and cook for about one hour, stirring occasionally to avoid sticking.

Gulash should be rather spicy and is best served with boiled or roast potatoes.

Lepre in salmì

JUGGED HARE (Veneto)

Preparation: 24 hours
Cooking time: 2 hours 30 minutes

Ingredients for 4 people:

3 cups red wine
4 bay leaves
4 cloves
pepper
salt
1 tenderized hare
2 onions
5 tablespoons olive oil
5 tablespoons butter
3 tablespoons sugar
grated lemon rind
4 juniper berries
(1 tablespoon flour)
(cup of red wine)

1. Boil the wine for 20 minutes with the bay leaves, cloves, a few grains of pepper, and a pinch of salt. Take the "marinade" off the heat after 20 minutes and set aside to cool.
2. In the meantime, prepare the hare as necessary (it is preferable to buy it ready to cook) and cut into pieces. When the marinade has cooled a little, add the pieces of hare and marinate for about 24 hours.
3. Slice the onions and sauté in the oil in a casserole large enough to hold the jugged hare.
4. Gently fry the pieces of hare in butter in another pan.
5. Add the pieces of hare to the onions and cover completely with the marinade. Add the sugar, the grated lemon rind, and the juniper berries. Boil over low heat for two and a half hours. Check cooking progress and stir occasionally.
6. When cooked, arrange the pieces of hare on a serving dish.
7. Strain the cooking sauce; if is too liquid, add a tablespoon of flour and mix well. If it is too thick, add a little red wine. When serving, pour the hot sauce over the pieces of hare.

▼ *Lepre in salmì*

Lonza di maiale al latte
PORK LOIN IN MILK (Various regions)

Preparation: 10 minutes
Cooking time: 1 hour

Ingredients for 4 people:

2 onions
3 ounces cured ham cut into 3
slices
4 tablespoons olive oil
2 tablespoons butter
1 bay leaf
1-1½ pounds loin of pork
1¾ cup milk
salt
nutmeg
3 tablespoons grated Parmesan
cheese

1. Finely slice the onions.
2. Cut the ham into strips
3. Heat the oil and the butter with the bay leaf, the onions and the ham. When hot, gently fry the pork to brown it all over.
4. Heat the milk separately and then add it hot to the meat. Add salt, a pinch of grated nutmeg, and Parmesan cheese. Then cover and cook on medium heat for about one hour, turning the meat occasionally.
5. When cooked, pass the sauce through a blender.
6. Allow the pot roast to cool and then slice (if cut while still hot, the meat will disintegrate). Serve the hot slices (you can warm in a little cooking sauce before serving) and pour the hot sauce over the meat.

Polenta côncia
POLENTA WITH CHEESE (Piedmont)

Preparation: 20 minutes resting for the polenta; 20 minutes
Cooking time: 1 hour

Ingredients for 4 people:

5 cups water
salt
1 pound cornmeal (polenta)
7 ounces fontina cheese
7 tablespoons butter
7 ounces gorgonzola cheese
1 cup white wine

1. Boil the water and add salt. As soon as it comes to a boil (but do not bring to a rolling boil, otherwise, the polenta will form lumps) sprinkle the cornmeal (polenta) into the water. Mix well and whip to avoid forming lumps. When well mixed, stir with a wooden spoon and cook for at least one hour over high heat, stirring frequently.
2. When cooked, pour onto a wooden serving board or similar surface and allow to set for 20 minutes.
3. Cut the fontina cheese into 8 slices.
4. Grease a pan with a little butter.
5. If the polenta has set sufficiently well, cut it into 8 slices and arrange in the pan; otherwise simply place the polenta whole on the base of the pan. Spread the gorgonzola cheese over the polenta and then arrange the slices of fontina cheese.
6. Heat the oven to 350°F.
7. Melt the remaining butter.
8. Sprinkle the melted butter and wine over the polenta.
9. Heat in the oven until the cheese melts. Serve piping hot.

◀ *Lonza di maiale al latte*

Polenta taragna
BUCKWHEAT FLOUR POLENTA (Lombardy)

Cooking time: 1½ hours

Ingredients for 4 people:

5 cups water
salt
1 pound buckwheat flour
¼ cup corn flour
14 tablespoons butter
7 ounces fontina cheese

1. Boil the water and add salt. As soon as it comes to a boil (but do not bring to a rolling boil, otherwise, the polenta will form lumps) sprinkle the two types of flour (polenta) into the water. Mix well with a whisk to avoid forming lumps. When well mixed, stir with a wooden spoon and cook for at least one hour over high heat, stirring frequently.
2. Ten minutes before the polenta is ready, add the butter and mix well.
3. Dice the cheese and mix with the polenta off the heat. Pour the polenta on to a wooden serving board and serve piping hot.

This polenta dish is a meal in itself, but can be served with sausages if preferred.

Polenta tirolese
TYROLEAN POLENTA (Alto Adige)

Cooking time: 1 hour

Ingredients for 4 people:

5 ounces smoked *pancetta*
5 ounces Italian sausages
3 tablespoons butter
5 cups water
salt
1 pound corn flour
3 tablespoons grated Parmesan cheese

1. Cut the *pancetta* into cubes and slice up the sausages.
2. Cook the *pancetta* and sausage meat in 2 tablespoons butter.
3. Boil the water and add salt. As soon as it comes to a boil (but do not bring to a rolling boil; otherwise the polenta will form lumps) sprinkle the flour (polenta) into the water. Mix well with a whisk to avoid forming lumps. When well mixed, stir with a wooden spoon and cook for 15 minutes over a high heat.
4. Add the well-fried *pancetta* and sausage, mix well, and cook for a further 30 minutes.
5. In the meantime, grease an oven-proof dish with the remaining butter and heat the oven to 350°F.
6. Remove the polenta from heat and mix in Parmesan cheese.
7. Pour the polenta into the dish and bake for 15-20 minutes. Serve piping hot.

Rosticciata

PORK LOIN WITH SAUSAGES (Lombardy)

Preparation: 10 minutes
Cooking time: 20 minutes

Ingredients for 4 people:

**14 ounces pork loin cut into thin
slices
a little flour
1 pound onions
14 ounces Italian sausages
2 tablespoons butter
1 tablespoon tomato sauce
salt**

1. Mix the slices of pork in the flour.
2. Finely chop the onions and cut the sausages into pieces. Gently fry the onions and the sausages in the butter.
3. Add the tomato sauce, 2 tablespoons water, and a pinch of salt (the sausages are already salted so be careful not to add too much salt).
4. Add the slices of pork and cook for 15 minutes. Halfway through the cooking, turn the slices of pork over.
5. Serve piping hot with polenta.

Salsiccia con i crauti

SAUSAGES AND CABBAGE (Trentino-Alto Adige)

Preparation: 5 minutes
Cooking time: 1 hour

Ingredients for 4 people:

**1 onion
2 ounces smoked *pancetta* (one
slice)
2 tablespoons olive oil
2 tablespoons butter
1 apple
1 pound cabbage
1½ cups vegetable stock
a few dill seeds
salt
4 Italian sausages**

1. Prepare the cabbages as shown in the recipe on page 84.
2. Cut the sausages into 4-5 pieces and add to the cabbage after 30 minutes cooking time; then cook for another 30 minutes. Serve hot.

Pollo alla contadina
YEOMAN'S CHICHEN (Various regions)

Preparation: 5 minutes
Cooking time: 40 minutes

Ingredients for 4 people:

1 chicken cut into 4 pieces
a little flour
2 ounces *pancetta*
1 tablespoon olive oil
1 sprig of rosemary
½ cup dry white wine
1 bouillon cube
salt
pepper
10½ ounces Brussel sprouts
½ pound small, flat onions
1 tablespoon chopped parsley

1. Dip the chicken pieces in the flour.
2. Cut the *pancetta* into strips and gently fry in the oil with the sprig of rosemary.
3. Heat one and a half cups of water.
4. Add the pieces of chicken to the *pancetta* and sprinkle with white wine. Evaporate the wine over high heat, then reduce heat to low.
5. Remove the sprig of rosemary and moisten with the boiling water.
6. Break the bouillon cube into the chicken, add salt and pepper, and mix. Cook over low heat 30 minutes, turning occasionally.
7. In the meantime, boil a pot of water for the vegetables.
8. Clean the sprouts and the small onions.
9. When the water comes to a boil, add salt and the vegetables. Cook for 15 minutes.
10. Drain the vegetables and add to the chicken. Cook together for a further 10 minutes.
11. Serve hot and sprinkle with chopped parsley.

Scaloppine al prezzemolo
VEAL CUTLETS WITH PARSLEY (Lombardy)

Preparation: 5 minutes
Cooking time: 8 minutes

Ingredients for 4 people:

21 ounces thin slices of veal
a little flour
4 tablespoons butter
lemon juice
2 tablespoons chopped parsley
salt

1. Dip the veal slices in the flour.
2. Melt the butter in a pan and cook the slices of veal on one side.
3. When cooked on the first side, turn and add the lemon juice and the parsley. Salt and serve hot.

◀ *Pollo alla contadina*

75

Spezzatino di manzo con le verze

BEEF STEW WITH GREEN CABBAGE (Various regions)

Preparation: 10 minutes
Cooking time: 40 minutes

Ingredients for 4 people:

1¼–1½ pounds rump of beef
half a green cabbage
1 large onion
1 clove of garlic
4 tablespoons olive oil
2 tablespoons butter
3½ ounces tomato purée
salt
pepper

1. Cut the beef into 1¼-inch cubes.
2. Remove the cabbage core and carefully wash the leaves, then cut into strips.
3. Slice the onion finely and sauté with the clove of garlic in the oil and butter.
4. Add the meat and fry gently for a few minutes.
5. Add the tomato, salt, and pepper, and cook for 40 minutes.
6. After the first 10 minutes, add the cabbage.
7. Serve the stew piping hot.

Vitello tonnato

VEAL IN TUNA SAUCE (Lombardy)

Preparation: 30 minutes
Cooking time: 1 hour 15 minutes

Ingredients for 4 people:

1 carrot, peeled
1 stalk of celery
1 onion
1½ pounds rump of veal

for the sauce:
2 egg yolks at room temperature
salt
1 cup peanut oil at room temperature
juice of half a lemon
5 ounces tuna in oil
4 anchovies in oil
2 ounces capers

1. Clean the carrot and celery and remove the outer leaves of the onion. Cut these into 3-4 pieces.
2. Place the vegetables in plenty of water and when it comes to a boil add the veal and cook for one hour.
3. In the meantime, prepare the tuna sauce. First prepare the mayonnaise as follows: beat the egg yolks with a pinch of salt in a bowl using a wooden spoon, stirring slowly and always in the same direction; add the oil a drop at a time until a firm and regular mixture is made; then add the lemon juice. Chop the tuna finely with the anchovies and the capers. Mix this carefully with the mayonnaise.
4. When the meat is cooked, cool and cut into thin slices.
5. Arrange the slices of veal on a serving dish and cover completely with the tuna sauce. Garnish with a few capers and serve cold.

There are many variants of this recipe in Lombardy and Piedmont; this is one of the most common.

Luccio arrosto
ROAST PIKE (Various regions)

Preparation: 10 minutes
Cooking time: 35 minutes

Ingredients for 4 people:

2¼ pounds whole pike
(a freshwater fish), cleaned and
scaled
salt
1 bay leaf
1 sprig of parsley
1 sprig of rosemary
olive oil
pepper
½ cup dry white wine

1. Heat the oven to 350°F.
2. Season the inside of the pike with salt, bay leaf, parsley, and rosemary.
3. Rub the outside with oil and sprinkle with salt and pepper.
4. Grease an oven-proof dish and arrange the pike; sprinkle with the wine and cook for 35 minutes.

Pesce Persico alla Lombarda
PERCH LOMBARD-STYLE (Lombardy)

Preparation: 10 minutes
Cooking time: 10 minutes

Ingredients for 4 people:

1 egg
salt, pepper
2¼ pounds fillets of perch
(a freshwater fish), cleaned
and scaled
flour
breadcrumbs
6 tablespoons butter

1. Beat the egg with salt and pepper.
2. Dip the fillets in the flour, then in the egg, and then in the breadcrumbs.
3. Heat the butter and then fry the fillets for 5 minutes per side.

Sgombri con i piselli

MACKEREL WITH PEAS (Various regions)

Preparation: 10 minutes
Cooking time: 30 minutes

Ingredients for 4 people:

salt
4 medium mackerel (sea fish),
cleaned and scaled
pepper
1 onion
3 tablespoons olive oil
2 tablespoons butter
14 ounces frozen or canned peas
1 tablespoon chopped parsley
½ cup tomato sauce, homemade or
canned

1. Salt the inside of the mackerel and sprinkle the outside with salt and pepper.
2. Slice the onion thinly and sauté in the oil and butter in a large pan.
3. Gently fry the mackerel in the onion.
4. Add the peas and parsley.
5. Dilute the tomato sauce with a little hot water and pour over the mackerel. Cover the pan and cook for 30 minutes. Check progress and turn occasionally.

Trota bollita

BOILED TROUT (Various regions)

Preparation: 1 hour
Cooking time: 25 minutes

Ingredients for 4 people:

1 carrot, peeled
1 onion
salt
1 stalk of celery
1 sprig of parsley
1 bay leaf
2¼ pounds whole rainbow trout
(freshwater fish), cleaned and scaled

1. Cut the carrot, celery, and onion into pieces.
2. Fill an oval fish pan (or other suitable pan) with water, salt, add the vegetables, parsley, and bay leaf.
3. Boil for an hour on low heat.
4. When the stock has boiled for an hour, place the trout in the pan and cook for about 25 minutes (the cooking time depends on the size of the fish).
5. Serve the trout piping hot, accompanied by boiled vegetables.

◀ *Trota bollita*

Trota al forno con patate

TROUT BAKED WITH POTATOES (Various regions)

Preparation: 30 minutes
Cooking time: 15 minutes

Ingredients for 4 people:

6 potatoes
8 fillets of trout (about 2¼
pounds)
3 tablespoons olive oil
2 tablespoons butter
salt
pepper
½ cup dry white wine
1 tablespoon chopped parsley

1. Boil the potatoes whole but do not cook entirely.
2. Fry the trout fillets well in the oil and butter.
3. Heat the oven to 350 °F.
4. Peel the potatoes and cut into thin slices.
5. Grease an oven-proof dish and arrange alternating layers of trout fillets and potatoes, finishing with potatoes. Sprinkle with salt, pepper, and white wine. Bake for 15 minutes.
6. Serve the trout fillets hot, sprinkled with chopped parsley.

Bietole alle acciughe
BEETS WITH ANCHOVIES (Various regions)

Preparation: 15 minutes
Cooking time: 20 minutes

Ingredients for 4 people:

2¼ pounds fresh beets
salt
3 tablespoons butter
1 clove of garlic
2 anchovy fillets

1. Peel the beets and place in a pot of water with a little salt and bring to a boil.
2. Boil the beets for 20 minutes.
3. When the beets are ready, drain well.
4. Fry the clove of garlic and the anchovy fillets in a pan until they dissolve.
5. Add the beets, mix, and leave to flavor for 5 minutes. Serve hot.

Spinach can be cooked in the same way.

*Carote allo speck**
CARROTS WITH *SPECK* (Various regions)

Preparation: 10 minutes
Cooking time: 50 minutes

Ingredients for 4 people:

1 pound carrots
2½ ounces smoked *speck*
1 chopped onion
4 tablespoons butter
1 bouillon cube
⅔ cup heavy cream
salt
pepper

1. Peel and clean the carrots and thinly slice.
2. Cut the *speck* into cubes.
3. Finely chop the onion and sauté in the butter.
4. Add the carrots and cook for 5 minutes.
5. Add the *speck*, a cup of water, and the bouillon cube.
6. Add the heavy cream, salt, pepper, and cook over low heat for 40 minutes.

*Speck is a kind of smoked ham available at Italian and German delicatessens.

Carciofi ripieni
STUFFED ARTICHOKES (Friuli-Venezia Giulia)

Preparation: 15 minutes
Cooking time: 45 minutes

Ingredients for 4 people:

4 young artichokes (without thorns)
juice of half a lemon
1 clove of garlic
1½ ounces slice of *pancetta*
6 tablespoons breadcrumbs
2 tablespoons grated Parmesan cheese
1 heaping tablespoon chopped parsley
salt
pepper
olive oil

1. Remove the tougher outer leaves of the artichokes. Cut off the tips and open out a little; then wash under running water and soak for a while in the water with the lemon juice so that they do not darken in color.
2. Cut the clove of garlic in half and chop finely.
3. Chop the *pancetta* finely.
4. Prepare the stuffing by mixing the breadcrumbs, the chopped garlic, the *pancetta*, the grated Parmesan cheese, the chopped parsley, and a pinch of salt and pepper.
5. Drain the artichokes and cut off the stalks at the base; then stuff the tops of the artichokes.
6. Arrange the artichokes upright and side by side in a pan. Add the stalks cut into pieces. Douse with plenty of olive oil, add a little water to the base, and cook for 45 minutes. Baste the artichokes occasionally with the cooking sauce.

Cipolline al forno in agro dolce
BAKED SWEET AND SOUR ONIONS (Veneto)

Preparation: 5 minutes
Cooking time: 20 minutes

Ingredients for 4 people:

1 pound onions
2 tablespoons butter
1 tablespoon oil
½ tablespoon sugar
salt
1 tablespoon vinegar

1. Remove the outer leaves of the small onions.
2. Rinse and place in an oven dish with butter and oil.
3. Sprinkle with sugar and add salt and vinegar. Mix well and bake for 20 minutes at 400°F. Mix the onions occasionally while cooking.

◀ *Carciofi ripieni*

Crauti
SOUR CABBAGE (Trentino-Alto Adige)

Preparation: 5 minutes
Cooking time: 1 hour

Ingredients for 4 people:

1 onion
2 ounces smoked *pancetta*
(one slice)
2 tablespoons olive oil
2 tablespoons butter
1 apple
1 pound sour cabbage
1½ cups vegetable stock
a few seeds of dill
salt

1. Slice the onion, cut the *pancetta* into cubes, and fry in the oil and butter in a pot large enough to contain the cabbage.
2. Peel the apple, remove the core, and cut into small pieces.
3. Add the cabbage, the apple, the cup of stock, a few seeds of dill, and a pinch of salt. Cook for one hour.

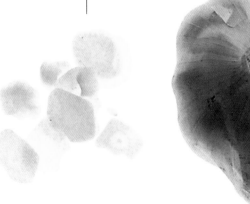

Fagiolini in salsa di pomodoro
GREEN BEANS IN TOMATO SAUCE (Various regions)

Preparation: 10 minutes
Cooking time: 40 minutes

Ingredients for 4 people:

1½ pounds green beans
half an onion
3 tablespoons olive oil
3½ ounces smoked *pancetta* in a thick slice
1⅓ cups stock
1 pound canned peeled tomatoes
salt

1. Top and tail the beans; wash.
2. Finely chop the onion and sauté in the oil. When the onion has browned, add 2 tablespoons water.
3. Add the beans and cook with the lid on about 10 minutes, stirring frequently.
4. Cut the *pancetta* into cubes.
5. Heat the stock.
6. Add the tomatoes, the *pancetta,* and the stock to the beans. Add salt and cook for 30 minutes over low heat.

Finocchi alla Piemontese

FENNEL PIEDMONT-STYLE (Piedmont)

Preparation: 5 minutes
Cooking time: about 45 minutes

Ingredients for 4 people:

8 fennel bulbs
milk
1 bay leaf
salt
3½ ounces fontina cheese
butter
breadcrumbs
2 tablespoons grated Parmesan
cheese

1. Wash the fennel carefully and remove the outer leaves if they are tough, then cut into quarters.
2. Place the fennel in a pan and cover with the milk, adding the bay leaf and salt. Stir frequently.
3. While the fennel is cooking, cut the fontina cheese into cubes and grease an oven-proof dish with butter.
4. When the fennel is cooked, remove from heat and remove the bay leaf. Heat the oven to 350°F.
5. Add the fontina cheese to the fennel, mix well, arrange in the dish, and smooth off. Sprinkle with the breadcrumbs and the grated Parmesan cheese and bake in the oven.
6. When the top has browned a little, take out of the oven and serve hot.

Mozzarella cheese can be used instead of fontina.

Funghi trifolati

TRUFFLED MUSHROOMS (Various regions)

Preparation: 15 minutes
Cooking time: 30 minutes

Ingredients for 4 people:

1¾ pounds fresh white mushrooms
1 clove of garlic
3 tablespoons butter
2 tablespoons olive oil
½ cup beef stock
salt
pepper
1 tablespoon chopped parsley

1. Clean the mushrooms carefully and cut into thin slices.
2. Sauté the clove of garlic in 2 tablespoons butter and the oil.
3. Add the mushrooms and a little stock. Add salt and pepper and cook on low heat for 30 minutes.
4. A minute or two before the mushrooms are ready, add remaining butter and parsley, and mix well.

Cavolfiore alla besciamella
CAULIFLOWER IN WHITE SAUCE (Various regions)

Preparation: 20 minutes
Cooking time: 30 minutes to boil the cauliflower; 15 minutes in the oven

Ingredients for 4 people:

1 cauliflower (about 2¼ pounds)
salt
½ cup grated Parmesan cheese
2 tablespoons butter
2 tablespoons breadcrumbs

for the white sauce:
4 tablespoons butter
½ cup flour
2 cups cold milk
½ tablespoon salt

1. Remove the green leaves and the stalk from the cauliflower.
2. Bring water to a boil, add salt, and immerse the cauliflower. Cook for 30 minutes.
3. In the meantime, prepare the white sauce as illustrated on page 35; mix with the grated cheese.
4. Heat the oven to 400°F.
5. Grease an oven-proof dish with butter.
6. Drain the cauliflower and cut into 5-6 pieces.
7. Arrange the pieces of cauliflower in the dish and cover with the white sauce. Sprinkle with the breadcrumbs and add a few pats of butter; bake for 15 minutes.

◄ *Cavolfiore alla besciamella*

Patate alla Triestina
POTATOES TRIESTE-STYLE (Friuli-Venezia Giulia)

Preparation: 45 minutes
Cooking time: 10 minutes

Ingredients for 4 people:

2¼ pounds potatoes
1 onion
4 tablespoons butter
½ cup vegetable stock
salt
pepper

1. Place the potatoes in a pot of cold water, bring to a boil, and cook for 40 minutes.
2. In the meantime, chop the onion very finely.
3. Drain the potatoes, peel, and cut into pieces.
4. Sauté the onion in the butter and add the potatoes and stock when brown. Add salt and pepper.
5. Crush the potatoes with a fork and continue cooking over low heat. Serve piping hot.

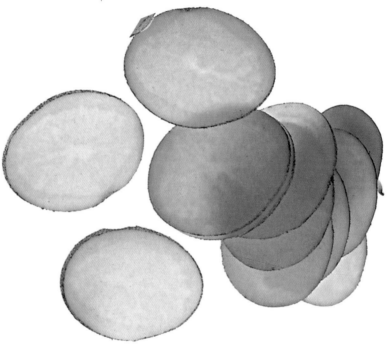

Patate al forno
ROAST POTATOES (Various regions)

Preparation: 10 minutes
Cooking time: 1½ hours

Ingredients for 4 people:

2½ pounds potatoes
3 pats of butter
3 tablespoons olive oil
1 sprig of rosemary
salt

1. Peel and wash the potatoes. Dry and cut into cubes.
2. Place the potatoes in an oven-proof dish with butter, oil, and the sprig of rosemary. Add salt.
3. Cook at 400°F for 1 hour 30 minutes.

Patate al formaggio parmigiano
Boiled potatoes with Parmesan cheese (Various regions)

Cooking time: 45 minutes

Ingredients for 4 people:

2¼ pounds potatoes
6 tablespoons butter
¾ cup grated Parmesan cheese
salt
pepper

1. Place the potatoes in a pot of cold water, bring to a boil, and cook for 40 minutes.
2. When cooked, drain and peel the potatoes.
3. Heat the butter in a small pan.
4. Arrange the potatoes on a serving plate and crush with a fork. Sprinkle with Parmesan cheese and pour the melted butter over them. Salt and pepper. Mix well and serve hot.

Spinaci alla Genovese
Spinach Genoa-style (Liguria)

Preparation: 20 minutes
Cooking time: 10 minutes

Ingredients for 4 people:

⅓ cup raisins
2¼ pounds spinach
salt
2 anchovy fillets
4 tablespoons olive oil
⅓ cup pine nuts
pepper

1. Soften the raisins in lukewarm water.
2. Clean the spinach carefully.
3. Bring a pot of water to a boil and then add salt and the spinach. Cook for 10 minutes. Drain and squeeze when cooked.
4. Heat the anchovy fillets in the oil and when they have dissolved, add the spinach, the well-squeezed raisins, and the pine nuts. Add salt and pepper, mix well, and cook for 10 minutes.

Peperonata
MIXED BELL PEPPERS (Veneto)

Preparation: 20 minutes
Cooking time: 1 hour

Ingredients for 4 people:

1 green bell pepper
1 red bell pepper
1 yellow bell pepper
1 eggplant
2 onions
2 tomatoes
1 potato
1 clove of garlic
1 tablespoon chopped parsley
olive oil
½ cup vegetable stock
salt
pepper
½ tablespoon sugar

1. Wash and cut all the vegetables into cubes (peel and grate the potato).
2. Place in a pot and add the whole clove of garlic, the parsley, olive oil, stock, salt, and pepper. Cook with the lid on for 30 minutes, stirring occasionally.
3. Remove the lid, add the sugar, and cook until all the liquid is absorbed (at least 30 minutes). Serve hot or at room temperature.

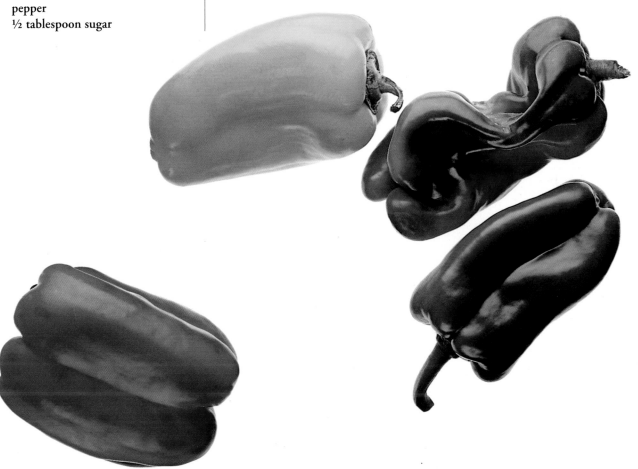

◀ *Peperonata*

Amaretti

ALMOND COOKIES (Piedmont)

*Preparation: 30 minutes; 2 hours
    resting*
Cooking time: 40 minutes

Ingredients for 30-40 amaretti:

10 ounces whole almonds
1⅓ cups sugar
¼ cup white flour
2-3 egg whites
½ cup powdered sugar

1. Heat the oven to 200°F.
2. Bring a pot of water to a boil.
3. Scald the almonds in the boiling water, peel them, and dry in the oven.
4. Chop the almonds with a little sugar (you can use a blender).
5. Mix the chopped almonds, the remaining sugar, the flour, and add the egg whites a little at a time. Mix for 10 minutes.
6. Place a sheet of aluminum foil over a baking sheet.
7. Place little heaps of the mixture spaced out on the foil (they will expand as they cook).
8. Sprinkle with the powdered sugar and set aside for 2 hours.
9. Heat the oven to 250°F.
10. Bake in the hot oven for 40 minutes.

Biscotti all'uvetta

ALPINE COOKIES (Various regions)

Preparation: 20 minutes
Cooking time: 15 minutes

Ingredients for 60 cookies:

⅔ cup raisins
10 tablespoons butter
4 heaping tablespoons sugar
1 whole egg and 1 egg yolk
2 cups flour
2 teaspoons baking powder

1. Soften the raisins in lukewarm water.
2. Work the butter and sugar together well.
3. Add the whole egg, the yolk, and the flour and mix well.
4. Squeeze the raisins and mix with the other ingredients.
5. Add the baking powder and mix well.
6. Heat the oven to 350°F.
7. Grease a baking sheet with butter or cover with foil.
8. Pour spoonfuls of the mixture on the sheet to make about 60 cookies.
9. Bake for about 15 minutes.

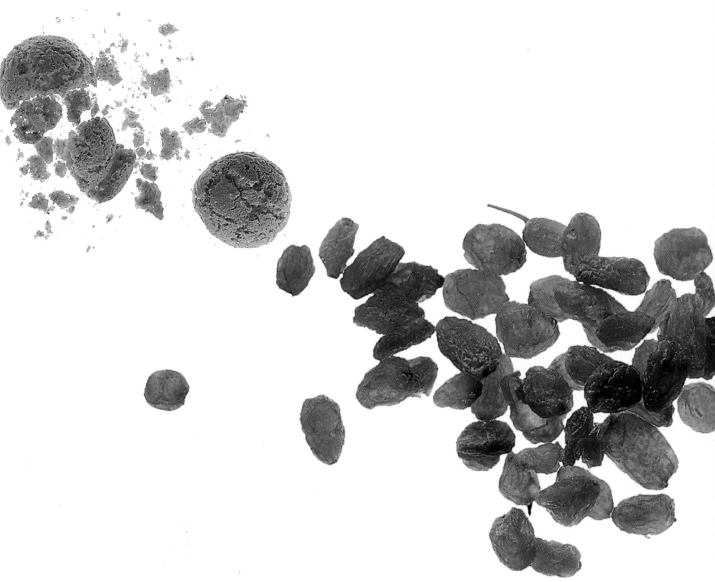

Crostoli

FRIED PASTRIES (Friuli-Venezia Giulia)

Preparation: 1 hour
Cooking time: frying time

Ingredients for 6 people:

2 cups flour
2 eggs
4 tablespoons softened butter
¼ cup superfine sugar
½ cup milk
3 tablespoons grappa (a liqueur like
schnapps); you can also use
sherry or port, marsala, or rum
a pinch of salt
plenty of frying oil
½ cup powdered sugar

1, Arrange a heap of flour on the table top and make a hollow in the top; pour in the eggs, the softened butter, the superfine sugar, the milk, the liqueur, and a pinch of salt. Work the dough for some time until it can be rolled out.
2. Roll out the dough to a thickness of about 1/10 inch.
3. Use a pastry wheel to cut out various rectangular shapes about 1.5 inches wide by 3 inches long and make a cut in the middle. If you prefer, you can cut out strips two fingers wide and "knot" them.
4. Heat the oil in a wide pan and fry 2-3 crostoli at a time without browning them excessively.
5. When cooked, remove from the oil and place on paper towels.
6. Arrange on a serving plate and sprinkle with powdered sugar.

These crisp pastries are made all over Italy but every region has its own shape and name ("galani" in the Veneto, "bugie" in Piedmont and Liguria, "chiacchiere" or "cenci" in Tuscany, "frappe" or "flappe" in Umbria, to mention only a few).

Mele al forno

BAKED APPLES (Various regions)

Preparation: 15 minutes
Cooking time: 30 minutes

Ingredients for 4 people:

4 round, tart baking apples
(Granny Smith, Cortland, etc.)
1½ ounces almonds
1½ ounces pecans or walnuts
3 tablespoons butter
3 tablespoons sugar
3 tablespoons brandy

1. Wash, dry, and core the apples (making a hole only at the top).
2. Peel the almonds after scalding them for a few moments in boiling water, then chop them together with the pecan or walnuts.
3. Work the butter with a wooden spoon until it is soft, add the sugar, almonds, chopped nuts, and brandy.
4. Heat the oven to 400°F.
5. Fill the apples with this mixture. Decorate with a few slivers of almond.
6. Grease an oven-proof dish with butter and sprinkle with sugar; arrange the apples and bake for about 30 minutes.
7. Serve lukewarm or cold.

◀ *Crostoli*

Dolce di mele
APPLE PIE (Various regions)

Preparation: 50 minutes
Cooking time: about 45 minutes

Ingredients for 6-8 people:

2 pounds baking apples
3 tablespoons sugar
a little lemon rind
2 cups flour
½ cup sugar
1 whole egg
7 tablespoons butter, softened
2 teaspoons baking powder
1 teaspoon rum
a pinch of salt
a little butter
a little flour
1 egg yolk

2. Cook the apples in very little water with the sugar and the lemon rind for 20 minutes. Then remove the lemon rind and leave the apples to cool.
3. Mix the flour, sugar, the whole egg, butter, baking powder, rum, and a pinch of salt and knead well.
4. Butter and flour a medium size pie plate and heat the oven to 375°F.
5. Arrange two-thirds of the dough on the base and sides of the pie plate.
6. When the apples are cool, place them in the pie plate.
7. Shape the remaining dough into a round piece and cover the pie, making sure to close the edges well so that the apples remain inside the pie itself.
8. Beat the egg yolk and brush over the top of the pie.
9. Then prick the top with a fork and bake for about 45 minutes.

Frittelle di mele
APPLE FRITTERS (Alto Adige)

Preparation: 20 minutes
Cooking time: frying time

Ingredients for 6 people:

4 apples
¾ cup flour
1 egg
2 tablespoons sugar
1 cup milk
a pinch of cinnamon
a pinch of salt
1½ teaspoons baking powder
cooking oil for frying
½ cup powdered sugar

1. Peel and core the apples and cut into very thin round slices.
2. Prepare a batter with the flour, egg, sugar, milk, pinch of cinnamon, pinch of salt, and the baking powder. Mix well.
3. Heat the frying oil well.
4. When the oil boils, immerse the apple rings in the batter and fry on one side and then the other. As soon as they are golden, remove with a slotted spoon and drain on paper towels.
5. Arrange on a serving plate and sprinkle with powdered sugar. Serve hot.

Fritole
FRITTERS (Veneto)

Preparation: 30 minutes; 3 hours rising
Cooking time: frying time

Ingredients for 6 people:

1 cup raisins
1 package (2¼ tsp) active dry yeast
2 cups milk
17½ ounces (about 3½ cups) flour
2 eggs
6 tablespoons grappa (you can also use rum)
scant ½ cup sugar
grated lemon rind
a pinch of powdered cinnamon
a pinch of salt
cooking oil for frying
¼ cup vanilla sugar

1. Soften the raisins in lukewarm water.
2. Dissolve the yeast in a little lukewarm milk.
3. Use a wooden spoon to mix well in a bowl the flour, eggs, the remaining milk, the grappa or rum, sugar, grated lemon rind, a pinch of cinnamon, and a pinch of salt.
4. Add to this dough the well-squeezed raisins and the yeast dissolved in the milk and mix until it is very soft. Cover the mixing bowl with a cloth and allow to rise for three hours in a warm place.
5. When the dough has risen, mix the ingredients again and add a little water or milk if it is not fluid enough.
6. Heat the frying oil in a pan and then add spoonfuls of the mixture, well-separated so that they do not stick together. Fry the fritole on one side and then turn over until they become nut-colored. Remove with a slotted spoon and drain on paper towels. Continue in the same way to fry all the mixture.
7. Arrange on a serving plate and sprinkle with vanilla sugar. They are best eaten warm but are just as delicious when a little cooler.

Pere cotte al vino rosso
PEARS BAKED IN RED WINE (Piedmont)

Preparation: 15 minutes
Cooking time: 40 minutes

Ingredients for 6 people:

6 pears
½ cup sugar
¾ cup red wine (Barolo is best)
½ cup of water

1. Peel the pears but do not cut off the stem.
2. In a pan tall enough to hold the pears upright, dissolve the sugar in the wine and water over medium heat.
3. When the syrup begins to boil, add the pears. Sprinkle the pears with sugar and cook for 40 minutes, basting them every now and then with the syrup.
4. Serve cold.

Pesche ripiene
STUFFED PEACHES (Piedmont)

Preparation: 15 minutes
Cooking time: 40 minutes

Ingredients for 6 people:

6 peaches
12 amaretti biscuits
¾ cup sugar
¼ cup unsweetened cocoa
½ cup wine
butter

1. Wash the peaches, cut them in half, and remove the pit.
2. Chop the amaretti and mix with the sugar, cocoa, and wine.
3. Butter an oven-proof dish and arrange the peach halves with the cut part upward.
4. Heat the oven to 350°F.
5. Fill each peach with the mixture.
6. Add a pat of butter to each peach.
7. Add a little water to the base of the dish and bake for 40 minutes.

Salame di cioccolato
CHOCOLATE SALAMI (Various regions)

Preparation: 20 minutes; 4 hours in the refrigerator

Ingredients for 6 people:

7 ounces Italian biscotti
7 tablespoons butter, at room temperature
¾ cup powdered sugar
⅔ cup unsweetened cocoa
3 egg yolks
4 tablespoons sweet liqueur as preferred

1. Break the biscotti into pieces.
2. Work the butter with a wooden spoon until it is creamy.
3. Add the sugar, cocoa, egg yolks, and liqueur and mix well.
4. Then add the broken biscotti.
5. Shape the mixture into a salami shape by hand.
6. Wrap the "salami" in foil and place in the refrigerator for 4 hours.
7. Remove the foil and serve sliced.

Children love this treat; you can leave out the liqueur if making it for them.

◄ *Salame di cioccolato*

99

Torta al cioccolato

CHOCOLATE CAKE (Various regions)

Preparation: 20 minutes
Cooking time: 40 minutes

Ingredients for 6-8 people:

6 tablespoons butter
3 eggs, separated
½ cup plus 1 tablespoon sugar
½ cup unsweetened cocoa
3 tablespoons milk
4½ ounces potato starch
a pinch of salt
2 teaspoons baking powder
a little butter
a little flour
¼ cup powdered sugar

1. Melt the butter.
2. Work the egg yolks and sugar together to make a cream.
3. Add the cocoa, milk, potato starch, a pinch of salt, and the baking powder and mix well.
4. Add the butter (not too hot) and mix.
5. Heat the oven to 375°F.
6. Whip the egg whites and then blend delicately with the rest of the mixture.
7. Butter and flour a medium size cake pan.
8. Pour the mixture into the cake pan and bake for 40 minutes.
9. When baked, sprinkle with powdered sugar.

Torta alle mandorle semplice

ALMOND CAKE (Veneto)

Preparation: 25 minutes
Cooking time: 30 minutes

Ingredients for 6-8 people:

7 ounces almonds
4 eggs, separated
1 scant cup sugar
½ cup cornstarch
2 teaspoons baking powder
a pinch of salt
juice of 1 orange
grated rind of half an orange
a little butter
a little flour
¼ cup powdered sugar

1. Chop the almonds.
2. Work the egg yolks and sugar together to make a cream.
3. Add the cornstarch, almonds, baking powder, a pinch of salt, the orange juice, and the grated orange rind.
4. Whip the egg whites and add to the mixture.
5. Heat the oven to 350°F.
6. Butter and flour a medium size cake pan.
7. Pour the mixture into the pan and bake for 30 minutes.
8. When baked, sprinkle with powdered sugar.

Torta alle nocciole

HAZELNUT CAKE (Piedmont)

Preparation: 20 minutes
Cooking time: about 30 minutes

Ingredients for 6-8 people:

7 ounces shelled and roasted
hazelnuts
4 tablespoons butter, softened
½ cup plus 1 tablespoon sugar
3½ ounces (about ¾ cup) flour
¾ cup cornstarch
2 eggs
½ cup milk
grated lemon rind
2 teaspoons baking powder
a little butter - a little flour
¼ cup powdered sugar

1. Chop the nuts finely.
2. Mix the butter and sugar well in a bowl.
3. Stir in the flour, cornstarch, eggs, milk, grated lemon rind, and baking powder. Add the nuts and mix well. Add more milk if the ingredients do not blend properly.
4. Heat the oven to 375°F.
5. Butter and flour a medium size cake pan.
6. Pour the mixture into the pan and bake for 25-30 minutes.
7. When baked, allow to cool and sprinkle with powdered sugar.

Strudel

APPLE STRUDEL (Trentino-Alto Adige)

Preparation: 1 hour
Cooking time: 1 hour

Ingredients for 8 people:

for the pastry:
4 tablespoons butter
9 ounces (about 1¾ cups) flour
1 tablespoon sugar
a pinch of salt
1 egg

for the filling:
⅓ cup raisins
1¾ pounds apples
2½ tablespoons pine nuts
2 tablespoons grated lemon rind
¼ cup sugar
a pinch of cinnamon
2 tablespoons butter
a little butter
¼ cup powdered sugar to garnish

1. Melt the butter.
2. Prepare a heap of flour and make a hole in the top; add the sugar, a pinch of salt, the egg, and the melted butter. Knead the dough for 20 minutes. If the dough is not soft enough, add a little water. Set aside to rise for 30 minutes in a warm place, covering the mixing bowl with a moist cloth and standing it on an upside-down pot.
3. While the dough rises, you can prepare the filling. First, soften the raisins in lukewarm water.
4. Peel and core the apples and cut into thin slices.
5. Mix the apples, well-squeezed raisins, pine nuts, grated lemon rind, sugar, and a pinch of cinnamon.
6. Dust a non-stick cloth with flour and roll out the pastry very thinly.
7. Melt butter and brush over the pastry.
8. Cover the pastry with the filling.
9. Heat the oven to 350°F.
10. Roll up the pastry inside the cloth. Close both ends well so that the filling cannot ooze out.
11. Butter a baking sheet, place the strudel on top, and remove the cloth. Bake for one hour.
12. When baked, cool and sprinkle with powdered sugar.

◀ *Strudel*

103

Torta autunnale

AUTUMN CAKE (Various regions)

Preparation: 40 minutes
Cooking time: 25 minutes

Ingredients for 6-8 people:

3 eggs, separated
⅓ cup sugar
1 teaspoon vanilla extract
3 ounces (about ¾ cup) flour
a little butter
a little flour

for the garnish:
6 tablespoons zabaione (see recipe on page 107)
1 bunch of seedless white grapes
1 bunch of seedless red grapes
2 tablespoons apricot jam

1. Work the egg yolks, sugar, and vanilla for some time with a wooden spoon until a foamy mixture is made.
2. Add the flour little by little.
3. Whip the egg whites and fold into the mixture.
4. Heat the oven to 350°F.
5. Butter and flour a medium size cake pan.
6. Pour the mixture into the pan and bake for 25 minutes.
7. In the meantime, prepare the zabaione following the recipe on page 107.
8. Wash the grapes.
9. When the cake is ready, pour the zabaione over it and then garnish with the white and red grapes in alternate rows.
10. Melt the jam in a small pan over medium heat with a tablespoon of water.
11. Brush the cake with the jam.

Torta genovese

CAKE GENOA-STYLE (Liguria)

Preparation: 25 minutes
Cooking time: 40 minutes

Ingredients for 6-8 people:

4 tablespoons butter
5 eggs
⅔ cup sugar
1 cup flour
1 teaspoon baking powder
a pinch of salt
1 teaspoon grated lemon rind
a little butter
a little flour
¼ cup powdered sugar

1. Melt the butter without over-heating it and then set aside to cool.
2. Beat the eggs and sugar in a bowl until well blended.
3. Warm the beaten eggs in a double-boiler, stirring continually. When they have doubled in volume, remove from the heat.
4. Gradually add the flour, baking powder, butter, a pinch of salt , and the grated lemon rind.
5. Heat the oven to 350°F.
6. Butter and flour a medium size cake pan.
7. Pour the mixture into the pan and bake for 40 minutes.
8. When baked, cool and sprinkle with powdered sugar.

Torta con le mandorle

ALMOND CAKE (Liguria)

Preparation: 40 minutes
Cooking time: 1 hour 15 minutes

Ingredients for 6-8 people:

for the shortcake:
3½ ounces (about ¾ cup) flour
¼ cup sugar
salt
a little grated lemon rind
4 tablespoons butter, softened
1 egg yolk

for the filling:
a little butter
a little flour
10½ ounces whole almonds
3 whole eggs and 3 egg yolks
1 cup plus 2 tablespoons sugar
1 scant cup cornstarch
2 teaspoons baking powder
½ cup milk
4 tablespoons butter, softened
¼ cup powdered sugar

1. Prepare the shortcake as follows. Prepare a heap of flour and make a hollow in the top. Add sugar, a pinch of salt, the lemon rind, the softened butter, and the egg yolk and knead carefully.
2. Butter and flour a large cake pan.
3. Arrange the shortcake on the base of the pan (it will be thin but serves only as a base).
4. Chop the almonds finely.
5. Whip the three whole eggs and the three egg yolks together with the sugar (use an electric blender). The mixture should be very foamy.
6. Heat the oven to 350°F.
7. Gradually and gently mix the whipped eggs with the cornstarch, the baking powder, the crushed almonds, milk, and 4 tablespoons butter.
8. Pour the mixture into the cake pan on top of the pastry and bake for one hour 15 minutes.
9. Leave the cake to cool and sprinkle with powdered sugar.

There are a great many variants to this recipe. Ours is a typical one.

Torta di mele

APPLE TART (Various regions)

Preparation: 25 minutes
Cooking time: 1 hour

Ingredients for 6-8 people:

⅔ cup raisins
4 large baking apples
9 ounces (about 2 cups) flour
1 cup sugar
4 tablespoons butter, softened
1 egg
1½ cups milk
2 teaspoons baking powder
grated lemon rind
salt
a little butter
a little flour
¼ cup powdered sugar

1. Soften the raisins in lukewarm water, and drain well.
2. Peel and core the apples and cut into thin slices.
3. Mix well together the flour, sugar, butter, egg, milk, baking powder, raisins, lemon rind, and a pinch of salt.
4. Heat the oven to 350°F.
5. Add two-thirds of the apple slices to the mixture and mix well.
6. Butter and flour a medium size cake pan.
7. Pour the mixture into the pan, arrange the remaining apple slices on top in a spoke-like pattern, and bake for one hour.
8. When baked, sprinkle with powdered sugar. The cake is best served hot.

◀ *Torta di mele*

Zabaione

WINE EGG CUSTARD (Piedmont)

Preparation: 10 minutes
Cooking time: about 20 minutes

Ingredients for 4 people:

2 egg yolks
⅓ cup sugar
⅓ cup marsala wine (or white wine)
1 egg white

1. Whisk the egg yolks together with the sugar and marsala wine for 10 minutes.
2. Heat this cream in a double-boiler, mixing continually without bringing to a boil.
3. When the mixture is properly whipped to a dense foam, remove from the heat.
4. Whisk the egg white to soft peaks and mix with the zabaione.
5. Pour the zabaione into 4 goblets. Garnish with Italian biscotti.

Zabaione is also delicious cold; keep in the refrigerator for a couple of hours and enjoy with whipped cream.

Torta marmorizzata
MARBLE CAKE (Alto Adige)

Preparation: 25 minutes
Cooking time: 50 minutes

Ingredients for 6-8 people:

14 tablespoons butter, at room
    temperature
1 scant cup sugar
3 eggs, separated
10½ ounces (about 2 cups) flour
½ cup milk
grated rind of half a lemon
2 teaspoons baking powder
a pinch of salt
2 tablespoons unsweetened cocoa
1 tablespoon rum

1. Work the butter and sugar together well with a wooden spoon.
2. Add the egg yolks one at a time and continue to mix.
3. Add a little flour, while still mixing, then the milk and the lemon rind. Add the rest of the flour, the baking powder and a pinch of salt.
4. Whisk the egg whites until firm but not dry.
5. Fold the egg whites into the flour mixture.
6. Divide the batter into two parts and add the cocoa to one part (if the cocoa is too bitter, add a little sugar) together with the rum.
7. Heat the oven to 350°F.
8. Butter a tube pan and dust with flour.
9. Pour in the white half of the mixture and then the dark mixture with the cocoa.
10. Bake for 50 minutes.

Tortelli alla Milanese
MILANESE CAKES (Lombardy)

Preparation: 25 minutes
Cooking time: frying time

Ingredients for 6-8 people:

1⅓ cup water
5 tablespoons butter
a pinch of salt
1 cup flour
3 tablespoons vanilla sugar
grated lemon rind
3 eggs
cooking oil for frying
⅓ cup powdered sugar

1. Heat the water, butter, and salt in a saucepan.
2. When this comes to a boil, remove from heat. Add the flour and mix well with a wooden spoon.
3. Return the mixture to the heat and continue mixing for about 10 minutes until it hardens and sticks to the sides of the saucepan.
4. Remove from the heat, add the vanilla sugar and the grated lemon rind, and mix well.
5. Add one egg at a time and mix well.
6. Heat plenty of cooking oil in a pan.
7. When the oil is hot but not boiling, add small, cherry-sized pieces of the mixture a little apart from each other. When browned, remove with a slotted spoon and drain on paper towels. Fry the rest of the mixture in the same way.
8. Arrange the cakes on a serving dish and sprinkle with powdered sugar.

Torta paradiso
PARADISE CAKE (Lombardy)

Preparation: 25 minutes
Cooking time: 45 minutes

Ingredients for 6-8 people:

14 tablespoons butter
1⅔ cups powdered sugar
4 eggs, separated
¾ cup flour
¾ cup finely ground cornmeal
a pinch of salt
grated rind of one lemon
a little butter
a little flour
¼ cup powdered sugar

1. Work the butter into a cream with a wooden spoon.
2. Gradually add the sugar and mix well.
3. Beat the 4 egg yolks and 2 egg whites.
4. Slowly blend the beaten eggs with the rest of the mixture making sure it is completely absorbed.
5. Sift together the flour, cornmeal, and salt. Gradually add to the batter.
6. Add the grated lemon rind.
7. Heat the oven to 350°F.
8. Butter and flour a medium size cake pan and pour in the mixture (make sure that it fills the pan by more than two-thirds).
9. Bake for 45 minutes.
10. Serve the cake sprinkled with powdered sugar.

This cake is an ideal snack for young children.

Ciambella con l'uva sultanina
RING-SHAPED CAKE WITH RAISINS (Various regions)

Preparation: 15 minutes
Cooking time: 50 minutes

Ingredients for 6-8 people:

⅔ cup raisins
14 tablespoons butter, softened
1 scant cup sugar
¾ cup finely ground cornmeal
about 1¾ cup flour
a pinch of salt
2 teaspoons baking powder
3 egg yolks
a little butter
a little flour
¼ cup powdered sugar

1. Soften the raisins in a bowl of lukewarm water and heat the oven to 350°F.
2. Mix the butter in a bowl with the sugar, cornmeal, flour, and salt.
3. Add the baking powder and, one at a time, the egg yolks (if the dough becomes too hard, add a little egg white). Last, add the well-drained raisins.
4. Butter and flour a tube pan and pour in the mixture; bake for about one hour.
5. Serve the cake sprinkled with powdered sugar.

Zelten

CANDIED FRUIT CAKE (Trentino-Alto Adige)

Preparation: 1 hour; 12 hours resting
Cooking time: 40 minutes

Ingredients for 8-10 people:

½ cup raisins
2 ounces dry figs
⅓ cup walnuts
⅓ cup pine nuts
⅓ cup almonds
1½ ounces candied lime
1½ ounces candied orange
2 oranges
1 cup rum
a pinch of cinnamon
6 tablespoons butter, softened
10½ ounces (about 2 cups) flour
⅔ cup sugar
3 egg yolks
2 teaspoons baking powder
½ cup milk
a little butter
a little flour
3 tablespoons honey
dried and candied fruits as
preferred for garnishing

1. Wash and dry the raisins.
2. Cut the dry figs into tiny pieces.
3. Chop the walnuts, the pine nuts, and the almonds (not too finely).
4. Cut the candied lime and orange into small pieces.
5. Squeeze the juice from two oranges.
6. Place the dry and candied fruit to marinate in the orange juice and rum, adding a pinch of cinnamon, for 12 hours.
7. When the fruit has marinated, prepare the pastry.
8. Mix the flour with the butter, sugar, egg yolks, and baking powder. Slowly add the milk. Knead the dough well.
9. Drain the fruit and mix with the dough.
10. Heat the oven to 350°F.
11. Butter and flour a medium baking sheet.
12. Divide the dough into 8 parts, flatten into oval shapes, and place on the baking sheet.
13. Warm the honey with a little water and baste over the zelten.
14. Bake for 40-45 minutes.
15. Remove from the oven and garnish with large pieces of fruit. Zelten are best enjoyed cold and even better a few days after they have been made.

You can make a large number of zelten because they store well if wrapped in aluminum foil or plastic wrap.

The Po Plains

Cape sante alla Veneziana
SCALLOPS VENETIAN-STYLE (Veneto)

Preparation: 25 minutes
Cooking time: 15 minutes

Ingredients for 4 people:

12 large scallops in the shell
1 clove of garlic
1 cup olive oil
a sprig of parsley
2 tablespoons dry white wine
1 lemon
salt
pepper

1. Open each shell with a knife holding the flat side upward.
2. Remove the meat from each shell and then eliminate the gray and black parts.
3. Carefully wash the meat to eliminate all residue of sand. Also wash 4 concave half-shells to serve the cooked dish.
4. Gently fry the garlic in the oil in a pan; when it begins to brown, remove.
5. Pour the sea food into the hot oil and brown well on both sides.
6. Add the chopped parsley, the wine, and a little lemon juice. Add a little salt and pepper.
7. Turn off the heat. Place the cooked sea food on the washed shells and serve immediately.

◀ *Carpaccio*

Carpaccio
THINLY SLICED RAW BEEF WITH MUSHROOMS (Veneto)

Preparation: 15 minutes

Ingredients for 4 people:

10½ ounces raw beef fillets
5 ounces whole Parmesan cheese
¼ pound white mushrooms
a little olive oil
1 lemon

1. Slice the fillets very thinly. Arrange the slices of meat on four plates.
2. Cut the cheese into paper-thin flakes and arrange over the meat.
3. Wash and dry the mushrooms; cut them into thin slices and arrange over the dish.
4. Add a little olive oil and lemon juice to each plate. Serve.

Crostini affumicati
SMOKED CROSTINI (Various regions)

Preparation: 15 minutes
Cooking time: 5 minutes

Ingredients for 4 people:

4 slices of smoked ham
4 slices of homemade bread
4 walnuts
2 ounces ricotta cheese
2 egg yolks
salt
pepper
1½ ounces provolone cheese

1. Heat the oven to 300°F.
2. Arrange a slice of ham on each slice of bread. Cut the ham so that it is the same shape as the bread.
3. Chop the remaining ham with the walnuts and then add the ricotta cheese and the egg yolks; add a little salt and pepper and mix well.
4. Spread the mixture on top of the ham on the slice of bread; sprinkle with grated provolone cheese.
5. Place the crostini in the oven for 4-5 minutes, until the cheese begins to melt. Serve immediately.

Formaggio fritto con le uova
FRIED CHEESE WITH EGGS (Friuli-Venezia Giulia)

Preparation: 5 minutes
Cooking time: 15 minutes

Ingredients for 4 people:

10½ ounces low-fat cheese
a little finely ground cornmeal
8 tablespoons butter
4 eggs

1. Cut the cheese into slices and turn in the meal.
2. Heat a pan and melt 6 tablespoons of butter; when the butter is hot, fry the cheese slices well.
3. In the meantime, melt the remaining butter in another pan and fry the eggs.
4. Serve the fried eggs with the cheese.

Uova farcite
STUFFED EGGS (Lombardy)

Preparation: 10 minutes
Cooking time: 15 minutes

Ingredients for 4 people:

4 boiled eggs
2 ounces tuna, preferably in olive oil
1 anchovy fillet
1 tablespoon mayonnaise

1. Place the eggs in a pot, cover with cold water, and bring to a boil. Boil for 6-8 minutes.
2. Cool the eggs under running water and then shell them and cut them in half.
3. Remove the hard-boiled yolks and mix them together well with the tuna and anchovies. Add mayonnaise and mix well.
4. Fill a pastry bag with this mixture and fill the hard-boiled egg whites. Keep in the refrigerator until served.

116

Piadina romagnola
PITA BREAD ROMAGNA-STYLE (Emilia-Romagna)

Preparation: 1 hour
Cooking time: about 30 minutes

Ingredients for 6 people:

17½ ounces (about 3½ cups) flour
1½ ounces brewer's yeast
salt
1 tablespoon cooking fat
5 ounces cured ham

1. Heap the flour on the work-top and make a hollow in the center. Dissolve the yeast in half a cup of lukewarm water and add to the flour.
2. Add salt and cooking fat and knead the ingredients well, adding lukewarm water until the dough is like that used to make bread.
3. Wrap the dough in a clean cloth and allow to rise for 30-40 minutes.
4. Roll out the dough 1/10 inch thick and prepare disks about 6 inches in diameter.
5. Cook these disks on a stone or cast iron griddle (or a heavy metal pan).
6. Remove the piadina from the pan, cover with ham slices, and serve immediately.

Polenta con formaggio e soppressa
POLENTA WITH CHEESE & COUNTRY STYLE SALAMI (Veneto)

Preparation: 5 minutes
Cooking time: 15 minutes

Ingredients for 4 people:

2 tablespoons butter
4 slices precooked polenta
(see page 71)
4 slices "soppressa" (country style salami)
4 slices cheese (such as "Asiago")

1. Melt the butter in a pan and gently fry the slices of polenta for 8-10 minutes, turning frequently.
2. Place a slice of "soppressa" on each piece of polenta and cover this with the cheese.
3. Cover with the lid and cook over a medium heat until the cheese melts (about 5 minutes). Serve immediately.

117

Sardelle "in saòr"

SAVORY SARDINES (Veneto)

Preparation: 30 minutes; 48 hours
marinating
Cooking time: 5 minutes; frying time

Ingredients for 4 people:

17½ ounces fresh sardines (or red
mullet or small sole)
a little white flour
olive oil
salt
2 large onions
1 cup vinegar

1. Carefully clean the sardines, remove the scales, the insides, the fins and, if you prefer, the head. Wash, drain well, and then dip in the flour.
2. Fry the sardines in plenty of hot oil until they are brown on both sides; remove them from the pan and dry on paper towels; add salt.
3. Remove the oil from the pan and wipe carefully with a paper towel; then pour half a cup of fresh oil into the pan.
4. Cut the onions into thin slices and then fry them gently in the oil on very low heat.
5. When the onions have browned, add the vinegar and boil for a few minutes to make a thick sauce.
6. Arrange a layer of sardines in a pan and cover with a layer of sauce; then add another layer of sardines and another layer of sauce and so on. The sardines should be completely covered by the sauce when the dish is ready.
7. Cover the pan and marinate in a cool place for about 48 hours.

If preferred, pine nuts and raisins can be added to the sardines before pouring the sauce over them (as the ancient Venetians used to do). "In saòr" means "savory."

Tigelle

STUFFED FOCACCIA WITH ROSEMARY AND GARLIC (Emilia-Romagna)

Preparation: 30 minutes; one hour
resting
Cooking time: frying time

Ingredients for 6 people:

2 teaspoons active dry yeast
14 ounces (about 3 cups) flour
⅓ cup cooking fat
1 teaspoon salt
plenty of oil for frying
1 sprig of rosemary
1 clove of garlic
1 tablespoon lard

1. Dissolve the yeast in 1 cup lukewarm water.
2. Heap the flour on the work-top and add the cooking fat, diluted yeast, and salt. Knead the dough well to a good consistency.
3. Wrap the dough in a kitchen towel and allow to rise for about one hour in a dry place.
4. Roll out the dough to about 1/10 inch in thickness. Cut out disks around 4 inches in diameter.
5. Heat plenty of oil in a pan and fry the disks until they begin to brown. Drain well and cut each disk in half.
6. Chop the rosemary together with the garlic, then add the lard and mix everything together well.
7. Spread this mixture over one of the halves, close with the other half, and serve hot.

◀ Tigelle

119

Cannelloni ripieni
FILLED CANNELLONI (Emilia-Romagna)

Preparation: 15 minutes
Cooking time: 1 hour

Ingredients for 4 people:

1 small onion
1 carrot, peeled
1 stalk of celery
⅓ cup olive oil
9 ounces ground beef
salt
pepper
1 pound cannelloni
2 tablespoons grated Parmesan cheese
1 egg
2 tablespoons butter

1. Chop the onion, the carrot, and the celery; place in a casserole with the oil and fry gently for a few minutes.
2. Add the ground beef. Add salt and pepper and cook on medium heat for about 30 minutes.
3. Heat plenty of water in a pot. When it comes to a boil, add salt and the cannelloni; cook until still firm to the bite and drain.
4. When the sauce is ready, remove from the heat and allow to cool slightly. Then add half of the Parmesan cheese and the egg and stir.
5. Heat the oven to 400°F.
6. Fill the cannelloni with three-quarters of the sauce. Butter an oven-proof dish and arrange the cannelloni in it. Cover with the remaining sauce; sprinkle with Parmesan cheese and pats of butter.
7. Bake in the oven for 15-20 minutes. Serve immediately.

Bigoli* con le sarde
BIGOLI PASTA WITH SARDINES (Veneto)

Preparation: 15 minutes
Cooking time: 25 minutes

Ingredients for 4 people:

7 ounces fresh sardines
2½ tablespoons olive oil
1 clove of garlic
salt
14 ounces bigoli

1. Clean the sardines, eliminating the scales, innards, and bones. Wash and dry carefully and then chop finely.
2. Boil plenty of water to cook the pasta.
3. Heat the oil in a small pan and sauté the garlic for 4-5 minutes.
4. Remove the garlic and add the chopped sardines. Cover and cook over low heat for about 10 minutes, stirring occasionally.
5. When the water comes to a boil, add salt and the pasta and cook until they are still a little firm to the bite (5-8 minutes). Drain and flavor with the fish sauce. Serve immediately.

*Bigoli are very thick spaghetti and are generally made at home. Spaghetti can be used instead.

◄ *Cannelloni ripieni*

Bigoli* all'anatra
BIGOLI PASTA WITH DUCK SAUCE (Veneto)

Preparation: 20 minutes
Cooking time: 1 hour 30 minutes

Ingredients for 4 people:

1 young duck, cut into 6-8 pieces,
with giblets
2 carrots, peeled
1 onion
1 stalk of celery
salt
4 tablespoons butter
5-6 sage leaves
pepper
14 ounces dark (whole wheat)
bigoli
4 tablespoons grated Parmesan
cheese

1. Place the duck in a pot with plenty of cold water. Add all the vegetables and salt and bring to a boil. Then boil for one hour.
2. Cut the giblets into small pieces. Gently fry in butter with the sage in a frying pan.
3. Add the chopped giblets and some of the liquid the duck is cooking in. Add salt and pepper and cook over low heat for about 30 minutes.
4. When the duck is cooked, remove from the pot and drain, reserving the liquid.
5. Bring the stock back to a boil and then add the bigoli. Cook for 5-8 minutes so that the bigoli are still a little firm to the bite.
6. Drain the bigoli, flavor with the giblets and Parmesan cheese. Mix well and serve.

*Bigoli are very thick spaghetti and are generally made at home. Spaghetti can be used instead.
The duck can be served as a main course with "pearà" bread sauce (see page 181).

Gnocchetti di ricotta
SMALL GNOCCHI WITH RICOTTA CHEESE (Veneto)

Preparation: 45 minutes
Cooking time: 3 minutes

Ingredients for 6 people:

1 cup white flour
1¼ cup grated Parmesan cheese
salt
1 pound fresh ricotta cheese
5 eggs
3 tablespoons butter

1. Bring plenty of water to a boil in a pot.
2. Heap the flour and 1 cup of Parmesan cheese on a work-top; add a pinch of salt, ricotta, four whole eggs, and one egg yolk. Knead the ingredients well.
3. Prepare rolls of dough (about ½ inch in diameter). Cut each roll into pieces about 1 inch long.
4. When the water boils, add salt and then cook the gnocchi for about 3 minutes.
5. Drain the gnocchi a few at a time and flavor with butter and Parmesan cheese; serve.

Crêpes di ricotta e spinaci

CRÊPES WITH RICOTTA CHEESE AND SPINACH (Various regions)

Preparation: about 1 hour
Cooking time: 30 minutes

Ingredients for 4 people:

for the crêpes:
1 cup flour
1¼ cups milk
2 eggs
1 tablespoon olive oil
salt
a little butter for frying

for the filling:
14 ounces frozen spinach
salt
14 ounces fresh ricotta cheese
½ cup grated Parmesan cheese
a pinch of nutmeg
pepper

plus:
2 tablespoons butter

1. Place the flour in a bowl and mix gradually with the milk.
2. Add the eggs, the oil, and a little salt; beat with a whisk. Set aside for about 30 minutes.
3. In the meantime, place the spinach in a pot with a little salted water and cook over medium heat.
4. When the spinach is ready, chop and place it in a bowl.
5. Add the ricotta cheese, the Parmesan cheese, nutmeg, salt and pepper. Mix well and place the bowl in the refrigerator.
6. When the batter is ready, prepare the crêpes. Lightly butter the base of a pan. Heat well and then pour in enough batter to cover the base of the pan.
7. Cook over low heat and turn the crêpe when almost ready on the first side. When ready, slide onto a serving plate. Prepare all the crêpes in this way.
8. Heat the oven to 400°F.
9. Spread a little of the ricotta and spinach mixture over the crêpes; roll them up and place them side by side in the oven tray.
10. Add pats of butter and bake in the oven for 15 minutes. Serve immediately.

▼ *Crêpes di ricotta e spinaci*

Gnocchi alla Veronese

GNOCCHI VERONESE-STYLE (Veneto)

Preparation: 1 hour 30 minutes
Cooking time: 20 minutes

Ingredients for 4 people:

1¾ pounds potatoes (preferably all the same size)
1½ cups flour
salt
6 tablespoons butter
a pinch of sugar
a pinch of cinnamon
½ cup grated Parmesan cheese

1. Boil the potatoes whole, peel, and mash.
2. Mix the mashed potatoes on a work-top with the flour and a pinch of salt. Knead the dough well.
3. Roll the dough into fingers and then cut into pieces about 1 inch long.
4. Roll these over the back of a cheese grater to shape.
5. Place the gnocchi separately on a cloth or floured work-top.
6. Bring plenty of salted water to a boil in a pot; add the gnocchi and cook until they float to the surface (about three minutes).
7. Remove the gnocchi from the water a few at a time with a slotted spoon. Leave them to drain and arrange on individual plates.
8. Melt the butter in a small pan and add 1½ tablespoons to each portion of gnocchi.
9. Add a pinch of sugar and a pinch of cinnamon; season with plenty of Parmesan cheese.

This is the original Veronese recipe, which is not so popular today. Tastes change over time and the modern preference is to prepare these gnocchi with tomato sauce (see page 333).

◀ *Gnocchi alla Veronese*

HOW TO PREPARE POTATO GNOCCHI

Lasagne al forno

BAKED LASAGNA (Emilia-Romagna)

Preparation: about 1 hour
Cooking time: about 2 hours

Ingredients for 6 people:

for the pasta:
14 ounces (about 3 cups) flour
4 eggs
salt

for the meat sauce:
1 medium onion
1 carrot, peeled
1 stalk of celery
1 clove of garlic
4 tablespoons butter
3 tablespoons olive oil
1 pound ground beef
½ cup dry white wine
½ cup stock
9 ounces canned peeled tomatoes
salt

for the white sauce:
4 tablespoons butter
⅓ cup flour
3 cups milk
salt
a pinch of nutmeg

plus:
½ cup grated Parmesan cheese
a little butter

1. Prepare the sauce. Wash and finely chop the onion, the carrot, the celery, and the garlic.
2. Melt the butter and oil in a casserole; then add the chopped vegetables and sauté over low heat for 5 minutes.
3. Add the ground beef and cook for 15 minutes, stirring frequently.
4. Add the wine to the meat and allow it to evaporate. Add the stock, the tomatoes, and a pinch of salt. Stir and replace the lid. Cook on a very low heat for at least 1 hour. Stir occasionally.
5. While the sauce cooks, prepare egg pasta (see page 10).
6. Roll out the pasta very thinly and cut out rectangles of the same size as the oven dish.
7. Boil plenty of water in a large, wide pot to cook the pasta.
8. In the meantime, prepare the white sauce as explained in the recipe on page 35.
9. When the water comes to a boil, add salt and cook the lasagne a few at a time. Drain on a clean cloth.
10. Heat the oven to 400°F.
11. When the sauce is ready, remove from the heat. Butter an oven-proof dish and place one piece of pasta inside. Spread a layer of meat sauce over the top.
12. Arrange another layer of lasagne and cover this with a little white sauce and Parmesan cheese. Continue in the same way until all the lasagne are used. Pour the meat and white sauces and plenty of Parmesan cheese on top of the last layer.
13. Bake in the oven for about 20 minutes and serve.

Lasagne verdi al forno
BAKED GREEN LASAGNA (Emilia-Romagna)

Preparation: about 1 hour
Cooking time: about 2 hours
15 minutes

Ingredients for 6 people:

for the pasta:
14 ounces (about 3 cups) flour
14 ounces spinach
4 eggs
salt

for the meat sauce:
see recipe on page 126

for the white sauce:
see recipe on page 126

plus:
½ cup grated Parmesan cheese
a little butter

1. Prepare the meat sauce as described in the recipe on page 126.
2. Prepare the pasta. Boil the spinach in salted water. When ready, squeeze well and purée in a blender.
3. Heap the flour on a work-top. Add the spinach, the eggs, and the salt. Knead the ingredients well and allow to rise for a few minutes.
4. Roll out the dough very thinly and cut out rectangles of the same size as the oven dish.
5. Boil plenty of water in a large, wide pot to cook the pasta.
6. In the meantime, prepare the white sauce (see page 126).
7. When the water comes to a boil, add salt and cook the lasagne a few at a time. Drain on a clean cloth.
8. Heat the oven to 400°F.
9. Butter an oven dish. Arrange the first layer of lasagne and cover with a layer of meat sauce. Arrange the second layer of lasagne and then add a layer of white sauce, sprinkle with Parmesan cheese.
10. Continue in the same way until all the lasagne are used; finally, cover the top with white sauce and plenty of Parmesan cheese.
11. Bake in the oven for about 20 minutes and serve.

▼ *Lasagne verdi al forno*

Maccheroni ai quattro formaggi
MACARONI WITH FOUR CHEESES (Lombardy)

Preparation: 5 minutes
Cooking time: 30 minutes

Ingredients for 6 people:

salt
1½ pounds grooved macaroni
3½ ounces gorgonzola cheese
3½ ounces fontina cheese
3½ ounces Emmenthal cheese
6 tablespoons butter
1 cup milk
a little nutmeg
½ cup grated Parmesan cheese

1. Bring plenty of water to a boil in a pot. When it boils, add salt and then cook the macaroni as required.
2. In the meantime, dice the gorgonzola, fontina, and Emmenthal.
3. Melt the butter in a non-stick pan. Add the diced cheeses and mix continuously.
4. Add ½ cup of lukewarm milk to this sauce. Add a little salt and a little nutmeg; mix well.
5. Drain the macaroni and arrange in a bowl. Flavor immediately with ½ cup hot milk and grated Parmesan cheese.
6. Then add the cheese sauce and mix quickly. Serve immediately.

Maccheroni al gorgonzola
MACARONI WITH GORGONZOLA CHEESE (Lombardy)

Preparation: 5 minutes
Cooking time: 30 minutes

Ingredients for 4 people:

salt
1 pound macaroni
4 tablespoons butter
10½ ounces gorgonzola cheese
½ cup milk

1. Bring plenty of water to a boil in a pot. When it boils, add salt and then cook the macaroni as required.
2. Melt the butter in a non-stick saucepan.
3. Dice the gorgonzola and add to the butter. Add the milk and a pinch of salt.
4. Mix with a wooden spoon until the gorgonzola melts.
5. Drain the macaroni and mix with the cheese sauce. Serve immediately.

Maccheroni alla Bolognese

MACARONI BOLOGNESE (Emilia-Romagna)

Preparation: 10 minutes
Cooking time: 50 minutes

Ingredients for 4 people:

½ onion
1 carrot, peeled
half a stalk of celery
2 ounces *pancetta*
4 tablespoons butter
¼ pound ground beef
2 cloves
salt
pepper
½ cup stock
1 pound macaroni
4 tablespoons grated Parmesan
cheese

1. Wash and finely chop the onion together with the carrot and celery. Chop the *pancetta*.
2. Place the butter and chopped vegetables in a pan and sauté for a few minutes on low heat.
3. Then add the ground beef, *pancetta*, and cloves. Add salt and pepper.
4. Add the stock, mix well, and cover. Cook for about 40 minutes, stirring occasionally.
5. Bring plenty of water to a boil. When the water comes to a boil, add salt and the macaroni; cook firm.
6. Then drain the macaroni, mix with the sauce and Parmesan cheese. Serve immediately.

Ofelle alla Triestina

HOMEMADE POTATO PASTA TRIESTE-STYLE (Friuli-Venezia Giulia)

Preparation: 1 hour 15 minutes
Cooking time: 45 minutes

Ingredients for 4 people :

for the pasta:
2¼ pounds potatoes
7 ounces (about 1½ cups) flour
1 tablespoon powdered yeast
salt
1 egg

for the filling:
1 pound spinach
5 ounces ground veal
3½ ounces Italian sausage
salt
1 small onion
2 tablespoons butter (approx.)

to flavor:
7 tablespoons butter
½ cup grated Parmesan cheese

1. Wash the potatoes and boil whole.
2. In the meantime, boil the spinach in salted water; when ready, drain and chop finely.
3. Place the spinach in a bowl; add the veal and sausage; salt and mix.
4. Chop the onion. Melt 2 tablespoons butter in a pan. Add the onion and sauté for a few minutes.
5. Then add the meat and the spinach and cook for 20-30 minutes, stirring occasionally.
6. Peel the boiled potatoes and blend them; arrange on a work-top.
7. Mix the potatoes with the flour, the yeast, salt, and egg. Mix well and then roll out.
8. Bring plenty of water to a boil in a pot to cook the ofelle.
9. Cut the rolled-out potato mixture into 3-inch squares and then make ravioli as explained on page 12.
10. Cook the ofelle in the boiling water for a few minutes.
11. Melt remaining butter separately.
12. Drain the ofelle, flavor with melted butter and Parmesan cheese.

The ofelle can also be cooked in boiling stock. Again, they should be drained and flavored with butter and Parmesan cheese.

Pasta in salsa di noci
PASTA WITH WALNUTS (Veneto)

Preparation: 10 minutes
Cooking time: 25 minutes

Ingredients for 4 people:

1 cup walnut pieces
1 tablespoon pine nuts
1 clove of garlic
a sprig of basil
4 tablespoon butter
salt
1 pound spaghetti (or other pasta)
⅓ cup grated Parmesan cheese
a little olive oil
pepper

1. Boil the water for the pasta.
2. Finely chop the walnut pieces together with the pine nuts. Chop the garlic and basil together on a separate plate.
3. Melt the butter in a small pan. Add the chopped walnuts and pine nuts and fry gently for a few minutes.
4. When the water comes to a boil, salt and cook the pasta.
5. Pour the nut sauce into a bowl; add the cheese, a little olive oil, and the chopped garlic and basil; salt and pepper lightly and mix well.
6. When the pasta is cooked firmly, drain and flavor with the sauce; serve immediately.

Ravioli di magro
RAVIOLI WITH SPINACH FILLING (Emilia-Romagna)

Preparation: about 1 hour
Cooking time: 25 minutes

Ingredients for 4 people:

for the pasta:
14 ounces (about 3 cups) flour
4 eggs
salt

for the filling:
14 ounces frozen spinach
salt
10½ ounces fresh ricotta cheese
½ cup grated Parmesan cheese
1 egg
a pinch of nutmeg
pepper

for the topping:
6 tablespoons butter
3 tablespoons grated Parmesan
cheese

1. Cook the spinach in a pot with a little salted water to thaw.
2. Prepare egg pasta following the recipe on page 10.
3. Drain and squeeze the spinach; chop and place in a bowl. Add all the other ingredients for the filling and mix well with a fork.
4. Roll out the pasta thinly, cut out 2-inch squares, and make ravioli as explained on page 12. When starting, cover the pasta with a clean cloth so that it does not dry too much.
5. Bring plenty of water to a boil in a pot.
6. Cook in boiling water (5-8 minutes, depending on the pasta). Drain a few at a time with a slotted spoon.
7. Flavor in layers with fresh butter and Parmesan cheese.

Another sauce for these ravioli is made by melting butter with five or six sage leaves.

◄ *Pasta in salsa di noci*

Spaghetti alla Veneta
SPAGHETTI VENETO-STYLE (Veneto)

Preparation: 15 minutes
Cooking time: 30 minutes

Ingredients for 6 people:

14 ounces softened dried cod
1 clove of garlic
1 small onion
¼ cup olive oil
12 ounces canned crushed tomatoes
salt
pepper
a pinch of cayenne pepper
1¼ pounds spaghetti

1. Arrange the dried cod in a casserole with cold water. Bring to a boil and boil for 3 minutes.
2. Drain the fish, remove the skin and bones, and cut into small pieces.
3. Chop the garlic and the onion finely.
4. Gently fry the garlic and onion in oil in a pan. Then add the tomatoes, salt and pepper, and sprinkle with cayenne pepper.
5. Add the fish, mix, and cook for 25 minutes on medium heat.
6. Bring plenty of water to a boil in a pot; when the water comes to a boil, add salt and cook the spaghetti to a firm bite.
7. Drain the pasta and flavor with the sauce; mix and serve.

Tagliatelle verdi ai piselli
GREEN TAGLIATELLE WITH PEAS (Emilia-Romagna)

Preparation: 5 minutes
Cooking time: about 20 minutes

Ingredients for 4 people:

1 small onion
4 tablespoons butter
7 ounces frozen or canned peas
salt
3 ounces boiled ham (single slice)
1 pound green tagliatelle

1. Bring plenty of water to a boil in a pot.
2. In the meantime, finely chop the onion; sauté with butter in a pan.
3. Add the peas and salt, mix well, and cook for about 15 minutes, adding a little hot water if required.
4. Dice the ham and add it to the peas; cook for a further 5 minutes.
5. When the water comes to a boil, salt, add the tagliatelle, and cook to a firm bite (about 5 minutes).
6. Drain the tagliatelle, top with the sauce, and serve immediately.

Rotolo ripieno
STUFFED PASTA ROLL (Emilia-Romagna)

Preparation: 1 hour 15 minutes
Cooking time: 45 minutes

Ingredients for 4 people:

for the pasta:
10½ ounces (about 2 cups) flour
3 eggs
salt

for the filling:
12 ounces frozen spinach
salt
3½ ounces boiled ham (one slice)
12 ounces fresh ricotta cheese
½ cup grated Parmesan cheese
1 egg
a pinch of nutmeg
pepper

for the topping:
6 tablespoons butter
3 tablespoons grated Parmesan
cheese

1. Cook the spinach in a pot with a little salted water.
2. Prepare the egg pasta (see page 10).
3. Dice the ham; place in a bowl together with the ricotta, Parmesan cheese, egg, and nutmeg. Add salt and pepper.
4. When the spinach is ready drain and squeeze; add to the other ingredients for the filling. Mix well.
5. Bring plenty of water to a boil in an oval or large round pot.
6. Roll out the pasta into a disk shape about 1/10 inch thick and place on a clean cloth.
7. Spread the filling over the pasta, leaving a border of about 2 inches.
8. Use the cloth to help you roll the pasta up. Wrap the pasta roll in the cloth and tie up well with a little string, closing the ends well.
9. When the water comes to a boil, salt and cook the pasta roll for 45 minutes.
10. When the pasta roll is ready, drain, remove the cloth, and cut into slices about ½ inch thick. Arrange the slices on a serving dish and keep warm.
11. Melt the butter and pour over the slices. Sprinkle with Parmesan cheese and serve.

▼ *Rotolo ripieno*

Tortelli di zucca

TORTELLI WITH PUMPKIN (Lombardy)

Preparation: about 1 hour
Cooking time: 40 minutes

Ingredients for 6 people:

for the pasta:
17½ ounces (about 3½ cups) flour
5 eggs
salt

for the filling:
2½ pounds fresh pumpkin
1¼ cup grated Parmesan cheese
1 teaspoon cinnamon
a little nutmeg

plus:
7 tablespoons butter
4 tablespoons grated Parmesan
cheese

1. Prepare the pasta following the recipe on page 10 and set aside.
2. Remove the hard skin, seeds, and filaments from the pumpkin.
3. Cut the pumpkin into pieces and place in a pan with a little water. Cover and cook on low heat.
4. When the pumpkin is soft, crush to a pulp and place in a bowl. Add the other ingredients for the filling and mix well with a wooden spoon.
5. Roll the pasta out thinly; cut into 3-inch squares. Prepare the tortelli following the explanation for tortellini (page 12).
6. Bring plenty of water to a boil in a pot and, when boiling, add the tortelli and cook (only a few minutes).
7. Drain the tortelli a few at a time and arrange in a large serving bowl. Add the butter and Parmesan cheese. Mix and serve immediately.

Tortellini

TORTELLINI (Emilia-Romagna)

Preparation: about 1 hour
Cooking time: 1 hour 45 minutes

Ingredients for 6 people:

for the pasta:
17½ ounces (about 3½ cups) flour
5 eggs
salt

for the filling:
3½ ounces mortadella
3 ounces cured ham
5 ounces ground pork
2 eggs
1¼ cup grated Parmesan cheese
a pinch of nutmeg
salt
pepper

1. Prepare the meat sauce following the recipe on page 126.
2. Dice the mortadella and chop the ham; place both in a bowl. Add the ground pork.
3. Incorporate the eggs, the Parmesan cheese, a pinch of nutmeg, salt and pepper. Mix well and leave to rest in the refrigerator.
4. Prepare the pasta following the recipe on page 10.
5. Roll out the pasta thinly and cut out 2-inch squares. Prepare the tortellini as explained on page 12.
6. Bring plenty of water to a boil in a pot. When it comes to a boil, add salt and cook the tortellini.
7. Drain after 3-4 minutes, flavor with the sauce and serve immediately.

Tortellini can also be served in a broth by boiling them in 6 cups of stock.

◀ *Tortelli di zucca*

Agnolini
MEAT-FILLED HOMEMADE PASTA (Lombardia)

Preparation: 30 minutes
Cooking time: about one hour

Ingredients for 4 people:

for the pasta:
10½ ounces (about 2 cups) flour
3 eggs
salt

for the filling:
1 medium onion
4 tablespoons butter
1 pork sausage
2 ounces smoked *pancetta*
½ pound ground beef
salt, pepper
½ cup dry white wine
1½ cups grated Parmesan cheese
a little nutmeg
1 egg

plus:
6 cups stock

1. Finely chop the onion. Melt the butter in a pan, add the onion, and sauté.
2. Dice the sausage and *pancetta*.
3. Place the ground beef in a pan with the sausage and *pancetta*. Salt and pepper. Add the wine, cover, and cook on low heat for about 30 minutes.
4. Prepare the pasta, following the recipe on page 10. Roll out thinly and cut out 2-inch squares. Cover with a clean cloth so that it does not dry out.
5. When the meat is ready, add the Parmesan cheese, nutmeg, and egg. Mix briskly.
6. Heat the stock in a pot.
7. Prepare the agnolini following the explanation on page 12.
8. When the stock comes to a boil, add the agnolini and cook for a few minutes. Serve piping hot.

▼ *Agnolini*

Bauletti di carne

HOMEMADE PASTA FILLED WITH HAM AND CHEESE (Friuli-Venezia Giulia)

Preparation: about 1 hour
Cooking time: 20 minutes

Ingredients for 6 people:

for the pasta:
17½ ounces (about 3½ cups) flour
5 eggs
salt

for the filling:
2 ounces gruyére cheese
2 ounces cured ham
2 ounces boiled ham
a sprig of parsley
10½ ounces fresh ricotta cheese
½ cup grated Parmesan cheese
3 eggs
a little nutmeg
salt, pepper

plus:
4 cups stock

1. Chop the gruyére cheese into large pieces with the two kinds of ham and the parsley.
2. Place the ricotta in a bowl and work with a fork. Add all the other ingredients and mix well.
3. Prepare the pasta (see page 10). Roll out half the pasta and place little heaps of filling on it at regular distances.
4. Roll out the rest of the pasta and arrange on top of the filling.
5. Press down the two pieces of pasta around the heaps so that they stick together well.
6. Bring a pot of stock to a boil.
7. Cut out the filled pasta in round-shaped ravioli (see page 12).
8. When the stock comes to a boil, add the bauletti and cook as required. Serve immediately.

Crema di carciofi e piselli

CREAM OF ARTICHOKES AND PEAS SOUP (Lombardy)

Preparation: 15 minutes
Cooking time: 1 hour 15 minutes

Ingredients for 6 people:

4 artichokes
1 lemon
1 medium onion
8 tablespoons butter
¾ cup flour
6 cups stock
9 ounces fresh shelled peas
salt
6 slices of homemade bread
3 eggs

1. Clean the artichokes and remove the tougher outer leaves and tips. Cut into quarters, removing the chokes, and place in a bowl of water with the lemon juice.
2. Finely chop the onion and sauté in a casserole with the butter.
3. Drain the artichokes, add them to the casserole, and leave to season for a few minutes.
4. Incorporate the flour with the stock and pour this over the artichokes.
5. Add the peas and salt and cook on low heat for about one hour, stirring occasionally.
6. Grill the bread in the oven or a toaster.
7. When everything is ready, blend all ingredients. Return the cream to the casserole; add an egg and two egg yolks and mix briskly.
8. Return the casserole to the heat and cook for a few minutes.
9. Arrange a slice of toasted bread in each serving dish, cover with the soup, and serve.

Crema di asparagi
CREAM OF ASPARAGUS SOUP (Lombardy)

Preparation: 5 minutes
Cooking time: about 1 hour

Ingredients for 6 people:

2¼ pounds asparagus
salt
7 cups stock
3 cups milk
5 tablespoons butter
¾ cup flour
6 slices of homemade bread
2 tablespoons grated Parmesan
cheese
2 egg yolks

1. Boil the asparagus in a pot of salted water. In the meantime, bring the stock and the milk to a boil in two separate pots.
2. Melt the butter in a large casserole. Gradually incorporate the flour, mixing well, and cook for 2 minutes on low heat.
3. Gradually add the milk and then the stock, mixing constantly.
4. Drain the asparagus, slice the tender parts, and blend; add to the casserole. Cover and cook for about 20 minutes.
5. Toast the slices of bread and place each one in a serving bowl. Remove asparagus mixture from the heat; add the Parmesan cheese and two egg yolks, mixing briskly. Pour the soup into the serving bowls and serve.

Minestrone di zucca
PUMPKIN SOUP (Lombardia)

Preparation: 10 minutes
Cooking time: about 1 hour

Ingredients for 4 people:

1¾ pounds fresh pumpkin
4 tablespoons butter
2 cups vegetable stock
3 cups milk
salt
pepper
a pinch of nutmeg
⅔ cup rice
4 slices of homemade bread
2 tablespoons grated Parmesan
cheese

1. Cut the pumpkin into pieces and remove the hard skin and seeds; cut into 1-inch cubes.
2. Gently fry the pumpkin in a casserole with half the butter, mixing continuously.
3. After 3 minutes, add the stock, cover, and cook on low heat for about 20 minutes.
4. In the meantime, boil the milk in a small pot.
5. Blend the pumpkin and return it to the casserole. Add the hot milk and season with salt, pepper, and nutmeg. Bring to a boil.
6. Add the rice to the pumpkin soup and cook on low heat for 20-25 minutes, stirring occasionally.
7. Grill the slices of bread (in a toaster or in the oven) and arrange each slice in a serving dish.
8. When the soup is ready, flavor with the Parmesan cheese and the remaining butter. Mix, pour into the four dishes, and serve.

◀ *Crema di asparagi*

Passatelli

HOMEMADE EGG PASTA (Emilia-Romagna)

Preparation: 10 minutes
Cooking time: about 30 minutes

Ingredients for 4 people:

5 cups meat stock
3 cups flour
1½ cups grated Parmesan cheese
1 lemon, grated
4 eggs
salt
pepper
a pinch of nutmeg
3 tablespoons grated Parmesan
cheese, for sprinkling

1. Bring the stock to a boil in a pot.
2. Mix in a bowl the flour and cheese; add the grated lemon rind, salt, pepper, and a pinch of nutmeg. Mix with a wooden spoon and incorporate the eggs one at a time.
3. When the mixture is firm, roll out to 1-inch thick. Cut out the passatelli with the appropriate kitchen tool and drop the pasta into the boiling stock.
4. When the passatelli rise to the surface, remove from the heat and serve sprinkled with Parmesan cheese.

If you don't have the utensil for making the passatelli, mash the pasta and add the pieces directly to the stock.

▼ *Passatelli*

Risi e bisi
RICE AND PEAS (Veneto)

Preparation: 5 minutes
Cooking time: 30 minutes

Ingredients for 4 people:

5 cups meat stock
1 medium onion
2 ounces *pancetta*
2½ tablespoons olive oil
4 tablespoons butter
10½ ounces fresh shelled peas
salt
pepper
1⅔ cups rice
a sprig of parsley
2 tablespoons grated Parmesan
cheese

1. Bring the stock to a boil in a pot. Chop the onion and dice the *pancetta*.
2. In a casserole, gently fry the *pancetta* and the onion with the oil and half the butter.
3. After a few minutes, add the peas and five tablespoons hot stock. Salt, pepper, and cook for 5 minutes.
4. Add the rice to the casserole and fry gently. Add a ladle of stock and mix until everything is absorbed. Continue adding stock and mix until the rice is cooked.
5. Wash and chop the parsley and sprinkle over the rice; add the remaining butter and grated cheese, mix and serve.

Riso con gli spinaci
RICE WITH SPINACH (Emilia-Romagna)

Preparation: 5 minutes
Cooking time: 35 minutes

Ingredients for 4 people:

7 ounces frozen spinach
5 tablespoons butter
5 cups stock
1⅔ cups arborio rice
2 eggs
salt
3 tablespoons grated Parmesan
cheese

1. Place the spinach and the butter in a casserole. Cook on low heat until thawed.
2. In the meantime, bring the stock to a boil in a pot.
3. Mix the rice in with the spinach and stir well. Add a ladle of stock and stir again. Add stock continuously until the rice is cooked (about 20 minutes).
4. When the rice is almost ready, break two eggs into a bowl, add salt, and whip.
5. Pour the eggs into the risotto, mix well, and turn off the heat. Sprinkle with Parmesan cheese and serve.

◄ *Riso con le erbe*

Riso con le erbe
RICE WITH MIXED VEGETABLES (Veneto)

Preparation: 10 minutes
Cooking time: 30 minutes

Ingredients for 6 people:

4 cups vegetable stock
10½ ounces fresh beets
10½ ounces fresh spinach
1 small onion
4 tablespoons butter
2½ cups arborio rice
2 tablespoons dry white wine
salt
3 tablespoons grated Parmesan cheese

1. Bring the stock to a boil in a pot.
2. Wash the beets and spinach carefully; dry and cut into thin, narrow strips.
3. Finely chop the onion and sauté with the butter in a casserole. Add the beets and spinach and cook for 5 minutes. Then add the rice and the wine and mix well.
4. Add a ladle of boiling stock to the casserole and mix until absorbed. Continue adding stock and mixing until the rice is completely cooked.
5. Turn off the heat and add salt as required; sprinkle with grated cheese and serve.

Riso con le patate
RICE WITH POTATOES (Veneto)

Preparation: 15 minutes
Cooking time: about 30 minutes

Ingredients for 4 people:

9 ounces potatoes
1 small onion
3½ ounces *pancetta*
8 leaves of rosemary
2 tablespoons butter
5 cups stock
salt
pepper
1 cup rice
2 tablespoons grated Parmesan cheese

1. Wash, peel, and cut the potatoes into pieces.
2. Chop the onion, *pancetta,* and rosemary.
3. In a casserole, gently fry these chopped ingredients in butter; then add the potatoes and stock. Add salt and pepper and cook for 5 minutes.
4. Add the rice and simmer for about 15 minutes, stirring occasionally.
5. When the rice is ready, sprinkle with grated cheese and serve immediately.

Riso e sedano

RICE AND CELERY (Veneto)

Preparation: 5 minutes
Cooking time: 35 minutes

Ingredients for 6 people:

5 cups meat stock
1 medium onion
10½ ounce bunch of celery
1 ounce *pancetta*
4 tablespoons butter
salt
pepper
1⅔ cups rice
2 tablespoons grated Parmesan cheese

1. Heat the stock in a pot.
2. Cut the onion and celery into pieces, chop the *pancetta*.
3. In a small pan, gently fry the *pancetta* in the butter; add the onion and the celery. Salt, pepper, and cook on low heat for 10-15 minutes.
4. When the stock comes to a boil, add the rice and cook as required.
5. After about 15 minutes, add the fried onion and celery. Mix well and complete the cooking. Then sprinkle with Parmesan cheese and serve.

Riso e zucca

RICE AND PUMPKIN (Lombardy)

Preparation: 10 minutes
Cooking time: 35 minutes

Ingredients for 4 people:

1 pound fresh pumpkin
4 tablespoons butter
½ onion
about 4 cups stock
1⅔ cups arborio rice
salt
pepper
3 tablespoons grated Parmesan cheese

1. Remove the hard outer skin, seeds, and filaments of the pumpkin. Cut into 1-inch cubes.
2. In a pan, melt half the butter; add the onion and the diced pumpkin. Fry gently for about 10 minutes.
3. In the meantime, bring the stock to a boil in a pot.
4. Remove the onion from the pumpkin sauce and then add the rice. Mix well, and add salt and pepper to taste.
5. Add a ladle of stock and stir again until absorbed. Continue adding stock and stirring until the rice is cooked (about 20 minutes).
6. Remove from the heat, mix with the remaining butter and the Parmesan cheese. Serve immediately.

Risotto alla Milanese
RISOTTO MILANESE (Lombardy)

Preparation: 5 minutes
Cooking time: 30 minutes

Ingredients for 4 people:

about 5 cups stock
1 small onion
4 tablespoons butter
1⅔ cups arborio rice
salt
½ teaspoon crushed saffron threads
3 tablespoons grated Parmesan cheese

1. Heat the stock in a pot.
2. Finely chop the onion and sauté with 3 tablespoons butter in a casserole.
3. Add the rice to the casserole and allow to flavor. Add a ladle of stock, salt, and stir. Continue adding stock and stirring until the rice is completely cooked (about 20 minutes).
4. At the last moment, add the saffron and mix well. Add the remaining butter and the Parmesan cheese; mix and serve immediately.

Risotto alla pilota
RISOTTO WITH SAUSAGES (Lombardy)

Preparation: 5 minutes
Cooking time: 35 minutes

Ingredients for 4 people:

2 cups arborio rice
1 medium onion
5 tablespoons butter
7 ounces Italian sausages
salt
4 tablespoons grated Parmesan cheese

1. Bring about 3½ cups of salted water to a boil.
2. Then add the rice so that it forms a cone or pyramid, with the top just emerging from the water (use a ladle to add or remove water as required). Simmer for 10-12 minutes.
3. Finely chop the onion and sauté in a pan with the butter.
4. Cut up the sausages and add to the frying onions. Cook on medium heat, stirring occasionally.
5. When the rice has been cooking for the time indicated, remove from the heat. Cover the pot with a couple of clean cloths and set aside for 15 minutes.
6. Add the sausages to the rice and mix. Sprinkle with Parmesan cheese, stir, and serve.

Risotto al radicchio rosso
RISOTTO WITH RADICCHIO (Veneto)

Preparation: 5 minutes
Cooking time: 35 minutes

Ingredients for 6 people:

1 pound radicchio
about 6 cups meat stock
½ onion
6 tablespoons butter
a pinch of sugar
2½ cups arborio rice
salt
4 tablespoons grated Parmesan cheese
pepper

1. Boil a little salted water in a pot.
2. Prepare and wash the radicchio and cook in the boiling water for 4-5 minutes. Drain and cut into strips.
3. Heat the stock in a pot.
4. Finely chop the onion and sauté with 4 tablespoons butter in a casserole.
5. Add the radicchio to the frying onions, add the sugar, stir, and cook for 5 minutes on low heat.
6. Add the rice to the casserole and allow it to flavor for a few moments. Add a little stock and cook until absorbed. Continue adding stock and mixing until the rice is completely cooked (about 20 minutes).
7. Remove from the heat, season with the remaining butter, Parmesan cheese, and a pinch of pepper. Mix and serve.

Risotto con le cicale
RISOTTO WITH CRAYFISH (Veneto)

Preparation: 10 minutes
Cooking time: 30 minutes

Ingredients for 4 people:

17½ ounces whole crayfish*
salt
½ cup dry white wine
2 cloves of garlic
a sprig of parsley
⅓ cup olive oil
1⅔ cups arborio rice

1. Carefully wash the crayfish*; place them in a pot with 5 cups boiling salted water and the wine. Boil the shellfish for about 3 minutes.
2. Finely chop the garlic with the parsley.
3. When the shellfish have boiled as indicated, drain them from the stock, open the shells, and remove the meat.
4. In a casserole, gently fry the chopped garlic and parsley in the oil. Add the shellfish, salt, and cook for 10 minutes.
5. Add the rice, a ladle of fish stock, and stir. Continue adding broth and mixing until the rice is ready (about 20 minutes). Serve immediately.

* Can also be prepared with jumbo shrimp, sea crayfish, or langoustines.

◀ *Risotto con le cicale*

Risotto con le zucchine

RISOTTO WITH ZUCCHINI (Veneto)

Preparation: 10 minutes
Cooking time: 35 minutes

Ingredients for 4 people:

10½ ounces zucchini
1½ ounces smoked *pancetta*
half a clove of garlic
1 small onion
about 5 cups stock
2 tablespoons butter
salt
pepper
1⅔ cups arborio rice
a sprig of parsley
2 tablespoons grated Parmesan cheese

1. Wash the zucchini, top and tail, and cut into round slices.
2. Chop the *pancetta*. Cut the garlic in half, and chop together with the onion.
3. Bring the stock to a boil in a pot.
4. In a pan, sauté the chopped onion and garlic with the butter. After a couple of minutes, add the zucchini. Salt, pepper, and fry gently on medium heat, until the zucchini are browned.
5. Then add the rice and a ladle of boiling stock; stir until the stock is absorbed. Continue adding stock and stirring until the rice is completely cooked (about 20 minutes).
6. In the meantime, chop the parsley finely.
7. When the rice is ready, add the parsley and the Parmesan cheese. Mix well and serve immediately.

▼ *Risotto con le zucchine*

Risotto con seppie nere
RISOTTO WITH BLACK CUTTLEFISH (Veneto)

Preparation: 25 minutes
Cooking time: 50 minutes

Ingredients for 4 people:

17½ ounces cuttlefish with ink sac
1 small onion
1 clove of garlic
⅓ cup olive oil
salt
pepper
1 cup dry white wine
3 cups fish stock
1⅓ cups arborio rice
2 tablespoons butter

1. Prepare the cuttlefish by removing the skin and the hard white shell inside. With a knife or your thumbs, remove the innards between the eyes and the eyes themselves. Carefully remove the sac with the black ink and place in a bowl.
2. Rinse the cuttlefish well and cut into strips.
3. Chop the onion and place in a casserole. Add the garlic and the oil and cook over medium heat.
4. When the garlic begins to brown, remove and add the cuttlefish. Salt, pepper, and cook for a few minutes.
5. Add the wine, raise the heat, and allow the wine to evaporate.
6. In the meantime, squeeze the black ink from the sac into the casserole with 2-3 tablespoons water. Cook for about 20 minutes on medium heat.
7. Also bring the fish stock to a boil in another pot.
8. When the black ink sauce has cooked sufficiently, add the rice and leave to flavor. Add the stock gradually, mixing continually until the rice is cooked.
9. Add the butter, mix well, and allow to set for a couple of minutes before serving.

Zuppa di cavolfiore
CAULIFLOWER SOUP (Various regions)

Preparation: 10 minutes
Cooking time: about 1 hour 30 minutes

Ingredients for 4 people:

5 ounces potatoes
1 medium onion
1 carrot, peeled
1 stalk of celery
⅓ cup olive oil
2 tablespoons butter
1 medium cauliflower
3½ ounces canned peeled tomatoes
salt, pepper
7 cups stock
2 ounces boiled ham
2 tablespoons grated Parmesan cheese

1. Wash, peel, and dice the potatoes. Chop the onion, slice the carrot finely, and cut the celery into large pieces.
2. In a casserole, heat the oil and the butter; add the vegetables, cover and cook for 10 minutes on low heat.
3. In the meantime, wash the cauliflower and separate into pieces.
4. Add the peeled tomatoes and cauliflower to the casserole. Salt, pepper, and cook for another 10 minutes.
5. Heat the stock in another pot and add to the casserole with the vegetables. Keep on low heat, and simmer for about one hour.
6. Chop the ham. Ten minutes before the soup is ready, add the ham and the Parmesan cheese. Stir, finish cooking, and serve.

149

Ali di pollo alle verdure

CHICKEN WINGS WITH VEGETABLES (Lombardy)

Preparation: about 10 minutes
Cooking time: 1 hour 10 minutes

Ingredients for 4 people:

7 ounces fresh shelled peas
salt
5 ounces carrots
8 chicken wings (about 1¾ pounds)
a little flour
4 tablespoons butter
pepper
1 small onion
1 clove of garlic
½ cup stock

1. Boil the peas in a small pot with a little salted water. Peel the carrots and cut into pieces about ½-inch in size and boil in another pot with salted water.
2. Wash and dry the chicken wings and dip in the flour.
3. Melt half the butter in a pan and add the chicken; fry gently.
4. When the chicken is browned, arrange in an oven dish. Salt, pepper, and mix.
5. Drain the vegetables when cooked.
6. Finely chop the onion and garlic; sauté with the remaining butter in the pan used to brown the chicken.
7. Add the boiled vegetables; salt, pepper, and cook for 5 minutes.
8. Add the stock, stir, and cook for a further 10 minutes.
9. Add the chicken wings to the vegetables, cover, and cook on medium heat until ready (30-40 minutes). Serve immediately.

Anatra ai sapori dell'orto

DUCK WITH GARDEN VEGETABLES (Veneto)

Preparation: 15 minutes
Cooking time: 1 hour 30 minutes
(approx.)

Ingredients for 4 people:

1 duck, about 2¼ pounds
½ onion
1 carrot, peeled
1 stalk of celery
3½ ounces *pancetta*
5 sage leaves
⅓ cup olive oil
salt
pepper
a little nutmeg
½ cup of dry white wine
½ cup of stock
14 ounces canned crushed
   tomatoes

1. Rinse and dry the duck pieces, and trim off the excess fat.
2. Chop together the onion, the carrot, and the celery. Dice the *pancetta*.
3. Place the chopped vegetables in a casserole; add the *pancetta* and five sage leaves and fry gently in the oil.
4. Then add the pieces of duck; sprinkle with salt, pepper, and nutmeg. Mix and cook on medium heat for 15 minutes.
5. Add the wine and allow to evaporate; skim off the fat produced by the duck skin.
6. Add the stock and the crushed tomatoes; cover and cook for about one hour. Serve hot.

◄ *Anatra ai sapori dell'orto*

Rotolo di vitello arrosto
ROAST OF ROLLED VEAL (Emilia-Romagna)

Preparation: 20 minutes
Cooking time: 1 hour 15 minutes

Ingredients for 6 people:

2¼ pounds roasting veal
(suitable for tying up)
salt
pepper
3½ ounces thin sliced *pancetta*
3 tablespoons chopped mixed herbs
(parsley, marjoram, thyme, rosemary
and sage)
½ cup grated Parmesan cheese
6 tablespoons butter

1. Pound the meat on a work-top; lightly salt and pepper.
2. Cover the veal with the slices of *pancetta*. Leave an edge of about 1 inch and sprinkle with the chopped herbs and cheese.
3. Roll up the meat and close the ends with a large needle and kitchen string. Then tie up the rest of the roast.
4. Melt the butter in a large casserole and gently fry the meat on all sides.
5. Pour in a cup of water, add a little more salt, and cover tightly. Cook for about 40 minutes.
6. Turn the meat and cook for another 30 minutes.
7. Arrange the meat on a serving dish, remove the string, and cut into slices. Serve immediately.

Asparagi alla Veneta
ASPARAGUS VENETIAN-STYLE (Veneto)

Preparation: 10 minutes
Cooking time: 20-30 minutes

Ingredients for 4 people:

8 eggs
4½ pounds asparagus
olive oil
salt
pepper
bread crumbs
grated Parmesan cheese
vinegar

1. Hard boil the eggs (cover with water in a pot and boil for six minutes when the water starts to boil).
2. Remove the stringy parts of the asparagus with a knife and cut off the woody stem at the bottom. Wash well.
3. Steam the asparagus for 20-30 minutes depending on size.
4. Drain and shell the eggs. Crush two eggs and mix with a little oil, salt, pepper, breadcrumbs, and grated cheese to form a spread.
5. Drain the asparagus, place them on a serving dish, and garnish with this spread, a little olive oil, and a little vinegar.
6. Cut the other hard-boiled eggs in half and arrange them around the asparagus. Garnish with oil, salt, and pepper (you can also add a little vinegar).

Busecca

OMELETTE IN TOMATO SAUCE (Lombardy)

Preparation: 10 minutes
Cooking time: 30 minutes

Ingredients for 4 people:

5 eggs
salt
2 tablespoons butter
3 ounces *pancetta*
1 small onion
2½ tablespoons olive oil
5 ounces canned crushed tomatoes

1. Break the eggs into a bowl, salt, and beat with a fork until foamy.
2. In a pan, heat the butter and pour in a little beaten egg, to form a thin omelette.
3. Cook the omelette on both sides and then place on a plate. Cook other omelettes until the egg is used up.
4. Dice the *pancetta*; chop the onion. Gently fry the onion and *pancetta* in the oil in a casserole.
5. Add the tomato and salt and cook for 10 minutes on medium heat.
6. In the meantime, roll up the omelettes and cut into slices.
7. Add the omelette slices to the sauce. Cook for 5 minutes and serve.

Cazzoela

PORK RIB STEW (Lombardy)

Preparation: 10 minutes
Cooking time: about 2 hours

Ingredients for 6 people:

2 pig's feet
salt
3½ ounces salt pork rind
1 small onion
2 tablespoons olive oil
25 ounces pork spareribs
12 ounces sausages
½ cup dry white wine
2 stalks celery
2 carrots, peeled
pepper
½ cup stock
3½ pounds green cabbage

1. Wash the pig's feet and cut lengthwise; place in a pot with salted water together with the salt pork rind. Bring to a boil and cook for about one hour.
2. Chop the onion and sauté in a wide casserole in the oil.
3. When the onion has browned, add the spareribs and the sausage to the casserole and fry gently until well browned.
4. Pour the wine over the meat and allow to evaporate; remove the meat from the casserole. Turn off the heat.
5. Wash the celery and carrots and chop into large pieces.
6. Add these to the casserole with salt and pepper. Add the stock and stir; cover and cook on low heat.
7. Wash the cabbage; detach the leaves and, without drying them, place in a pot with a little salted water. Simmer on low heat, mixing frequently.
8. As soon as the cabbage is ready, add it to the carrots and celery and stir. Add the spareribs, sausages, pig's feet, and pork rind on top of the vegetables. Mix well.
9. Cover the casserole and cook for about one hour, stirring occasionally and skimming off the fat that forms during the cooking.
10. Serve piping hot.

Brasato di manzo
BRAISED BEEF (Lombardy)

Preparation: 15 minutes
Cooking time: 3 hours 15 minutes

Ingredients for 4 people:

1 small onion
1 clove of garlic
1 stalk of celery
2 carrots, peeled
⅓ cup olive oil
1¾ pounds beef (leg or rump)
1 cup red wine
1 bay leaf
1 sprig of rosemary
2 cloves
¼ cup tomato sauce
½ cup of stock
salt
pepper

1. Chop the onion and the garlic; slice the celery and carrots thinly.
2. Heat the oil in a casserole and gently fry the meat, turning several times.
3. Add the wine and allow it to evaporate. Add the bay leaf, chopped vegetables and herbs. Add the tomato sauce and the stock. Salt and pepper to taste.
4. Cover the casserole and cook on very low heat for about 3 hours.
5. When ready, slice the meat and arrange on a serving dish.
6. Blend the sauce and the vegetables and pour over the meat. Serve immediately.

Cotolette di vitello alla Milanese
VEAL CUTLETS MILANESE (Lombardy)

Preparation: 15 minutes
Cooking time: 15 minutes

Ingredients for 4 people:

4 veal cutlets (10½ ounces each)
2 eggs
salt
14 ounces breadcrumbs
14 tablespoons butter

1. Prepare the cutlets, removing any excess fat. Tenderize well with a tenderizing mallet.
2. Break the two eggs into a dish, salt slightly, and mix well.
3. Dip the cutlets in the beaten eggs and then in the breadcrumbs.
4. Heat the butter in a non-stick pan and, when hot, add the cutlets.
5. Cook on a medium heat for about 5 minutes; turn and cook the other side for a further 5 minutes. Salt and serve immediately.

◄ *Brasato di manzo*

Fegato alla Veneziana
LIVER VENETIAN-STYLE (Veneto)

Preparation: 5 minutes
Cooking time: 20 minutes

Ingredients for 4 people:

2 large white onions
½ cup olive oil
2 tablespoons butter
17½ ounces thin sliced veal liver
salt

1. Finely slice the onions and blanch on low heat in a pan with the oil and the butter. Cover and cook for 10 minutes.
2. Add the liver slices, raise the heat, and cook for 3 minutes.
3. Turn the liver slices and cook for a further 2 minutes. Salt, and serve piping hot.

Frittata con fiori di zucca
OMELETTE WITH ZUCCHINI FLOWERS* (Lombardy)

Preparation: 15 minutes
Cooking time: about 15 minutes

Ingredients for 4 people:

9 ounces zucchini flowers
a little flour
¾ cup olive oil
4 eggs
salt
pepper

1. Wash and dry the zucchini flowers and dip in the flour.
2. Heat the oil in a pan and fry the flowers until they brown on all sides.
3. Break the eggs into a bowl; salt, pepper, and beat with a whisk.
4. Pour the eggs into the pan over the fried zucchini flowers; cook the omelette and serve immediately.

*Zucchini flowers are available at specialty Italian grocers and most farmers' markets.

Frittata con spinaci
SPINACH OMELETTE (Veneto)

Preparation: 5 minutes
Cooking time: about 30 minutes

Ingredients for 4 people:

14 ounces frozen spinach
salt
1 clove of garlic
2 tablespoons butter
a pinch of nutmeg
5 eggs

1. Cook the spinach in a little salted water to thaw. Then drain and chop into large pieces.
2. Sauté the garlic in the butter in a non-stick pan.
3. Place the spinach in the pan and cook on medium heat for 10 minutes.
4. In the meantime, beat the eggs in a bowl together with a pinch of salt and nutmeg.
5. Pour the beaten eggs over the spinach; cover and cook on a medium heat until the eggs are ready. Serve immediately.

Cotechino con purè

PEPPERONI SAUSAGE WITH MASHED POTATOES (Veneto)

Preparation: 10-12 hours (resting)
Cooking time: about 3 hours

Ingredients for 4 people:

1 pepperoni sausage (about 25 ounces)
1¼ pound potatoes
½ cup milk
4 tablespoons butter
salt

1. Place the sausage in a bowl, cover with cold water, and set aside for 10-12 hours.
2. After this time, arrange the sausage in a pot full of water, prick with a fork in several places, and bring to a boil.
3. When the water comes to a boil, cover and cook on low heat for about 3 hours.
4. Prepare the mashed potatoes following the recipe on page 181.
5. When the sausage is ready, drain and slice. Arrange on a serving dish and garnish with the mashed potatoes. Serve.

Frittata ai carciofi

ARTICHOKE OMELETTE (Various regions)

Preparation: 20 minutes
Cooking time: 40 minutes

Ingredients for 4 people:

8 medium size artichokes
a little flour
⅓ cup olive oil
5 eggs
salt

1. Clean the artichokes, eliminating the tips and the harder outer leaves. Wash, dry, and cut into thin slices.
2. Dip the artichoke slices in the flour and then cook in the oil in a non-stick pan.
3. Break the eggs into a bowl and beat with a pinch of salt.
4. When the artichokes are ready, pour the beaten eggs over them. Cover and cook. Serve immediately.

◄ *Frittata ai carciofi*

Involtini

MEAT ROLLS (Lombardy)

Preparation: 25 minutes
Cooking time: 25 minutes

Ingredients for 4 people:

4 turkey cutlets
(about 14 ounces)
salt
pepper
4 lettuce leaves
(as large as the cutlets)
4 slices of boiled ham
4 cheese slices
4 sage leaves
3 tablespoons butter

1. Tenderize the cutlets, salt and pepper. Wash and dry the lettuce leaves.
2. Arrange on each cutlet a leaf of lettuce, a slice of ham, a slice of cheese, and a leaf of sage.
3. Tightly roll up each slice of meat and tie with kitchen string.
4. Gently fry the involtini in the butter in a pan; cover and cook on medium heat for about 20 minutes, stirring occasionally.
5. When ready, remove the string and serve immediately.

Manzo bollito con la pearà

BOILED BEEF WITH PEARÀ BREAD SAUCE (Veneto)

Preparation: 5 minutes
Cooking time: 2 hours 30 minutes

Ingredients for 4 people:

salt
2 pounds boneless chuck, round, or rump roast
1 medium onion
1 carrot, peeled
1 stalk of celery

for the pearà sauce:
see page 181

1. Boil plenty of salted water in a pot.
2. When the water comes to a boil, cook the meat together with the vegetables.
3. Boil for at least two hours, skimming off the foam occasionally.
4. In the meantime, prepare the pearà bread sauce, recipe on page 181.
5. When ready, drain the boiled meat, arrange on a serving plate, and serve with the bread sauce.

Melanzane alla Parmigiana

Eggplant parmigiana (Emilia-Romagna)

Preparation: 30 minutes; 30 minutes for the eggplants

Cooking time: frying time; 30 minutes

Ingredients for 6 people:

5 large eggplants
salt
olive oil for frying
12-15 leaves of basil
7 ounces mozzarella cheese
14 ounces canned crushed tomatoes
2 tablespoons grated Parmesan cheese

1. Wash the eggplant and cut them lengthwise into very thin slices. Salt and set aside for 30 minutes.
2. Rinse the eggplant slices and dry thoroughly with paper towels.
3. Heat the oil in a pan and fry the eggplant a few at a time. Dry on paper towels.
4. Chop the basil roughly. Cut the mozzarella cheese into slices. Heat the oven to 350°F.
5. Grease an oven-proof dish with oil and arrange a layer of eggplant; cover with a layer of tomato and a little salt. Add a few slices of mozzarella and a little basil. Continue in this way until the ingredients are used up.
6. Add a little tomato and Parmesan cheese over the top.
7. Cook in the oven for about 30 minutes and serve immediately.

Ossibuchi alla Milanese

OSSO BUCO MILANESE (Lombardy)

Preparation: 10 minutes
Cooking time: about 1 hour 30 minutes

Ingredients for 4 people:

4 ossibuchi (veal shanks) cut rather thickly (about 1 inch)
a little flour
1 stalk of celery
1 small carrot, peeled
½ onion
6 tablespoons butter
2 cloves of garlic
½ cup dry white wine
1 cup stock
salt
pepper
9 ounces canned peeled and chopped tomatoes
a sprig of parsley
½ lemon

1. Dip the ossibuchi in the flour. Chop the celery, carrot, and onion.
2. Melt the butter with a clove of garlic in a rather large pan; remove the garlic when it begins to brown.
3. Gently fry the ossibuchi on both sides in the melted butter.
4. Add the chopped fresh vegetables. When the vegetables begin to blanche, add the wine.
5. When the wine has evaporated, cover and continue cooking on low heat for 30 minutes. Add a little wine or stock to the ossibuchi every now and then. Salt and pepper to taste.
6. Add the tomato and cook for a further 45 minutes, adding a little stock occasionally as required. The sauce should not be too liquid but rather thick.
7. Chop a clove of garlic, the parsley, and the rind of half a lemon. Add this mixture a few minutes before taking the ossibuchi off the heat.
8. Serve the ossibuchi piping hot, preferably with seasonal vegetables.

◀ *Ossibuchi alla Milanese*

Polenta e aringa
POLENTA AND HERRINGS (Veneto)

Preparation: 15 minutes
Cooking time: 10-15 minutes

Ingredients for 6 people:

3 smoked herring
1 cup olive oil
polenta (see page 71)

1. Place the herring in a casserole with a little water; cover and boil for 10-15 minutes.
2. Drain the fish and clean (cut off the head, fins, and tail). Remove the skin and bones.
3. Cut up the herring fillets and arrange on a plate; cover with oil and mix. Serve with slices of polenta.

Polenta e osei
POLENTA AND GAME BIRDS (Veneto)

Preparation: 30 minutes
Cooking time: 40 minutes

Ingredients for 4 people:

polenta (see page 71)
12 very small game birds
8-10 sage leaves
8 tablespoons butter
salt

1. Prepare the polenta following the recipe on page 71.
2. Arrange the birds in a pan; sprinkle with chopped sage leaves and half the butter in pats. Cook for about 10 minutes, turning frequently.
3. Then add the remaining butter, a pinch of salt, and continue cooking for a further 10 minutes. Serve immediately, together with the polenta.

Lumache alla Bobbiese

SNAILS BOBBIESE-STYLE (Emilia-Romagna)

Preparation: 10 days; 1 day
Cooking time: 2 hours 30 minutes; 4
  hours

Ingredients for 6 people:

1 small onion
1 cup olive oil
7 tablespoons butter
3 dozen canned snails
2 ounces canned crushed tomatoes
salt
1½ pounds carrots
1¼ pounds leeks
1¼ pounds celery

1. Chop the onion and fry gently in the oil and the butter in a casserole. Add the snails and fry gently for a few minutes, stirring continuously.
2. Add tomato and enough water to cover the snails. Salt, mix, and cook for 2 hours.
3. Then leave the snails to marinate for 24 hours.
4. Add some more water to the casserole and cook the snails for a further 2 hours.
5. Wash and chop the carrots, leeks, and celery. Add the vegetables to the snails and cook further for 2 hours (adding a little hot water if necessary). Serve immediately.

▼ *Lumache alla Bobbiese*

Pollo ripieno

STUFFED CHICKEN (Lombardy)

Preparation: 30 minutes
Cooking time: 1 hour 30 minutes

Ingredients for 6 people:

2 cloves of garlic
1 small onion
2 tablespoons butter
3 ounces *pancetta*
¼ pound ground beef
1 egg
3 tablespoons grated Parmesan
cheese
⅓ cup breadcrumbs
½ cup milk
salt
pepper
1 whole chicken
(about 5-6 pounds)
4-5 sage leaves
⅓ cup olive oil

1. Heat the oven to 375°F.
2. Finely chop the garlic and the onion and sauté in the butter in a small pan.
3. Dice the *pancetta* and place in a bowl. Add the ground beef, egg, cheese, breadcrumbs, and milk.
4. Transfer the fried garlic and onion into the bowl. Salt, pepper, and mix well.
5. Stuff the chicken with this mixture; tie up the open end.
6. Chop the sage, place the chicken in an oven dish; add the oil and sage.
7. Cook in the oven for as long as required (to check if the chicken is ready, prick a leg with a fork; if the liquid that emerges is clear, then the chicken is cooked properly). Serve immediately.

Rambasicci

CABBAGE ROLLS WITH PORK AND BEEF (Friuli-Venezia Giulia)

Preparation: 15 minutes
Cooking time: 30-40 minutes

Ingredients for 6 people:

14 ounces ground pork
14 ounces ground beef
2 cloves of garlic
a pinch of paprika
salt
1 green cabbage
1 medium onion
4 tablespoons butter
1½ cups stock
1 tablespoon grated Parmesan
cheese

1. Mix the two kinds of ground meat in a bowl.
2. Chop the garlic and add to the meat; add the paprika, a little salt, and stir.
3. Bring about 3 cups of water to a boil in a pot.
4. Separate 12 large cabbage leaves and cook in the boiling water for 2-3 minutes. Dry well.
5. Arrange a little of the meat mixture on each cabbage leaf; roll up and secure with kitchen string.
6. Chop the onion and sauté in a pan with the butter.
7. When the onion has browned, place the meat rolls in the pan. Add a little stock, cover, and cook on medium heat, stirring occasionally.
8. When cooked, sprinkle with Parmesan cheese and serve.

◄ *Pollo ripieno*

Rane fritte

FRIED FROG LEGS (Lombardy)

Preparation: 25 minutes
Cooking time: frying time

Ingredients for 4 people:

24 large frog legs
salt
3 eggs
1 cup all-purpose flour
1 cup milk
plenty of oil for frying

1. Clean the frog legs and boil in 3 cups of salted water for 10-15 minutes.
2. Break the eggs into a bowl and whisk. Add the flour a little at a time.
3. Salt the mixture and add enough milk to make a thick batter.
4. Drain the frog legs when ready and dry thoroughly.
5. Heat the oil in a pan. Dip the frog legs in the batter; take one pair at a time with a spoon and fry.
6. When golden, place the frog legs to dry on paper towels. Serve hot.

Stinco di manzo

BEEF SHANK (Emilia-Romagna)

Preparation: 10 minutes
Cooking time: 4 hours

Ingredients for 6-8 people:

½ cup olive oil
4½ pounds shank beef
2 bay leaves
2 sprigs of rosemary
5-6 sage leaves
salt
½ tablespoon black pepper
2 cups stock
2 cups dry white wine

1. Heat the oven to 500°F.
2. Pour the oil into an oven dish and arrange the shank of beef.
3. Add the bay leaves, rosemary, sage, salt, and pepper. Add the stock and the wine and place in the hot oven.
4. When the cooking liquid begins to bubble, lower the oven to 350°F.
5. Cook for 3½-4 hours, turning the shank frequently and basting with the cooking sauce.
6. Remove the meat from the oven and cut into thin slices. Season with the strained sauce and serve.

Rifreddo

MIXED COLD MEAT (Emilia-Romagna)

Preparation: 30 minutes; 2-3 hours resting
Cooking time: 2 hours

Ingredients for 4 people:

a little butter
4 slices of veal (about 17½ ounces)
pepper
¾ cup grated Parmesan cheese
10½ ounces boiled ham (2 slices)
7 ounces mortadella (2 slices)
2 eggs
salt

1. Butter a medium size cake pan.
2. Tenderize the slices of meat and cut to the same size as the cake pan.
3. Arrange a slice of meat on the base of the pan and sprinkle with a little pepper and cheese.
4. Place a slice of ham on top, followed by a slice of mortadella and another slice of veal; flavor each layer with pepper and cheese.
5. Beat the lightly salted eggs with 2 tablespoons Parmesan cheese and pour over the meat.
6. Then add slices of veal, ham, mortadella, and meat again, sprinkling each layer with pepper and cheese.
7. Heat oven to 300°F. Cover the cake pan with aluminum foil and place in a roasting pan filled halfway with water. Bake for 2 hours.
8. When ready, drain the liquid from the cake pan and turn the meat loaf over into a deep serving pan.
9. Leave to cool and then place in the refrigerator for 2-3 hours.
10. Slice the rifreddo and serve on an oval platter.

Polpettone
MEAT LOAF (Emilia-Romagna)

Preparation: 15 minutes
Cooking time: 50 minutes

Ingredients for 4 people:

1 pound ground beef
2 eggs
1 tablespoon breadcrumbs
1 tablespoon grated Parmesan
cheese
salt
pepper
a little flour
1 pat butter
a little olive oil
½ cup dry white wine

1. Place the ground beef in a bowl; mix in a whole egg and 1 egg yolk, the breadcrumbs, and the Parmesan cheese; salt and pepper. Mix all the ingredients well.
2. Pour the mixture on to a work-top and work by hand to form the polpettone (a meat roll about 4 inches in diameter). Dip in a little flour.
3. Melt the butter and oil in an oval or rectangular pan on low heat.
4. Place the polpettone in the pan. Pour in the wine and raise the heat for a moment to evaporate the liquid.
5. Cover the pan and cook for about 45 minutes on medium heat.

Polpettone alla ricotta
MEAT LOAF WITH RICOTTA CHEESE (Veneto)

Preparation: 20 minutes
Cooking time: about 1 hour

Ingredients for 6 people:

1 pound fresh ricotta cheese
9 ounces ground turkey
9 ounces ground pork
salt
7 ounces thin-sliced cured ham
⅓ cup olive oil
1 cup white wine

1. Mix the ricotta cheese in a bowl with the two kinds of ground meat and a pinch of salt. Pour the mixture onto a work-top and work by hand to form the polpettone (a roll about 4 inches in diameter).
2. Wrap the slices of ham around the polpettone (you can overlap them). Tie up well with kitchen string.
3. Heat the oil in an oval pan and gently fry the polpettone. Turn 2-3 times.
4. Add the wine and, before it evaporates, cover with a lid. Cook for about one hour on medium heat, turning occasionally.
5. When the polpettones is ready, remove the kitchen string. Cut into slices and arrange on a serving dish.

◀ *Polpettone*

171

Tortino di verdure alla ricotta

Vegetable pie with ricotta cheese (Emilia-Romagna)

Preparation: 10 minutes
Cooking time: about 50 minutes

Ingredients for 4 people:

½ pound carrots
salt
½ pound zucchini
½ pound fresh ricotta cheese
3 tablespoons grated Parmesan cheese
4 eggs
a pinch of nutmeg
6 ounces canned peas
a little butter
some breadcrumbs

1. Peel the carrots, cut into pieces, and simmer in a small pan with a little salted water.
2. Wash the zucchini, top and tail; cut into round slices and simmer in another pan with a little salted water.
3. Mix the ricotta cheese, Parmesan, eggs, and nutmeg in a bowl; salt; mix all ingredients well.
4. Heat the oven to 350°F.
5. When tender, drain the zucchini and carrots thoroughly and rinse the peas.
6. Place the three kinds of vegetables in the cheese mixture and stir.
7. Butter an oven dish and sprinkle with breadcrumbs. Add the mixture and place in the oven.
8. Cook until the eggs are firm (about 30 minutes). Take out of the oven and serve.

Zampone con lenticchie

Pig's foot with lentils (Emilia-Romagna)

Preparation: 10 hours (marinating)
Cooking time: 3 hours

Ingredients for 4 people:

1 pig's foot (about 2¼ pounds)
12 ounces dry lentils
1 small onion
2 ounces pancetta (single slice)
2½ tablespoons olive oil
3-4 sage leaves
salt

1. Prick the rind of the pig's foot; place in a bowl with cold water and marinate overnight.
2. Then place the pig's foot in a large pot and cover with cold water. Simmer for about 3 hours.
3. Prepare the lentils (see page 179).
4. Drain the meat, arrange on a serving dish, and cover with the lentils. Serve immediately.

Acciughe marinate

MARINATED ANCHOVIES (Veneto)

Preparation: 30 minutes; 2 days in the refrigerator
Cooking time: 5 minutes for the anchovies; 10 minutes for the marinade

Ingredients for 4 people:

21 ounces salted anchovies
1 onion
1 cup white vinegar
2 cloves of garlic
1 bay leaf
10 black peppercorns
2 cloves

1. Bone the anchovies, wash and dry. Slice the onion.
2. Place the anchovies and slices of onion in alternating layers in a bowl.
3. Prepare the marinade for the anchovies as follows: Cook the vinegar, garlic, bay leaf, peppercorns, and cloves for 5 minutes on low heat.
4. Pour the hot marinade over the anchovies and marinate for two days in the refrigerator. Serve cold.

Baccalà alla Vicentina

DRIED CODFISH VICENZA-STYLE (Stockfish - Veneto)

Preparation: 30 minutes
Cooking time: 4 hours 30 minutes

Ingredients for 6 people:

2¼ pounds softened dried codfish ("Baccalà")
1 pound white onions
2 cloves of garlic
2 sprigs of parsley
4 anchovy fillets
1 cup olive oil
salt, pepper
¼ cup flour
1 cup milk

1. Cut the dried codfish into slices of about 2 inches. Split each slice and bone.
2. Finely chop the onion, garlic, parsley, and anchovies.
3. Gently fry these chopped ingredients in a large casserole with half of the oil; salt, pepper, and cook for 3-4 minutes, stirring frequently.
4. Dip the dried cod slices in flour and arrange in the casserole. Add the milk and remaining oil.
5. Cover and simmer for at least 4 hours on very low heat. Serve hot with slices of polenta (see recipe on page 71).

Seppie ripiene
STUFFED CUTTLEFISH (Veneto)

Preparation: 35 minutes
Cooking time: 50 minutes

Ingredients for 4 people:

1¾ pounds cuttlefish
2 cloves of garlic
a sprig of parsley
¼ cup olive oil
1 cup breadcrumbs
salt
pepper
2 eggs

1. Prepare the cuttlefish by removing the skin and pulling out the hard white bone. Use a sharp knife to remove the beak between the tentacles. Remove the eyes. Wash thoroughly. Detach the tentacles.
2. Heat the oven to 350°F.
3. Chop the garlic together with parsley and the tentacles. Fry gently in the oil for 4-5 minutes.
4. Add the breadcrumbs, a little salt and pepper, and mix well. Cook for 3-4 minutes, stirring.
5. Leave to cool, add the eggs, and mix quickly.
6. Stuff the cuttlefish with the filling and close with a little kitchen string or a toothpick.
7. Grease an oven dish with a little oil and arrange the stuffed cuttlefish. Cover with foil.
8. Place in the oven and cook for 35-40 minutes. Serve hot.

Seppie con piselli
CUTTLEFISH WITH PEAS (Veneto)

Preparation: 15 minutes
Cooking time: 50 minutes

Ingredients for 4 people:

1¾ pounds prepared cuttlefish
2 cloves of garlic
a sprig of parsley
¼ cup olive oil
7 ounces canned crushed tomatoes
salt
14 ounces freshly shelled peas

1. Wash the cuttlefish, dry, and cut into pieces.
2. Chop the garlic and parsley and fry gently in a casserole with the oil.
3. Add the cuttlefish, tomatoes, and half a cup of water. Salt, mix, and cover. Cook for about 25 minutes.
4. Then add the peas and stir, salt if necessary, and continue cooking for a further 20 minutes. Serve immediately.

◀ *Seppie ripiene*

Gamberetti bolliti

BOILED SHRIMP (Veneto)

Preparation: 30 minutes
Cooking time: 15-20 minutes

Ingredients for 6 people:

2¼ pounds fresh shrimp
1 lemon
2 cloves of garlic
a large sprig of parsley
½ cup olive oil
salt
pepper

1. Carefully wash the shrimp and place in a pot with cold water. Add the lemon juice and bring to a simmer.
2. When foam begins to form on the top, remove from the heat. Drain and shell the shrimp.
3. Chop garlic finely together with the parsley.
4. Arrange the shrimp on a serving dish; flavor with the oil, chopped garlic and parsley, salt and pepper. Serve hot or cold.

Luccio stufato

BRAISED PIKE (Lombardy)

Preparation: 30 minutes
Cooking time: 1 hour 15 minutes

Ingredients for 4 people:

7 ounces onions
5 ounces carrots, peeled
1 stalk of celery
⅓ cup olive oil
1 pike (about 21 ounces), cleaned and scaled
a little flour
½ cup dry white wine
salt
pepper

1. Clean the vegetables and chop into large pieces; fry gently with the oil in an oval casserole.
2. Dip the pike in the flour and fry gently in the casserole, turning frequently.
3. Add the wine and allow it to evaporate. Then add 1 cup water, salt and pepper, and lower the heat. Simmer for about one hour.
4. Arrange the pike on an oval serving dish and flavor with the strained cooking sauce. Serve.

Anguilla alla Veneziana

EEL VENETIAN-STYLE (Veneto)

*Preparation: 30 minutes; 2 hours for
the marinade*
Cooking time: 40 minutes

Ingredients for 6 people:

2¼ pounds eel
2 cups vinegar
4 bay leaves
salt
pepper
2 cloves of garlic
⅓ cup olive oil
2 tablespoons butter
½ cup dry white wine
3½ ounces canned crushed
   tomatoes

1. Prepare the eel, removing the skin and innards; cut into pieces about 3 inches in size and place in a bowl.
2. Cover with vinegar and half a cup of water; add the two bay leaves, a little salt and pepper, and marinate for about 2 hours.
3. When ready, gently fry the garlic in a saucepan with oil and butter.
4. When the garlic browns, remove it from the pan and add the eel; fry gently for a couple of minutes.
5. Pour in the wine and allow it to evaporate. Then add the tomato, the remaining bay leaves, and a few tablespoons water. Salt and pepper.
6. Cook on low heat for about 30 minutes, stirring occasionally. Serve piping hot with slices of polenta (see page 71).

▼ *Anguilla alla Veneziana*

◀ *Fiori di zucchini fritti*

Fiori di zucchini fritti
FRIED ZUCCHINI FLOWERS* (Lombardy)

Preparation: 25 minutes
Cooking time: frying time

Ingredients for 4 people:

16 zucchini flowers
1 cup flour
1 scant cup milk
3 eggs
salt
plenty of cooking oil

1. Open the zucchini flowers and remove the pistils. Wash and dry very delicately.
2. Place the flour in a bowl and add the cold milk a little at a time.
3. Beat the eggs together with a little salt in another bowl. Add the flour and milk to the eggs and mix well.
4. Heat the oil in a pan.
5. Dip the flowers in the batter and fry a few at a time, browning on both sides.
6. Drain on paper towel and serve hot.

* Zucchini flowers are available at specialty Italian grocers and most farmers' markets.

Lenticchie in umido
COOKED LENTILS (Lombardy)

Preparation: ½ hours (marinating)
Cooking time: about 1 hour 15 minutes

Ingredients for 4 people:

17½ ounces dry lentils
1 medium onion
3 ounces *pancetta* (one slice)
¼ cup olive oil
5-6 sage leaves
salt

1. Chop the onion and dice the *pancetta*.
2. Gently fry the onion and *pancetta* in a casserole with the oil; add the sage leaves.
3. Add the lentils to the casserole; add just enough water to cover completely.
4. Add salt, cover, and cook for about 1 hour, or until lentils are tender, on medium heat. Serve immediately.

Melanzane al prosciutto cotto

EGGPLANT WITH HAM (Emilia-Romagna)

Preparation: 10 minutes
Cooking time: about 1 hour

Ingredients for 6 people:

4 large eggplants
salt
1 medium onion
⅓ cup olive oil
2 tablespoons butter
4 ounces cured ham (2 slices)
pepper

1. Wash the eggplants and cut them into slices lengthwise.
2. Boil them in salted water. When ready, drain and dry on paper towels.
3. Finely chop the onion. Gently fry the onion with the oil and butter in a large pan.
4. Dice the ham and add to the frying onions. Fry gently for a few minutes.
5. Add the slices of eggplant, pepper lightly, and continue cooking over medium heat for about 30 minutes. Serve immediately.

Patate e carciofi in casseruola

POTATO AND ARTICHOKE STEW (Veneto)

Preparation: 1 hour
Cooking time: 1 hour

Ingredients for 4 people:

8 artichokes
1 lemon
4 medium potatoes
salt
1 tablespoon chopped parsley
2 tablespoons butter
2 tablespoons olive oil

1. Clean the artichokes, eliminating the harder outer leaves and the tips; hollow out slightly.
2. Place in a bowl with plenty of water and the lemon juice and set aside for at least 30 minutes.
3. In the meantime, peel and wash the potatoes, cut into quarters.
4. Drain the artichokes and cut off the stems; slice and keep the stems.
5. Place the artichokes upright in a casserole and arrange the sliced stems and potato quarters around them.
6. Sprinkle with salt and parsley. Cover with pats of butter and pour in the oil.
7. Add just enough water to cover the vegetables. Cover and cook on low heat for about 1 hour, stirring occasionally. Serve hot.

Purè di patate

MASHED POTATOES (Various regions)

Preparation: 15 minutes
Cooking time: 40 minutes to boil the
*   potatoes*

Ingredients for 4 people:

17½ ounces potatoes
1 cup milk
4 tablespoons butter
salt

1. Boil the potatoes in their skins (about 40 minutes).
2. When the potatoes are ready, drain and peel. Heat the milk.
3. In the meantime, blend the potatoes and place in a casserole.
4. Add the butter, warm milk, and salt to the hot potatoes and mix well with a wooden spoon.
5. Add milk as preferred to make a more or less dense purée. Mashed potatoes are best eaten hot; if they cool, warm in the oven for a few minutes.

Pearà

BREAD SAUCE (Veneto)

Preparation: 5 minutes
Cooking time: 2 hours 15 minutes

Ingredients for 4 people:

4 cups meat stock
4 tablespoons butter
9 ounces marrowbone
1 pound breadcrumbs
freshly ground pepper

1. Heat the stock in a pot.
2. Melt the butter and marrowbone in a casserole. Add the breadcrumbs and mix.
3. Gradually add the stock. Lower the heat and simmer for about 2 hours.
4. Add plenty of pepper 15 minutes before removing from the heat. Serve piping hot.

This sauce is an excellent accompaniment to boiled meats.

▼ *Pearà*

Fagioli in salsa
BEANS IN THICK SAUCE (Veneto)

Preparation: 12 hours (marinating)
Cooking time: about 1 hour 15
  minutes

Ingredients for 4 people:

21 ounces dry cannellini beans
2 cloves of garlic
⅓ cup olive oil
5-6 sage leaves
1 sprig of rosemary
10½ ounces canned crushed
tomatoes
salt
pepper

1. Place the beans in a bowl, cover with cold water, and allow to soften for about 12 hours.
2. When ready, gently fry the garlic in the oil in a casserole; add the sage and rosemary.
3. Drain the beans and add to the casserole. Add the crushed tomatoes, salt, and pepper.
4. Cover and cook over medium heat for about 1 hour, stirring occasionally. Serve immediately.

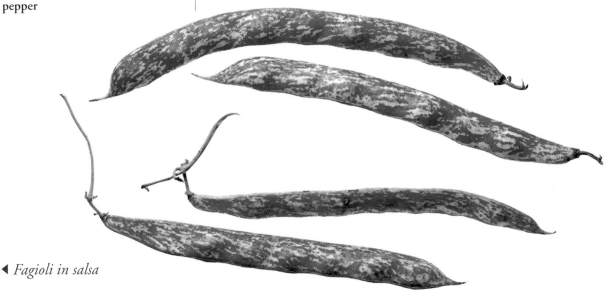

◀ *Fagioli in salsa*

Radicchio ai ferri
BRAISED RADICCHIO (Veneto)

Preparation: 15 minutes
Cooking time: about 10 minutes

Ingredients for 4 people:

28 ounces radicchio
1 cup olive oil
salt
pepper

1. Remove any damaged outer leaves; wash and dry carefully. Cut each piece of radicchio in half.
2. Heat a griddle.
3. Brush the radicchio with oil; add salt and pepper and cook on the griddle.
4. Turn after a few minutes, add more oil, and braise well. Serve hot.

Verze soffegà

STEWED CABBAGE (Veneto)

Preparation: 20 minutes
Cooking time: 1 hour 45 minutes

Ingredients for 4 people:

3 pounds cabbage
3½ ounces *pancetta* (1 slice)
1 large onion
2 cloves of garlic
2½ tablespoons olive oil
1 sprig of rosemary
1 bay leaf
1 tablespoon chopped parsley
salt
pepper
1 cup stock

1. Wash the cabbage and cut into thin strips.
2. Dice the *pancetta*; slice the onion and chop the garlic.
3. Gently fry the *pancetta* in oil in a pan. Add the garlic, onion, and herbs.
4. Add the cabbage, salt, pepper, and stock.
5. Cover and cook on low heat for about 1 hour 30 minutes, adding more stock if necessary. Serve lukewarm.

Zucca fritta

FRIED PUMPKIN (Lombardy)

Preparation: 15 minutes
Cooking time: frying time

Ingredients for 4 people:

21 ounces yellow pumpkin
a little flour
plenty of cooking oil for frying
salt

1. Remove the hard skin, seeds, and stringy pieces of the pumpkin. Cut into slices and dip in the flour.
2. Heat the oil in a pan and fry the pumpkin slices a few at a time.
3. Brown both sides and drain on paper towel. Add salt and serve.

Baìcoli veneziani

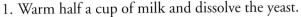

VENETIAN BISCOTTI (Veneto)

Preparation: 2 hours 15 minutes;
   2 days
Cooking time: 10 minutes;
   10 minutes

Ingredients for 6 people:

1½ cups milk
1 package (2¼ tsp) active dry yeast
14 ounces (about 3 cups) flour
4 tablespoons butter
1 egg white
¼ cup sugar
a pinch of salt
a little butter

1. Warm half a cup of milk and dissolve the yeast.
2. Place ¾ cup flour in a bowl; gradually add the milk and yeast and mix to a firm dough.
3. Wrap the dough in a cloth and set aside to rise in a warm place for about 30 minutes.
4. Dice and soften the butter. Warm the rest of the milk. Whisk the egg whites into soft peaks.
5. Mix the remaining flour and sugar in a bowl. Add the leavened dough, salt, butter, and egg whites.
6. Mix everything well and gradually add the milk until a bread-like dough is made.
7. Pour the dough onto a work-top and knead. Prepare rolls about 3 inches in diameter and 10 inches in length.
8. Lightly butter a large baking sheet and arrange the rolls of dough. Flatten slightly and cover with a cloth; set aside to rise for 1 hour 30 minutes.
9. After 1 hour 15 minutes, heat the oven to 350°F.
10. Place the rolls of dough in the oven and bake for about 10 minutes.
11. Take the cookies out of the oven and store for 2 days.
12. After this time, heat the oven to 350°F. Cut the rolls into thin slices.
13. Arrange the slices on the oven tray and bake for 10 minutes. Cool and serve.

If placed in a well-sealed container, baìcoli will keep for even 2-3 months.

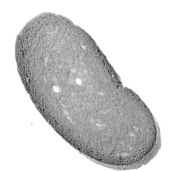

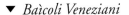
▼ *Baìcoli Veneziani*

Biscotti milanesi

MILANESE COOKIES (Lombardy)

Preparation: 1 hour
Cooking time: about 10 minutes

Ingredients for 4-6 people:

9 ounces (about 2 cups) flour
½ cup sugar
2 egg yolks
3 tablespoons very soft butter
grated rind of half a lemon
a little butter
a little flour

1. Heap the flour on a work surface.
2. In the hollow of the flour add the sugar, egg yolks, and two half eggshells of water. Knead the ingredients a little and then add the softened butter and the grated lemon rind.
3. Knead the ingredients carefully until a smooth, uniform dough is made. Set aside to rise for 30 minutes covered by a cloth.
4. In the meantime, butter and flour the cookie sheet and heat the oven to 350°F.
5. Roll out the dough very thinly and cut out cookies of various shapes and sizes as preferred (this is easier if you have cookie cutters).
6. Arrange the cookies on the sheet and place in the oven. The cookies bake very quickly, so keep a close eye on baking and remove from the oven as soon as they begin to brown.

Budino

CHOCOLATE CUSTARD (Friuli-Venezia Giulia)

Preparation: 10 minutes; 1 hour resting
Cooking time: about 10 minutes

Ingredients for 4 people:

3 cups milk
3 ounces (about ¾ cup) flour
⅓ cup sugar
2 ounces unsweetened cocoa
½ cup Marsala wine or dry white wine

1. Warm half a cup of milk.
2. Mix the flour, sugar, and cocoa in a bowl. Gradually add the lukewarm milk and blend well.
3. Gradually add the remaining milk, stirring constantly.
4. Place on medium heat and continue stirring until thick.
5. Pour the wine into 4 serving goblets and pour in the chocolate cream. Cool and serve.

This custard can be accompanied with zabaione (see page 107).

◀ *Budino*

"Bussolà" vicentino
VICENZA RING CAKE (Veneto)

Preparation: 30 minutes
Cooking time: 45 minutes

Ingredients for 4 people:

10½ ounces (about 2 cups) flour
⅓ cup superfine sugar
1½ teaspoons baking powder
1 pinch of salt
4 tablespoons butter
4 eggs
2 tablespoons grappa (or other liqueur)
a little butter
1 cup large sugar crystals

1. Heat the oven to 350°F.
2. Mix the flour with the sugar, baking powder, and salt; arrange on a work-top and make a hollow in the top.
3. Dice the butter and place in the hollow. Add three eggs and one egg yolk (keep the egg white).
4. Knead the ingredients and, when they are blended, add the grappa. Continue kneading the dough until it is smooth.
5. Lightly grease a doughnut-shaped cake dish with butter and add the dough. Brush with the egg white and sprinkle with large sugar crystals.
6. Place in the oven and bake about 45 minutes. Cool and serve.

▼ *Bussolà Vicentino*

Croccante

ALMOND CANDY (Various regions)

Preparation: 10 minutes; 2 hours resting
Cooking time: 5-10 minutes

Ingredients for 4 people:

⅓ cup sugar
2 teaspoons butter
1 lemon
14 ounces peeled almonds
a little cooking oil

1. Heat the sugar in a pan on low heat. Add the butter and the lemon juice and dissolve the sugar, stirring occasionally.
2. Roughly chop the almonds.
3. When the sugar has caramelized, add the almonds. Cook for a few minutes, stirring frequently.
4. Grease a round cake pan; add the mixture and press down with a spoon.
5. Place the cake pan in a container of cold water and set aside for about 2 hours.
6. After this time, remove the croccante from the cake pan, break into pieces, and serve.

The croccante will keep for several months if kept tightly sealed in a container.

Frittelle di polenta

POLENTA FRITTERS (Veneto)

Preparation: 10 minutes; 2 hours resting
Cooking time: frying time

Ingredients for 4 people:

10½ ounces yellow cornflour (polenta)
1 cup flour
⅔ cup superfine sugar
⅔ cup raisins
½ cup pine nuts
2 eggs
1 lemon
2 tablespoons grappa
1½ teaspoons baking powder
plenty of cooking oil for frying
¼ cup powdered sugar

1. Sift the cornflour and pour into a bowl. Add all the other ingredients and mix well for 5-10 minutes.
2. Cover the bowl with a cloth and allow to rise for about 2 hours.
3. Heat the oil in a pot. When it is very hot, fry spoonfuls of the batter.
4. Brown the fritters and drain on paper towels.
5. Sprinkle with powdered sugar and serve lukewarm.

Castagnole
Miniature doughnuts (Emilia-Romagna)

Preparation: 45 minutes
Cooking time: frying time

Ingredients for 6 people:

7 ounces (about 5½ cups) flour
½ cup plus 1 tablespoon sugar
2 teaspoons baking powder
salt
2 eggs
2 tablespoons olive oil
½ cup grappa (or other liqueur)
plenty of cooking oil for frying
⅓ cup powdered sugar

1. Arrange the flour on a work-top. Make a well in the center of the flour and add the sugar, baking powder, a pinch of salt, and the eggs. Mix well and then add the olive oil and liqueur.
2. Knead carefully to make a smooth, regular dough.
3. Prepare several long rolls from this dough, similar to "gnocchi," about 1 inch thick. Cut into small pieces about 1 inch long and roll between the palms of your hands.
4. Heat plenty of oil in a pan. When the oil is very hot (but not boiling) fry a few pieces of dough at a time.
5. Turn the dough so that it cooks on all sides and remove with a slotted spoon when browned.
6. Wipe off the excess oil with paper towels.
7. Serve the castagnole hot or cold, sprinkled with plenty of powdered sugar.

This is a typical Carnival treat.

◀ *Castagnole*

Frittelle di semolino

SEMOLINA FRITTERS (Emilia-Romagna)

Preparation: 15 minutes
Cooking time: about 15 minutes;
frying time

Ingredients for 4 people:

3½ ounces (about ½ cup) semolina
  (pasta flour)
¼ cup sugar
grated rind of half a lemon
2 cups of milk
3 eggs
a pinch of baking powder
plenty of cooking oil for frying
a little sugar

1. Mix the semolina with the sugar and grated lemon rind in a bowl.
2. Add the milk, blending it gradually with the other ingredients.
3. Bring the mixture to a boil and simmer for 4-5 minutes, stirring continually.
4. Remove from the heat and add the eggs one at a time, mixing briskly. Add the baking powder and mix well.
5. Heat the oil in a pot and fry a few spoonfuls of batter at a time.
6. Drain the fritters on paper towel, sprinkle with a little sugar, and serve.

Crostata alla marmellata

JAM TART (Various regions)

Preparation: 20 minutes; 30 minutes
resting
Cooking time: 20 minutes

Ingredients for 6 people:

7 ounces (about 3½ cups) flour
a pinch of salt
a scant ½ cup sugar
7 tablespoons butter, softened
2 egg yolks
grated rind of half a lemon
2 teaspoons baking powder
a little butter
a little flour
9 ounces apricot jam

1. Arrange the flour in a heap on the work-top.
2. In the hollow of the flour, add a pinch of salt, sugar, butter, egg yolks, grated lemon rind, and baking powder. Knead together quickly. Form the dough into a ball, cover with a cloth, and allow to rise for 30 minutes (our grandmothers always used to leaven dough under an upside-down pot heated for a minute or two on the oven burners).
3. Heat the oven to 375°F.
4. Butter and flour a medium size cake pan.
5. Place a third of the dough to one side. Work the remaining dough over the base of the pan forming an edge about 2½ inches high. Prick the dough with a fork and cover with the jam.
6. Prepare strips about 2½ inches wide from the remaining dough. Arrange these strips criss-cross fashion over the tart.
7. Place in the oven for about 20 minutes. Allow the tart to cool before serving.

Crostata alla ricotta

RICOTTA CHEESECAKE (Emilia-Romagna)

*Preparation: 15 minutes; time needed
to make the dough*
Cooking time: 45 minutes

Ingredients for 4 people:

1 shortcake (see page 192)
14 ounces fresh ricotta cheese
⅓ cup milk
½ cup shelled walnuts
⅔ cup sugar
1 ounce diced candied fruit
⅛ cup unsweetened cocoa
a little butter
a little flour

1. Drain the ricotta, place in a bowl, and add the milk. Mix well.
2. Chop the walnuts and add to the cheese; add the sugar, candied fruit, and cocoa. Blend the ingredients well.
3. Heat the oven to 350°F.
4. Butter and flour a cake pan; spread out the shortcake over the base.
5. Pour the filling over the dough and level off well with a spoon.
6. Bake for 45 minutes. Cool and serve.

▼ *Crostata alla ricotta*

Pan di Spagna
SPONGE CAKE (Various regions)

Preparation: 1 hour 30 minutes
Cooking time: 1 hour

Ingredients for 4 people:

6 eggs, separated
1 rounded cup powdered sugar
grated lemon rind
a pinch of salt
1 cup sifted flour
a little butter
a little flour

for the filling:
12 ounces strawberries
¼ cup sugar
juice of half a lemon
6 tablespoons Alchermes (or other dessert liqueur)

for the zabaione (see the recipe on page 107):
2 egg yolks
⅓ cup sugar
½ cup Marsala (or white wine)
1 egg white

1. Heat the oven to 350°F.
2. Whisk the egg yolks for about 20 minutes together with the sugar until they are almost white.
3. In a separate bowl, whisk the egg whites firmly and then fold into the egg yolks.
4. Add the lemon rind, a pinch of salt, and the flour. Mix carefully with a wooden spoon.
5. Butter and flour a cake pan and pour in the mixture. Smooth off the surface and bake for 1 hour.
6. In the meantime, wash and slice the strawberries (keep a few whole strawberries aside to garnish the cake). Add ¼ cup sugar and the juice of half a lemon and mix well. When the cake is ready, let cool. When cool, cut the cake into two or three disks. Place the first disk on a serving dish, sprinkle with the liqueur, and add the strawberries and zabaione. Garnish the other layers in the same way and finish with a layer of zabaione. Decorate the cake as preferred with the remaining strawberries.

Pan di Spagna (sponge cake) is the basic ingredient for many cakes. It can be garnished, for example, with whipped cream and strawberries, chocolate or vanilla filling (budino), or even pastry-chef's cream. It is always a good idea to sprinkle with a liqueur or fruit juice so that the sponge is not too dry.

▼ *Pane all'uva*

Panettone di Milano

PANETTONE MILANESE (Lombardy)

Preparation: 1 hour 30 minutes
Cooking time: 50 minutes

Ingredients for 6 people:

1 package (2¼ tsp) active dry yeast
1 cup milk
16 ounces (about 3¼ cups) flour
a pinch of salt
½ cup sugar
⅔ cup raisins
9 tablespoons butter, softened
2 eggs
2 ounces candied fruit in small
pieces
a little butter
a little flour
¼ cup powdered sugar

1. Dissolve the yeast in half a cup of warm milk.
2. Place the flour in a bowl; add a pinch of salt and a tablespoon of sugar. Mix the dissolved yeast with the milk. Set aside to rise for 1 hour.
3. In the meantime, soften the raisins in cold water for about 20 minutes.
4. After this time, heat the oven to 375°F.
5. Add the remaining sugar, butter, milk, and eggs to the dough. Blend all the ingredients well.
6. Add the drained raisins and candied fruit.
7. Butter and flour a deep cake pan and pour in the dough.
8. Place in the oven and bake for about 50 minutes.
9. Cool, sprinkle with powdered sugar, and serve.

Pane all'uva

RAISIN BUNS (Various regions)

Preparation: 2 hours
Cooking time: 1 hour

Ingredients for 6 people:

⅔ cup raisins
2 teaspoons active dry yeast
1 pound flour
⅔ cup sugar
4 tablespoons butter
1 cup milk
2 eggs
a pinch of salt

1. Soften the raisins in water for 20 minutes. Dissolve the yeast in a little lukewarm water.
2. Arrange the flour on a work-top. Add the sugar, butter, milk, one egg, the dissolved yeast, and salt. Knead well.
3. Drain the raisins and add to the dough. Cover with a clean cloth and set aside to rise for 30 minutes.
4. Then divide the dough into buns and allow to rise in a warm place for about 1 hour.
5. After 50 minutes, heat the oven to 350°F.
6. Beat the egg and brush over the buns.
7. Arrange the buns on a baking sheet and bake for 1 hour. Serve hot or cold.

195

Pesche ripiene

FILLED PEACHES (Various regions)

Preparation: 40 minutes
Cooking time: 45 minutes

Ingredients for 6 people:

6 firm yellow peaches
2 tablespoons butter
½ cup whole almonds
¼ cup sugar
1 egg
a pinch of cinnamon
½ cup dry white wine

1. Heat the oven to 350°F.
2. Wash the peaches, cut in half, and remove the pit. Cut out some of the pulp and set aside.
3. Chop the peach pulp and cook for 5 minutes in a pan with butter.
4. Chop the almonds and place in a bowl. Add the sugar, egg, and cinnamon and mix well.
5. Place a little of this mixture in the peach halves until they are filled.
6. Butter an oven-proof dish and arrange the peaches in it.
7. Pour the wine over and bake for 45 minutes. Serve immediately.

Tiramisù

TIRAMISÙ (Emilia-Romagna)

Preparation: 30 minutes

Ingredients for 4 people:

5 eggs
a scant ½ cup sugar
17½ ounces soft mascarpone cheese
2 tablespoons rum
1 cup strong coffee
3½ ounces sponge cake
a little unsweetened cocoa

1. Separate the whites and yolks of the eggs and place in two separate bowls.
2. Add the sugar to the egg yolks and whip into a soft cream.
3. Add the mascarpone, mixing gently with a wooden spoon. Then add the liqueur.
4. Whisk the egg whites until stiff but not dry, and fold into the the cream.
5. Pour the coffee into a bowl and dilute with 1 cup water. Add a little sugar.
6. Moisten some sponge cake with the coffee and squeeze well; arrange it on the base of a cake dish.
7. Cover this layer of sponge cake with a layer of cream.
8. Repeat until all the ingredients are used, topping with a layer of cream.
9. Sprinkle the top with cocoa and keep in the refrigerator until served.

◀ *Pesche ripiene*

Torta al latte
MILK TART (Emilia-Romagna)

Preparation: 25 minutes
Cooking time: 30 minutes

Ingredients for 4 people:

6 eggs
¼ cup sugar
½ cup flour
1 teaspoon vanilla extract
a pinch of cinnamon
a pinch of salt
3 cups milk
a little butter

1. Heat the oven to 350°F.
2. Break the eggs into a bowl and work together with the sugar.
3. Sift the flour and add gradually to the eggs; also add the vanilla, cinnamon, and a pinch of salt.
4. Add the milk a little at a time, mixing well.
5. Butter a cake pan and pour in the mixture.
6. Bake for about 30 minutes. Cool and serve.

▼ *Torta al latte*

Torta di ricotta e amaretti
RICOTTA AND AMARETTI TART (Emilia-Romagna)

Preparation: 45 minutes
Cooking time: 40-45 minutes

Ingredients for 6 people:

for the dough:
10½ ounces (about 2 cups) flour
2 teaspoons baking powder
10 tablespoons margarine
⅔ cup sugar
1 egg
a pinch of salt

for the filling:
½ cup sugar
10½ ounces ricotta cheese
2 eggs, separated
3½ ounces broken amaretti cookies
3 ounces raisins softened in hot water
1 drop of rum
a pinch of cinnamon
a little butter

1. Heap the flour and baking powder on a work-top and make a hollow in the top.
2. Dice the margarine and add to the flour. Add the sugar, egg, and salt. Knead all these ingredients well and set aside to rise for 15 minutes.
3. Prepare the filling. Place the sugar and ricotta in a bowl; add the egg yolks (keep the egg whites). Whisk until well blended.
4. Add the amaretti cookies, raisins, rum, and cinnamon and mix well.
5. Heat the oven to 350°F.
6. Butter a large cake pan and arrange three quarters of the dough over the base and sides.
7. Add the filling. Prepare strips about 1 inch in diameter from the remaining dough and arrange criss-cross fashion over the filling.
8. Bake for 40-45 minutes. Cool and serve.

Torta di tagliatelle
TAGLIATELLE CAKE (Emilia-Romagna)

Preparation: 20 minutes; 30 minutes resting
Cooking time: 40 minutes

Ingredients for 4 people:
¾ cup flour
1 egg
1 cup whole almonds
⅔ cup sugar
⅓ cup lime liqueur

for the shortcake:
5 tablespoons butter
1 cup flour
salt
⅓ cup sugar
1 egg
1 teaspoon baking powder
a little butter, a little flour

1. Prepare the shortcake as explained in the recipe on page 192 and allow to rise for 30 minutes.
2. In the meantime, mix ¾ cup flour with the egg and knead for 10 minutes. Prepare the tagliatelle as explained on page 10.
3. Chop the almonds and mix with the sugar.
4. Heat the oven to 350°F.
5. Butter and flour a medium size cake pan. Arrange the shortcake over the base and sides and then prick with a fork.
6. Pour a little almond and sugar mixture over the shortcake, baste with a little liqueur, and cover with a layer of tagliatelle. Continue in the same way until all the ingredients are used.
7. Place in the oven for 40 minutes. When baked, let the pie cool and then remove from the dish.

Torta di rose

ROSE-SHAPED-CAKE (Emilia-Romagna)

Preparation: about 1 hour
Cooking time: 45 minutes

Ingredients for 6-8 people:

½ cup milk
1 package (2¼ tsp) active dry yeast
16 ounces (about 3¼ cup) flour
6 tablespoons butter
¾ cup sugar
2 eggs
a pinch of salt
grated rind of half a lemon
a little butter

1. Warm the milk and dissolve the yeast.
2. Pour ¾ cup flour into a bowl and mix in the yeast dissolved in the milk. Allow to rise for about 30 minutes.
3. In the meantime, cut the butter into pieces, place in a bowl, and work with ½ cup sugar to form a paste.
4. Heat the oven to 350°F.
5. When the dough has leavened, add the remaining flour, eggs, a pinch of salt, grated lemon rind, and the remaining sugar.
6. Work these ingredients together well and roll out the dough to about 1/10 inch thick.
7. Spread the butter paste over the dough and roll up. Cut the roll into 8-9 slices.
8. Butter a cake pan and arrange the slices (the "roses"), keeping them separate.
9. Place in the oven and bake for about 45 minutes. Cool and serve.

◄ *Torta di rose*

Zaleti

CORN BISCUITS (Veneto)

Preparation: about 1 hour
Cooking time: 25 minutes

Ingredients for 6 people:

3½ ounces raisins
1 package (2¼ tsp) active dry yeast
1 cup milk
3 eggs
⅔ cup sugar
10½ ounces (about 2 cups) flour
14 ounces finely ground cornmeal
10 tablespoons butter
a pinch of salt
½ cup pine nuts
grated lemon rind
1 teaspoon vanilla extract
a little butter
¼ cup powdered sugar

1. Soften the raisins in a full cup of water. Dissolve the yeast in the lukewarm milk.
2. Work the eggs and sugar together in a bowl to form a cream.
3. Mix flour and meal together and incorporate with the cream, alternating with the yeast dissolved in the milk.
4. Melt the butter and then add to the other ingredients.
5. Drain the raisins and add to the mixing bowl. Add the salt, pine nuts, grated lemon rind, and vanilla. Knead to a soft dough.
6. Heat the oven to 350°F.
7. Divide the dough into small buns about 1½ inches in diameter.
8. Butter a baking sheet and arrange the biscuits separately on it.
9. Place in the oven and bake for about 25 minutes. Cool, sprinkle with powdered sugar, and serve.

Zuppa emiliana

EMILIAN TRIFLE (Emilia-Romagna)

Preparation: about 1 hour; the time needed to make the sponge; 2-3 hours rising

Cooking time: the time needed to bake the sponge

Ingredients for 4 people:

1 Pan di Spagna (sponge cake, see page 194)
3 eggs
⅓ cup sugar
⅓ cup flour
2 cups milk
2 ounces sweet cocoa powder
½ cup rum
½ cup Alchermes liqueur
½ cup plum jam

1. Prepare the sponge cake as explained in recipe on page 194.
2. Break the eggs and pour the yolks into a bowl; work well with the sugar.
3. Add the flour, alternating with small amounts of milk. Last, add the rest of the milk.
4. Place the mixture in a pan, place over low heat, and bring to a boil, stirring constantly.
5. Place half the cream in a bowl. Blend the cocoa with the remaining cream in the mixing bowl.
6. Mix the two kinds of liqueur. Cut the sponge cake in half horizontally. Moisten the bottom half with the liqueurs.
7. Spread the yellow cream over this and then the cocoa cream. Last, spread with the plum jam.
8. Moisten the other half of the sponge cake with the liqueurs and place on top of the other half.
9. Cool in the refrigerator for 2-3 hours and serve.

Torta sabbiosa
CRUMB CAKE (Veneto)

Preparation: 30-40 minutes
Cooking time: 30 minutes

Ingredients for 4 people:

10½ ounces (2 sticks plus 5 tablespoons) butter
1⅓ cups sugar
3 eggs, separated
1 cup flour
5 ounces potato starch
4 teaspoons baking powder
a pinch of salt
a little butter

1. Dice the butter and place in a bowl. Add the sugar and work together for some time to form a paste.
2. Add the egg yolks one at a time (keep the egg whites).
3. Mix together the flour, potato starch, baking powder, and salt; then mix these with the butter and sugar cream.
4. Heat the oven to 350°F.
5. Whisk the eggs whites until stiff but not dry, and fold into batter.
6. Butter a cake pan and pour in the mixture.
7. Place in the oven and bake for about 30 minutes. Cool and serve.

◀ *Torta sbrisolona*

Torta sbrisolona
CRUMB CAKE (Lombardy)

Preparation: 30 minutes
Cooking time: 30 minutes

Ingredients for 6 people:

10 tablespoons butter
7 ounces (about 5½ cups) flour
7 ounces (about 5½ cups) yellow cornmeal
⅔ cup sugar
1 egg
1 tablespoon dry white wine
a little butter
a little breadcrumbs

1. Heat the oven to 375°F.
2. Melt the butter and cool a little.
3. Mix the flour, cornmeal, and sugar in a bowl. Gradually add the butter.
4. Add the egg and wine and blend well.
5. Butter a large cake pan and sprinkle with breadcrumbs.
6. Pour the mixture into the cake pan and bake for about 30 minutes. Serve cold.

Central Italy

Antipasto di mare

SEAFOOD APPETIZER (Various regions)

Preparation: 40 minutes
Cooking time: 1 hour 15 minutes

Ingredients for 4 people:

10½ ounces shrimp in their shells
(3 ounces shelled)
7 ounces baby octopus
17½ ounces clams
17½ ounces mussels
bay leaf
¼ pound fresh green beans
½ red bell pepper
olive oil
juice of 1 lemon
salt
pepper
1½ tablespoons chopped parsley
1 chopped clove of garlic

1. Shell and rinse the shrimp as follows. First, remove the head and cut off the legs with scissors. Cut the shell along its length with the scissors and delicately remove the meat. Last, tweeze out the intestines.
2. Turn the baby octopus inside out to remove the innards; use a knife or your fingers to remove the beak (between the tentacles and the eyes).
3. Scrape the shells of the mussels and clams with a hard brush under running water; then remove the "beard."
4. Heat plenty of salted water with the bay leaf.
5. When the water comes to a boil, add the shrimp and cook until they change color. Remove the shrimp with a slotted spoon and keep warm.
6. Use a spoon to skim off the foam from the surface of the water and bring back to a boil.
7. When the water returns to a boil, add the baby octopus and cook for about 20-25 minutes (depending on size). When ready, drain and keep warm with the shrimp.
8. In the meantime, heat another pot of salted water.
9. Place the mussels and clams in a very wide pan (ideally, the pan should be large enough to hold all the shells in a single layer; if it is not large enough, shake the pan frequently while cooking), cover and cook over a medium-high heat for about 10-15 minutes until the shells open.
10. In the meantime, the second pot of water will have come to a boil; add the green beans and boil for 20 minutes.
11. When the mussels and clams have opened, turn off the heat; discard any shells that have not opened because these may not be fresh. Keep the cooking water.
12. Drain the beans when ready.
13. Wash the pepper, remove the seeds and the white fibers; cut into strips.
14. Add the baby octopus, shrimp, mussels and clams in their shells, beans, and strips of uncooked bell pepper to a bowl.
15. Strain the water used to cook the mussels and clams.
16. Season the seafood salad with a little strained cooking juice, olive oil, lemon juice, salt, pepper, and well-chopped parsley and garlic. Serve hot or cold as preferred.

◀ *Antipasto di mare*

Bruschetta
GRILLED GARLIC BREAD (Abruzzo-Molise)

Preparation: 2 minutes
Cooking time: 5 minutes

Ingredients for 4 people:

4 slices homemade bread
1 clove of garlic
salt, pepper, olive oil

1. Toast the slices of bread.
2. Rub the toasted bread with the clove of garlic.
3. Season each slice with salt, pepper, and oil. Serve hot.

Crostini ai fegatini
CHICKEN LIVERS ON TOAST (Tuscany)

Preparation: 15 minutes
Cooking time: 35 minutes

Ingredients for 4 people:

¼ pound chicken livers
piece of celery
piece of carrot, peeled
3 tablespoons oil
2 tablespoons butter
1 tablespoon chopped onion
2 tablespoons tomato sauce
½ cup white wine
salt, pepper
4 slices country bread, preferably
unsalted Tuscan bread

1. Rinse the livers.
2. Chop the celery and carrot.
3. Sauté the chopped carrot, celery, and onion in the oil and butter.
4. Add the livers, tomato sauce, and white wine. Salt, pepper, and cook for 30 minutes.
5. Toast the bread and dice.
6. Chop the livers and cooking sauce and spread over the toast. Serve hot.

Antipasto rustico autunnale
RUSTIC AUTUMN APPETIZER (Tuscany)

Preparation: 10 minutes
Cooking time: 1 hour

Ingredients for 4 people:

1 pound red cabbage
4 slices country bread, preferably
unsalted Tuscan bread
1 clove of garlic
olive oil
salt, pepper

1. Wash the cabbage leaves.
2. Boil the cabbage for 1 hour in plenty of salted water.
3. In the meantime, toast the slices of bread.
4. Rub the slices of bread with the clove of garlic.
5. Quickly dip the slices of bread in the water the cabbage is cooking in without soaking.
6. When the cabbage is cooked, drain and arrange over the slices of bread.
7. Season the slices of bread with a little olive oil, salt, and pepper and serve piping hot.

◀ *Antipasto rustico autunnale*

Involtini di peperoni alla crescenza

BELL PEPPER ROLLS WITH CHEESE (Various regions)

Preparation: 10 minutes

Ingredients for 4 people:

6 large pieces of sweet roasted peppers (under oil)
7 ounces ricotta cheese
1 tablespoon milk
8 pickled gherkins
1 tablespoon chopped parsley

1. Drain the pieces of pepper and cut in half lengthwise.
2. Soften the ricotta with a fork, adding a tablespoon of milk to make the task easier.
3. Chop two gherkins and add to the cheese with the chopped parsley.
4. Spread the cheese over the pieces of pepper.
5. Cut the remaining gherkins in half and arrange on top of the peppers.
6. Roll up the peppers and close with a toothpick.

Melanzane farcite

STUFFED EGGPLANT (Various regions)

Preparation: 40 minutes
Cooking time: 50 minutes

Ingredients for 4 people:

1 large eggplant
salt
3½ ounces green olives
1 small tablespoon pickled capers
3 anchovy fillets (in oil)
5 basil leaves
1 tablespoon chopped parsley
olive oil
7 ounces canned crushed tomatoes

1. Wash the eggplant and slice lengthwise, sprinkle the slices with salt and allow to sit for 30-60 minutes.
2. In the meantime, pit and halve the olives and chop with the capers, anchovies, and basil. Add the chopped parsley.
3. Heat the oven to 350°F.
4. Dry the eggplant and place in the hot oven for 10 minutes.
5. Grease an oven dish with olive oil.
6. Stuff the eggplant with the mixture; then roll up and secure with a couple of toothpicks. Place in the oven dish.
7. Pour the tomato over the "rolls," add a little salt, and bake for 40 minutes. Serve hot or cold as preferred.

◀ *Melanzane farcite*

213

Olive ascolane
ASCOLI OLIVES (Marches)

Preparation: 1 hour 30 minutes
Cooking time: frying time

Ingredients for 4 people:

4 tablespoons butter
2½ ounces ground pork & 2½ ounces ground beef, mixed together
2 tablespoons tomato sauce
5-6 chicken livers
breadcrumbs
2 eggs
2 tablespoons grated Parmesan cheese
cinnamon
nutmeg
salt
pepper
40 pitted green olives in brine
olive oil
1 lemon

1. Melt the butter in a pot, then add the ground meat and fry gently for a few minutes.
2. Add the tomato sauce and cook well, adding a drop of hot water if sauce is too dry.
3. When the meat is ready, add the chicken livers and cook for a further 5 minutes.
4. Remove from the heat and chop finely.
5. Add a tablespoon of breadcrumbs to the mixture, as well as an egg, the grated Parmesan cheese, a pinch of cinnamon and nutmeg, salt and pepper, and mix well to blend the ingredients.
6. Stuff the olives with this mixture.
7. Beat the remaining egg with a fork.
8. Dip the olives in the egg and then in the breadcrumbs.
9. Heat plenty of olive oil.
10. Fry the stuffed olives in the oil. As soon as they are golden, drain and dry on paper towels.
11. Serve the stuffed olives piping hot, garnishing the serving plate with quarters of lemon; if preferred, you can also squeeze lemon juice over the olives to make them easier to digest.

Pizzette veloci
QUICK SMALL PIZZAS (Various regions)

Preparation: 10 minutes
Cooking time: 5 minutes

Ingredients for 4 people:

4 slices of white bread
4 tablespoons tomato sauce
½ pound mozzarella cheese
salt
marjoram
olive oil

1. Heat the oven to 300°F.
2. Slice the bread.
3. Spread the tomato sauce over each square of bread.
4. Dice the mozzarella into small pieces and distribute over the bread.
5. Season with salt, marjoram, and a little oil and bake for a few minutes. When the mozzarella melts, remove from the oven and serve hot.

Mozzarella ai ferri
GRILLED MOZZARELLA CHEESE (Abruzzo-Molise)

Preparation: time to prepare the charcoal fire
Cooking time: 5 minutes

Ingredients for 4 people:

1 large mozzarella cheese
pepper

1. Prepare the barbecue.
2. Cut the mozzarella cheese into slices.
3. When the charcoal is ready, place the slices of cheese on the grill and cook not too close to the heat.
4. When the cheese slices begin to soften, remove from the heat, add pepper, and serve hot (if the cheese cools, it hardens and is not so appetizing).

Panzerotti

FRIED HAM AND CHEESE CALZONE (Lazio)

Preparation: 1 hour
Cooking time: 20 minutes

Ingredients for 4 people:

3½ ounces ricotta cheese
2½ ounces boiled ham in thick
slices
1 tablespoon grated Parmesan
cheese
3 eggs
salt
pepper
4 tablespoons butter, softened
10½ ounces (about 2 cups) flour
cooking oil for frying

1. Dice the cheese and ham.
2. In a bowl mix the grated Parmesan cheese, a whole egg, the diced cheese and ham, with a pinch of salt and pepper.
3. Prepare dough for the panzerotti as follows: heap the flour on a work-top and place pieces of softened butter in the middle, two egg yolks (keep the whites), and a drop of water; then knead well by hand. When the dough is uniform, roll out very thinly and then cut out disks about 4½ inches in diameter.
4. Fill each disk with the first mixture.
5. Beat the egg whites and brush around the edges of the disks.
6. Fold the disks over into a half-moon shape.
7. Heat plenty of cooking oil in a wide pan.
8. Fry the panzerotti in the hot oil and drain as soon as they become golden. Drain on paper towels and serve piping hot.

Schiacciata con le cipolle

ONION FOCACCIA (Umbria)

Preparation: 30 minutes; 3 rising
Cooking time: 30 minutes

Ingredients for 6 people:

2 teaspoons active dry yeast
10½ ounces (about 2 cups) flour
salt
olive oil
1½ onions
a few fresh sage leaves

1. Prepare the dough for the bread as follows: dissolve the yeast in water, heap the flour on the work-top and knead with the yeast, a pinch of salt, 1 tablespoon oil and, if necessary, a bit of water. Knead well to form a uniform dough. Set aside to rise covered with a cloth in a warm place for 3 hours.
2. In the meantime, finely slice the onion and dry on a cloth sprinkled with salt.
3. Chop the sage.
4. When the dough has risen, heat the oven to 375°F and grease a pizza pan or a large cake pan with a little olive oil.
5. Spread out the dough in the pan. Baste the surface with olive oil and cover with the sliced onion and chopped sage.
6. Bake for 30 minutes. Serve piping hot.

This schiacciata is also an excellent snack.

◀ *Panzerotti*

217

Bavette al pesce

BAVETTE PASTA WITH FISH (Tuscany)

Preparation: 20 minutes
Cooking time: 30 minutes

Ingredients for 4 people:

14 ounces red mullet, cleaned and scaled
1½ onions
1 stalk of celery
1 carrot, peeled
salt
4 tablespoons olive oil
1 clove of garlic
1 red chili pepper or ⅛ teaspoon cayenne pepper
⅓ cup dry white wine
1 cup chopped parsley
14 ounces bavette pasta

1. Boil 1½ quarts of water with onion, celery, carrot, and a little salt. When the water comes to a boil, add the fish and cook for 5 minutes.
2. Drain the fish but keep the cooking liquid.
3. Strain this liquid.
4. Remove the head, tail, bones, and skin from the red mullet. Chop the fillets into pieces.
5. Bring water to a boil to cook the pasta.
6. Chop the remaining ½ onion, then sauté in the oil in a large pan with the clove of garlic and the whole chili pepper (if you use cayenne pepper, add later).
7. When the onion is blanched, add the fish and fry gently for a moment or two. Remove the chili pepper and then add the white wine. Evaporate the wine over high heat.
8. In the meantime, when the water for pasta comes to a boil, add salt and the bavette.
9. Add the parsley to the fish (plus the cayenne pepper if used), a pinch of salt, and a couple of tablespoons of the fish stock. Mix and cook for a few minutes.
10. Drain the pasta when cooked to a firm bite and add to the pan with the fish. Mix well, season with a little olive oil, and heat for few minutes. Serve piping hot.

◀ *Bavette al pesce*

Bucatini all'Amatriciana
BUCATINI WITH AMATRICIANA SAUCE (Latium)

Preparation: 5 minutes
Cooking time: 30 minutes

Ingredients for 4 people:

5 ounces bacon
1 tablespoon olive oil
salt
1 pound bucatini
⅓ cup grated pecorino cheese

1. Boil the water to cook the pasta.
2. Cut the bacon into thin strips.
3. Fry the bacon gently in the oil.
4. When the water for the pasta comes to a boil, add salt and the pasta.
5. When the pasta is cooked to a firm bite, drain and season with bacon and the grated pecorino cheese. Mix well and serve piping hot.

This dish originates from Amatrice, a small town in the Sabina region, and has become the symbol of regional cooking in Latium.

Farfalle alle zucchine
BOW-TIE PASTA WITH ZUCCHINI SAUCE (Various regions)

Preparation: 15 minutes
Cooking time: 30 minutes

Ingredients for 4 people:

1 pound zucchini
3½ ounces smoked *pancetta*
6 tablespoons olive oil
1 clove of garlic
salt
pepper
1 pound farfalle
3 tablespoons grated Parmesan cheese

1. Boil the water for the pasta.
2. Cut the zucchini into thin slices.
3. Dice the *pancetta* finely.
4. Fry the *pancetta* gently in the oil with the clove of garlic.
5. Add the zucchini to the *pancetta*, a pinch of salt and pepper, 3 tablespoons water, and cook for 20-25 minutes.
6. In the meantime, when the water comes to a boil add salt and the pasta.
7. When the pasta is ready, drain and season with the zucchini.
8. Heat for a few minutes and serve hot, sprinkled with grated cheese.

Cacciucco di ceci

CHICK PEA SOUP (Tuscany)

Preparation: 35 minutes
Cooking time: 2 hours 10 minutes

Ingredients for 6 people:

10½ ounces fresh beets
2 onions
⅓ cup olive oil
1 clove of garlic
2 salted anchovies
1 pound dry chick peas (softened
in water for at least 12 hours) or 16
ounce can chick peas
1 tablespoon tomato sauce
salt, pepper
4 slices of country bread, preferably
unsalted Tuscan bread
3 tablespoons grated pecorino cheese

1. Carefully wash the beets and boil for 20-25 minutes.
2. Finely chop the onions.
3. Sauté in the oil the onion, clove of garlic, and the well-washed and boned anchovies.
4. When the onion begins to blanch and the anchovies turn into a paste, add the chick peas and the beets and cover with water. Add the tomato sauce, salt, and pepper and cook for 2 hours with the lid on, stirring occasionally.
5. In the meantime, toast the bread (or grill on the barbeque).
6. Arrange the slices of bread on serving dishes and, when ready, pour the soup on top. Sprinkle with grated pecorino cheese and serve piping hot.

▼ *Cacciucco*

Cacciucco alla Livornese
SEAFOOD SOUP LIVORNESE-STYLE (Tuscany)

Preparation: 1 hour
Cooking time: about 50 minutes

Ingredients for 4 people:

21 ounces mixed fish (any of red
mullet, scorpion fish, sole, angler
fish (tails), moray, conger-eel)
17½ ounces mussels
12 ounces dog-fish
12 ounces cuttlefish
12 ounces octopus
12 large shrimp
1 onion
2 cloves of garlic
sprig of parsley
⅓ cup olive oil
1 red chili pepper ⅛ teaspoon
cayenne pepper
1 cup red wine
17½ ounces canned peeled
tomatoes
salt
6 slices of country bread, preferably
unsalted Tuscan bread

1. Carefully clean all the fish. Remove the scales, innards, fins, heads, and tails. Wash well and cut the larger fish into smaller pieces.
2. Clean the mussels and scrape the shells with a stiff brush; remove the "beard."
3. Skin the dog-fish and cut into small slices.
4. Remove the skin, bone, and beak (between the eyes) of the cuttlefish. Pull on the tentacles to remove the innards. Wash the cuttlefish well and cut into rings.
5. Turn the sac of the octopus inside out through the opening between the tentacles and eliminate the innards. Turn the sac back and skin. Remove the eyes and beak with the help of a knife or by pressing with your thumbs. Cut into pieces.
6. Rinse the shrimp.
7. Chop the onion, clove of garlic, and parsley together, then fry gently in the oil with the chili pepper (whole or powder) in a pan large enough to hold all the fish.
8. When the onion begins to blanch, add the wine and evaporate on high heat. When the wine has evaporated, add the cuttle fish and octopus.
9. After 5 minutes, add the tomato and ½ cup hot water, salt, and cook for another 10 minutes.
10. Then add all the other fish, starting with those that take longer to cook and ending with the mussels and shellfish. Cook slowly for about 30 minutes.
11. In the meantime, toast the slices of bread, rub them with a clove of garlic, and arrange on four serving dishes.
12. When the fish is cooked, pour the soup over each slice of bread. Make sure every serving has shrimp and discard any mussels that did not open during cooking, because they are probably not fresh.

This fish soup, with variants in different cities, is one of the great recipes in Tuscan regional cuisine from Viareggio to Grosseto. Although considered a first course, it can also be served as a main course, especially in summer.

◀ *Cacciucco alla Livornese*

Fusilli alla Marchigiana
FUSILLI MARCHES-STYLE (Marches)

Preparation: 10 minutes
Cooking time: 30 minutes

Ingredients for 4 people:

12 ounces peeled fresh tomatoes
2 ounces black olives
3½ ounces smoked *pancetta*
2½ tablespoons olive oil
a few sage leaves
salt
pepper
1 pound fusilli
1½ tablespoons vinegar
⅓ cup grated pecorino cheese

1. Chop the peeled tomatoes.
2. Pit the olives and chop.
3. Dice the *pancetta* and fry gently in the oil with the sage leaves.
4. Add the peeled tomatoes, olives, salt, and pepper and cook for 25 minutes.
5. Boil the water to cook the pasta.
6. When the water comes to a boil, add salt and the pasta.
7. A few minutes before the sauce is ready, remove the sage leaves, add the vinegar, and stir.
8. When the pasta is ready, drain and season with the sauce and grated pecorino cheese. Serve piping hot.

Fusilli con tonno e fagiolini
FUSILLI WITH TUNA AND GREEN BEANS (Various regions)

Preparation: 30 minutes
Cooking time: 30 minutes

Ingredients for 4 people:

9 ounces fresh green beans
1 clove of garlic
4 tablespoons olive oil
3 tablespoons tomato sauce
salt
3½ ounces tuna in oil
1 pound fusilli
1½ tablespoons chopped parsley
½ cup grated Parmesan cheese

1. Top and tail the green beans, wash, and then boil in salted water for 15 minutes.
2. Boil the water for the pasta.
3. Sauté the clove of garlic in the oil; when it blanches, remove.
4. Add the tomato sauce to the oil with salt and cook for 15 minutes.
5. Break up the tuna.
6. Drain the green beans and break into pieces.
7. When the water for the pasta comes to a boil, add salt and the fusilli.
8. After the first 20 minutes cooking the tomatoes, add the chopped green beans, tuna, and parsley and cook for another 10 minutes.
9. When the pasta is ready, drain and season with the sauce and grated cheese.

Linguine all'origano
LINGUINE WITH MARJORAM (Various regions)

Preparation: 10 minutes
Cooking time: 25 minutes

Ingredients for 4 people:

1 clove of garlic
1 onion
salt
1 pound linguine
8 tablespoons olive oil
2 tablespoons marjoram
2 tablespoons chopped parsley
pepper
3 tablespoons grated Parmesan
cheese

1. Boil the water for the pasta.
2. Chop the clove of garlic.
3. Finely chop the onion.
4. When the water comes to a boil, add salt and the linguine.
5. In a pan large enough to hold all the pasta, sauté the onion and garlic in the oil.
6. Add the marjoram, parsley, and a little pepper. Flavor for a few minutes and then remove from the heat.
7. When the pasta is ready, drain and add to the pan with the herbs. Heat for a few minutes and serve sprinkled with grated cheese.

Panzanella

MIXED VEGETABLES ON SOAKED BREAD (Tuscany)

Preparation: 25 minutes

Ingredients for 4 people:

8 slightly stale slices of country bread, preferably unsalted Tuscan bread
4 ripe tomatoes
1 cucumber
1 red onion
a few leaves of basil
salt
pepper
olive oil
vinegar

1. Place the slices of bread in a bowl and add a little water.
2. In the meantime, wash and slice the tomatoes.
3. Remove the outer leaves of the onion and then slice.
4. Peel the cucumber and cut into thin slices.
5. When the bread is soaked in water, squeeze.
6. Break the bread into another bowl.
7. Cover the bread with the slices of tomato, onion, and cucumber; add the basil, a pinch of salt, and a pinch of pepper. Season with oil and vinegar and mix well. Place in the refrigerator for 10 minutes before serving.

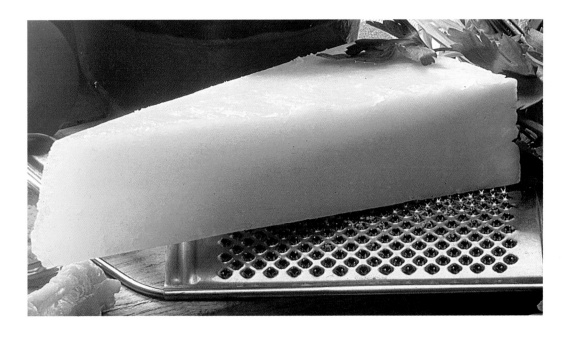

Gnocchi di semolino alla Romana

SEMOLINA GNOCCHI ROMAN-STYLE (Latium)

Preparation: 1 hour 15 minutes
Cooking time: 30 minutes

Ingredients for 4 people:

3 cups milk
salt
5 tablespoons butter
9 ounces semolina (pasta flour)
pepper
nutmeg
2 eggs
1 cup grated Parmesan cheese

1. Bring the milk to a boil with 2 cups of water, a pinch of salt, and a pat of butter.
2. When the milk comes to a boil, lower the heat and slowly add the semolina, stirring well to avoid forming lumps. Add salt and pepper and sprinkle with nutmeg. Cook for 20 minutes stirring continually.
3. Remove from the heat, add the eggs and ½ cup Parmesan cheese, and mix well.
4. Pour this mixture onto a work-top. Use a rolling pin to roll out a piece of dough about ½ inch thick; set aside to cool.
5. When the semolina is cool, use a glass to cut out disks about 2 inches in diameter.
6. Heat the oven to 400°F.
7. Butter an oven-proof dish.
8. Melt the butter in a saucepan.
9. Place the strips of left-over semolina in the butter, sprinkle with a little grated cheese, and pour in a little melted butter.
10. Place the gnocchi in parallel rows slightly overlapping each other in the oven dish on top of the other semolina and sprinkle with cheese and the remaining melted butter.
11. Bake for 30 minutes. Serve piping hot.

Maccheroni alla chitarra

SQUARE SPAGHETTI IN TOMATO SAUCE (Abruzzo)

Preparation: 1 hour
Cooking time: 30 minutes

Ingredients for 4 people:

for the pasta:
15½ ounces (about 3 cups) durum wheat flour
3 eggs
salt

for the sauce:
½ onion
½ carrot, peeled
½ stalk of celery
1 clove of garlic
4 tablespoons butter
3 tablespoons olive oil
½ pound ground beef
½ cup dry white wine
½ cup stock
9 ounces canned peeled tomatoes
salt

1. To prepare this dish you must have the "chitarra," a square, guitar-like utensil with many taut steel wires used to prepare the pasta.
2. Heap the flour on a work-top.
3. Add a pinch of salt and the eggs to the hollow in the top of the flour.
4. Knead the dough firmly for 20 minutes until it is smooth and uniform.
5. Roll the dough into a ball and set aside for 15 minutes in the refrigerator covered with a cloth.
6. Roll out the pasta dough with a rolling pin as thick as the space between the wires on the cutting utensil (the pasta should be square in shape).
7. Cut out rectangles of the same size as the cutting utensil.
8. Place the rectangles of dough one at a time on top of the "guitar" and pass over with the rolling pin: the pasta will drop onto the base in thick strips.
9. Boil the water for the pasta.
10. Prepare the meat sauce as given in the recipe on page 126.
11. When the water comes to a boil, add salt and the pasta.
12. Drain the pasta when cooked to a firm bite. Season with the sauce, sprinkle with grated cheese, and serve immediately.

Maccheroni alla chitarra can be flavored with any kind of sauce—they are excellent, for example, with the lamb sauce described on page 232.

◄ *Maccheroni alla chitarra*

Pappardelle maremmane
PAPPARDELLE MAREMMA-STYLE (Tuscany)

Preparation: 20 minutes
Cooking time: 40 minutes

Ingredients for 4 people:

½ onion
1 carrot, peeled
1 stalk of celery
1 clove of garlic
1 ounce walnuts
2 ounces sliced *pancetta*
1 sausage
1 ounce fresh mushrooms
4 tablespoons olive oil
7 ounces chicken livers
½ cup red wine
9 ounces canned peeled tomatoes
salt
pepper
1 pound pappardelle
4 tablespoons grated Parmesan
cheese

1. Chop the onion, carrot, celery, garlic, and walnuts.
2. Dice the *pancetta* finely.
3. Skin the sausage and break into pieces.
4. Wash the mushrooms, then slice thinly.
5. Sauté the chopped vegetables and walnuts in the oil for 5 minutes.
6. Add the *pancetta*, sausage, livers, and wine to this mixture and cook for 10 minutes.
7. Add the tomatoes and mushrooms, salt and pepper and cook for 25 minutes.
8. Boil the water for the pasta. When the water comes to a boil, add salt and the pappardelle.
9. When the pasta is ready, drain and flavor with the sauce. Serve immediately, sprinkled with grated Parmesan cheese.

◀ *Pappardelle maremmane*

231

Pipe al sugo d'agnello
PIPE PASTA WITH LAMB SAUCE (Marches)

Preparation: 30 minutes
Cooking time: 1 hour 45 minutes

Ingredients for 4 people:

½ onion
3½ ounces slice of *pancetta*
10½ ounces lamb
2 tablespoons olive oil
2 tablespoons butter
1 clove of garlic
1 cup red wine
3 tablespoons tomato sauce
meat stock
salt
pepper
5 ounces fresh or frozen peas
1 pound pipe pasta
3 tablespoons grated Parmesan cheese

1. Chop the onion.
2. Cut the *pancetta* into thin strips.
3. Dice the lamb finely.
4. Fry the *pancetta* gently in the oil and butter for a few minutes.
5. Add the onion and clove of garlic.
6. When the onion begins to blanch, add the lamb and fry gently for a few minutes.
7. Add the wine and evaporate over high heat.
8. Add the tomato sauce, a ladle of stock, a pinch of salt and pepper, and cook for 1 hour 45 minutes, stirring frequently and adding stock if the sauce becomes too thick.
9. Once the sauce has been cooking for an hour, boil the water for the pasta.
10. Add the peas to the meat sauce and cook for the last 20 minutes.
11. In the meantime, when the water comes to a boil, add salt and the pasta.
12. When the pasta is ready, drain and flavor with the sauce. Serve hot, sprinkled with grated cheese.

Penne all'arrabbiata
PENNE IN A HOT TOMATO SAUCE (Tuscany)

Preparation: 10 minutes
Cooking time: 30 minutes

Ingredients for 4 people:

3½ ounces smoked *pancetta*, 2-3 slices
5 ounces fresh mushrooms
3 tablespoons butter
7 ounces canned tomato sauce
½ chili pepper
4 basil leaves
salt
1 pound penne
2 tablespoons grated Parmesan cheese
2 tablespoons grated pecorino cheese

1. Boil the water for the pasta.
2. Dice the *pancetta* finely.
3. Clean the mushrooms and slice finely.
4. Sauté the *pancetta* in the butter for a few minutes.
5. Add the mushrooms and cook for a few minutes.
6. Add the tomato, chili pepper, basil leaves, and salt and cook for 25 minutes.
7. In the meantime, when the water comes to a boil, add salt and the pasta.
8. When the pasta is ready, drain and season with the sauce.
9. Serve sprinkled with the grated cheeses.

Penne al rosmarino
PENNE WITH ROSEMARY (Various regions)

Preparation: 10 minutes
Cooking time: 30 minutes

Ingredients for 4 people:

1 onion
2 cloves of garlic
3 sprigs of rosemary
1 tablespoon pine nuts
4 tablespoons butter
3 tablespoons olive oil
1 cup dry white wine
1 bouillon cube
½ red chili pepper (or ⅛ teaspoon cayenne pepper)
salt
1 pound penne
3 tablespoons grated Parmesan cheese

1. Boil the water for the pasta.
2. Chop the onion, garlic, rosemary, and pine nuts.
3. Fry these chopped ingredients gently in a pan with butter and oil.
4. When it blanches, add the white wine, the bouillon cube, and chili pepper. Cook for 10 minutes on low heat.
5. In the meantime, when the water has come to a boil, add salt and the pasta.
6. When the pasta is ready, drain and flavor with the sauce. Serve sprinkled with grated cheese.

Penne agli asparagi

PENNE WITH ASPARAGUS (Various regions)

Preparation: 30 minutes
Cooking time: 30 minutes

Ingredients for 4 people:

1 pound asparagus
salt
1 pound penne
4 tablespoons butter
3 tablespoons grated Parmesan cheese
freshly ground pepper

1. Cut the base off the asparagus and keep only the green tips.
2. Steam until tender.
3. Boil the water for the pasta.
4. Drain the asparagus when ready.
5. When the water comes to a boil, add salt and the pasta.
6. Cut the asparagus into pieces.
7. Melt the butter in a pan and then add the asparagus.
8. When the pasta is ready, drain and add to the pan with the asparagus; heat for a few minutes. Serve sprinkled with grated Parmesan cheese and freshly ground pepper.

◄ *Penne agli asparagi*

Rigatoni gratinati

RIGATONI AU GRATIN (Various regions)

Preparation: 30 minutes
Cooking time: 50 minutes

Ingredients for 4 people:

1 eggplant
salt
½ onion
1 clove of garlic
5 tablespoons olive oil
9 ounces canned peeled tomatoes
basil
pepper
1 pound rigatoni
butter
⅓ cup grated Parmesan cheese
5 tablespoons breadcrumbs

1. Cut the eggplant into slices and sprinkle with a little salt to extract the bitter juice.
2. Chop the onion finely.
3. Dry and dice the eggplant.
4. Sauté the onion and clove of garlic in the oil.
5. When the onion blanches, add the eggplant and cook for 10 minutes.
6. Add the tomato, a few basil leaves, salt, and pepper and cook for 25 minutes.
7. Boil the water for the pasta; when it comes to a boil, add salt and the pasta.
8. In the meantime, butter an oven-proof dish.
9. Heat the oven to 400°F.
10. When the pasta is cooked to a firm bite, drain and flavor with the sauce.
11. Pour the pasta into the oven dish, add a drop of olive oil, and sprinkle with grated cheese and breadcrumbs. Bake for 15 minutes.

Spaghetti aglio, olio e peperoncino

SPAGHETTI WITH GARLIC, OIL, AND CHILI PEPPER (Molise)

Preparation: 5 minutes
Cooking time: 25 minutes

Ingredients for 4 people:

3 cloves of garlic
salt
1 pound spaghetti
1 red chili pepper
⅓ cup olive oil

1. Boil the water for the pasta.
2. Slice the garlic.
3. When the water comes to a boil, add salt and the pasta.
4. Heat the sliced garlic, chili pepper, and oil. When the garlic browns slightly, remove from the heat. Remove the garlic and chili pepper from the oil.
5. When the spaghetti is ready, drain and flavor with the savory oil and serve immediately.

◀ *Rigatoni gratinati*

Spaghetti ai peperoni
SPAGHETTI WITH BELL PEPPERS (Various regions)

Preparation: 10 minutes
Cooking time: 30 minutes

Ingredients for 4 people:

½ red bell pepper
½ yellow bell pepper
½ white onion
1 clove of garlic
6 tablespoons olive oil
6 anchovy fillets
salt
pepper
1 pound spaghetti
3 tablespoons grated Parmesan
cheese

1. Wash the peppers and remove the white fibers and seeds; cut into strips.
2. Finely chop the onion and sauté with the garlic in the oil.
3. Add the anchovies and break up with a fork.
4. Add the peppers, salt, and pepper and cook for 30 minutes. Stir occasionally and add a few tablespoons water if required.
5. Boil the water for the pasta. When the water comes to a boil, add salt and the pasta.
6. Drain the pasta when cooked to a firm bite and flavor with the sauce. Sprinkle with grated cheese and serve.

Spaghetti al sapore di granchio
SPAGHETTI FLAVORED WITH CRAB (Tuscany)

Preparation: 20 minutes
Cooking time: 45 minutes

Ingredients for 4 people:

17½ ounces soft-shelled crabs
½ onion
olive oil
1 clove of garlic
1 red chili pepper
1 cup chopped parsley
1 cup white wine
10½ ounces canned peeled
tomatoes
salt
1 pound spaghetti

1. Rinse the crabs and cut into large pieces.
2. Finely chop the onion.
3. In a large pan add the oil and sauté the chopped onion, clove of garlic, chili pepper, and chopped parsley.
4. When the onion blanches, remove the garlic and chili pepper and add the crab pieces. Moisten with the wine and cook for 15 minutes.
5. Add the peeled tomatoes and salt and cook for another 30 minutes.
6. Boil the water for pasta. When it comes to a boil, add salt and the pasta.
7. When the sauce is ready, squeeze the pieces of crab and then discard.
8. Drain the pasta when cooked to a firm bite and add to the pan of sauce. Heat for 5 minutes. Serve immediately.

◀ *Spaghetti al sapore di granchio*

Spaghetti alla carbonara
SPAGHETTI WITH EGG AND *PANCETTA* (Latium)

Preparation: 10 minutes
Cooking time: 25 minutes

Ingredients for 4 people:

3½ ounces smoked *pancetta*
a pat of butter
1 clove of garlic
3 eggs
2 tablespoons grated Parmesan cheese
2 tablespoons grated Roman pecorino cheese
freshly ground pepper
salt
1 pound spaghetti

1. Boil the water to cook the pasta.
2. Finely dice the *pancetta* and sauté in the butter with the clove of garlic. Remove the garlic when it begins to brown.
3. Break the eggs into a bowl and beat with the grated cheese and plenty of freshly ground black pepper.
4. When the water comes to a boil, add salt and the pasta.
5. Drain the pasta when cooked to a firm bite and mix with the eggs and *pancetta*. Mix well and serve.

Spaghetti alla Matriciana
SPAGHETTI WITH BACON AND TOMATO SAUCE (Marches)

Preparation: 10 minutes
Cooking time: 40 minutes

Ingredients for 4 people:

½ onion
3½ ounces thick sliced bacon
14 ounces canned peeled tomatoes
salt
pepper
stock
1 pound spaghetti

1. Finely chop the onion.
2. Fry the bacon over moderate heat in a casserole so that the fat dissolves slowly.
3. When the pork fat has dissolved completely, add the onion and continue frying.
4. As soon as the onion browns, add the tomatoes, salt, and pepper and cook for 30 minutes, stirring frequently. Add the stock if the sauce becomes too thick as it cooks.
5. Boil the water to cook the pasta and when it comes to a boil, add salt and the spaghetti.
6. Drain the spaghetti when cooked to a firm bite, mix with the sauce, and serve.

This recipe was "imported" to the Marches from Latium (it is similar to Bucatini all'amatriciana) and saw the addition of tomato. "Matriciana" and "amatriciana" are synonymous.

Spaghetti con tonno e capperi
SPAGHETTI WITH TUNA AND CAPERS (Various regions)

Preparation: 5 minutes
Cooking time: 25 minutes

Ingredients for 4 people:

salt
1 pound spaghetti
olive oil
4 ounces tuna in oil
2 heaping tablespoons pickled capers
3 tablespoons grated Parmesan cheese

1. Boil plenty of water; add salt and the pasta.
2. As the spaghetti cooks, pour 4 tablespoons oil into a saucepan and add the tuna and capers. Mix well so that the tuna breaks into pieces, and heat for a few minutes.
3. Drain the pasta when cooked to a firm bite, then flavor with the tuna and caper sauce; add a little olive oil, mix well, and sprinkle with the grated cheese; serve.

Tagliatelle con la ricotta romana
TAGLIATELLE WITH RICOTTA CHEESE (Latium)

Preparation: 5 minutes
Cooking time: 25 minutes

Ingredients for 4 people:

5 ounces ricotta cheese
5 ounces heavy cream
nutmeg
2 tablespoons butter
salt
12 ounces egg tagliatelle
3 tablespoons grated Parmesan cheese

1. Boil the water for the pasta.
2. Mix the ricotta and the cream with a wooden spoon until well blended. Add plenty of nutmeg.
3. When the water comes to a boil, add the pasta.
4. Melt the butter in a saucepan.
5. When the pasta is ready, drain and flavor with the melted butter. Add the cheese cream and mix well. Serve hot, sprinkled with the grated Parmesan cheese.

Tagliatelle al cinghiale
TAGLIATELLE WITH BOAR SAUCE (Tuscany)

Preparation: 10 minutes
Cooking time: 30 minutes

Ingredients for 4 people:

3 Italian boar sausages
3 tablespoons olive oil
salt
12 ounces egg tagliatelle
2 egg yolks
3 tablespoons grated Parmesan cheese
pepper
nutmeg

1. Boil the water for the pasta.
2. Skin and break up the sausages.
3. Gently fry the sausages for 10 minutes in the oil.
4. In the meantime, when the water comes to a boil, add salt and the pasta.
5. Beat the egg yolks together with the Parmesan cheese, a pinch of salt, pepper, and nutmeg.
6. When the pasta is ready, drain and add the beaten eggs and the sausages. Serve piping hot.

Tagliolini filanti alle erbe
TAGLIOLINI WITH MELTED CHEESE AND HERBS (Various regions)

Preparation: 5 minutes
Cooking time: 20 minutes

Ingredients for 4 people:

5 ounces mozzarella cheese
salt
1 pound tagliolini
1 clove of garlic
½ red chili pepper or a pinch of cayenne pepper
5 tablespoons olive oil
1½ tablespoons chopped fresh parsley
1½ tablespoons chopped fresh basil

1. Boil the water to cook the pasta.
2. Cut the mozzarella into thin strips.
3. When the water comes to a boil, add salt and the pasta.
4. Sauté the garlic with the chili pepper in the oil. When the garlic begins to brown, remove from the heat and remove the garlic and the pepper.
5. When the pasta is ready, drain and mix with the savory oil. Add the chopped parsley and basil and the mozzarella. Mix well and serve as soon as the mozzarella begins to melt from the heat of the pasta.

◄ *Tagliatelle al cinghiale*

243

Tagliolini al limone
TAGLIOLINI WITH LEMON (Various regions)

Preparation: 10 minutes
Cooking time: 20 minutes

Ingredients for 4 people:

2 lemons
4 tablespoons olive oil
salt
pinch of cayenne pepper
1 pound tagliolini
1 tablespoon chopped basil
1 cup chopped fresh parsley

1. Boil the water for the pasta.
2. Squeeze the lemons and strain the juice.
3. Add the oil and a pinch of salt and cayenne to the lemon juice. Mix well with a fork.
4. When the water comes to a boil, add salt and the pasta.
5. Drain the pasta when cooked to a firm bite and flavor with the sauce. Add the basil and parsley, mix well and serve immediately.

Zuppa di vongole
CLAM SOUP (Tuscany)

Preparation: 25 minutes
Cooking time: 25 minutes

Ingredients for 6 people:

4 pounds clams
1 pound fresh ripe tomatoes
olive oil
2 cloves of garlic
1 red chili pepper
1 cup chopped fresh parsley
1 cup white wine
salt
pepper
6 slices country bread, preferably unsalted Tuscan bread

1. Scrub the shells of the clams with a stiff brush under running water.
2. Wash the tomatoes, cut into pieces, and remove the seeds.
3. Sauté the clove of garlic in a large pan with 4 tablespoons olive oil, the chili, and parsley.
4. Just before the garlic browns, add the wine and allow it to evaporate.
5. Remove the garlic and chili pepper and add the tomatoes. Add salt and pepper and cook for 5 minutes.
6. Add the clams and cook for 15 minutes with the lid on, shaking the pan frequently.
7. In the meantime, toast or grill the slices of bread.
8. Rub the bread with a clove of garlic and arrange on serving plates.
9. When the soup is ready, pour it over the bread and serve immediately. Do not eat any clams that have not opened during the cooking process as they may not be fresh.

Cipollata

ONIONS AND SAUSAGES ON GRILLED BREAD (Tuscany)

Preparation: 30 minutes
Cooking time: 45 minutes

Ingredients for 4 people:

4 white onions
2 Italian sausages
2 ounces *pancetta*
5 cups stock
olive oil
salt
4 slices of country bread, preferably
unsalted Tuscan bread
3 tablespoons grated Parmesan
cheese
fresh ground pepper

1. Finely slice the onions.
2. Skin the sausages and cut into pieces.
3. Dice the *pancetta*.
4. Heat the stock.
5. Fry the onions in the oil with the sausages and *pancetta*.
6. When the onions are well-browned, add the stock and salt (be careful with the salt, since sausages are often rather salty themselves), mix, and cook for 45 minutes.
7. In the meantime, toast or grill the bread.
8. Arrange the bread on the serving plates. When the cipollata is ready, pour over the bread.
9. Serve sprinkled with grated cheese and freshly ground pepper.

▼ *Cipollata*

Minestra di fagioli alla Toscana
PASTA AND BEANS TUSCAN-STYLE (Tuscany)

Preparation: 15 minutes
Cooking time: about 1 hour 45
*   minutes*

Ingredients for 6 people:

salt
10½ ounces dry beans (cannellini
or borlotti) (soften in advance for
12 hours in water)
3 cloves of garlic
6 sage leaves
2 sprigs of rosemary
olive oil
1 red chili pepper
3 tablespoons tomato sauce
10½ ounces grooved ditalini pasta

1. Heat 6 cups of salted water, adding the beans, 2 whole cloves of garlic, 6 sage leaves, the rosemary, and 3 tablespoons oil. Cook for 1 hour 30 minutes.
2. In the meantime, sauté the remaining garlic and chili pepper in 3 tablespoons oil.
3. When the garlic begins to blanch, remove. Also remove the chili pepper and add a bit of water and the tomato sauce. Cook for 5 minutes.
4. When the beans are cooked, remove from the heat. Remove the garlic, sprigs of rosemary, and sage leaves.
5. Remove two-thirds of the beans and blend; then return to the pot with the whole beans.
6. Add the tomato sauce and return to a boil (add water if necessary).
7. When the soup comes to a boil, add the pasta.
8. When the pasta is cooked, remove from the heat and serve piping hot, seasoning with a little olive oil.

Minestra di farro umbra
SPELT SOUP UMBRIAN-STYLE (Umbria)

Preparation: 10 minutes
Cooking time: 2 hours 30 minutes

Ingredients for 4 people:

3½ ounces dry borlotti, bolita, or
pinto beans (soften in advance for
12 hours in water)
salt
1 onion
1 stalk of celery
1 carrot, peeled
5 tablespoons olive oil
2 tablespoons tomato sauce
9 ounces farro (spelt)
pepper
3 tablespoons grated pecorino
cheese

1. Place the beans in 6 cups of salted water and cook for 1 hour 30 minutes.
2. Chop the onion, celery, and carrot.
3. Sauté these in the oil. After 5 minutes add the tomato sauce and 2 tablespoons hot water and cook for another 10 minutes.
4. Pour this mixture into the stock.
5. Add the farro, salt, and pepper and cook for 1 hour.
6. Serve the soup lukewarm with a little olive oil and grated cheese.

◀ *Minestra di fagioli alla Toscana*

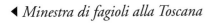

247

Pappa al pomodoro
TOMATO SOUP (Tuscany)

Preparation: 15 minutes
Cooking time: 35 minutes

Ingredients for 4 people:

21 ounces fresh ripe tomatoes
2 cloves of garlic
½ cup olive oil
6 basil leaves
salt
pepper
3 cups stock
9 ounces country bread, preferably unsalted Tuscan bread

1. Wash and peel the tomatoes; remove the seeds and cut into pieces.
2. Cut the cloves of garlic in half and sauté in the oil.
3. Add the tomatoes, basil, salt, and pepper and cook for 15 minutes.
4. In the meantime, heat the stock and cut the bread into thin slices.
5. Add the stock to the tomato sauce and cook for a further 15 minutes, stirring frequently, until creamy.
6. Serve this soup hot (but not boiling) or cold as preferred. Before serving, flavor with a little olive oil.

Minestrone alla Toscana
TUSCAN MINESTRONE (Tuscany)

Preparation: 1 hour
Cooking time: 1 hour 30 minutes

Ingredients for 4 people:

½ pound fresh beets
¼ pound fresh green beans
½ cabbage
2 zucchini
2 ripe tomatoes
2 potatoes
1 carrot
1 stalk of celery
1 onion
3½ ounces cannellini beans (if dry, soften in advance for 12 hours in water)
salt
1 clove of garlic
5 basil leaves
½ pound tagliatelle
olive oil
3 tablespoons grated Parmesan cheese

1. Wash and peel the beets and cut into pieces.
2. Top and tail the green beans, wash, and cut into pieces.
3. Remove the heart of the cabbage, wash, and cut into strips.
4. Top and tail the zucchini, wash, and cut into pieces.
5. Wash the tomatoes and chop into large pieces.
6. Peel the potatoes and the carrot. Wash and cut into pieces.
7. Remove the stringy fibers of the celery, wash, and cut into pieces.
8. Peel the onion and then chop finely.
9. Place all the vegetables in a pot, add salt, the clove of garlic, basil, and 4 cups of water. Cook for 1 hour once it comes to a boil.
10. Break up the tagliatelle.
11. After the soup has been cooking for 1 hour, add the broken tagliatelle.
12. When the pasta is ready, remove from the heat. Flavor with a little olive oil, sprinkle with grated cheese, and serve.

◄ *Pappa al pomodoro*

Ribollita
BREAD AND VEGETABLE SOUP (Tuscany)

Preparation: 1 hour 45 minutes
Cooking time: 1 hour 30 minutes

Ingredients for 4 people:

7 ounces cannellini beans (if dry, soften in advance for 12 hours in water)
½ red cabbage
½ green or white cabbage
2 potatoes
1 leek
1 stalk of celery
1 fresh ripe tomato
2 onions
1 carrot, peeled
olive oil
salt
pepper
9 ounces country bread, preferably unsalted Tuscan bread

1. Boil the beans in 3 cups water for 1 hour 30 minutes.
2. Remove the hearts from the cabbages, wash, and cut into strips.
3. Peel and wash the potatoes and then cut into large pieces.
4. Trim the leek of tough leaves, slice it, and rinse well of sand.
5. Remove the stringy fibers of the celery and cut into pieces.
6. Core the tomato and cut into pieces.
7. When the beans are cooked, drain (keeping the cooking stock). Reserve a ladle of beans and blend the rest. Return the bean purée to the cooking stock.
8. Finely chop 1 onion and the carrot and sauté in the oil in a large pot.
9. When the onion is tender, add all the vegetables, a ladle of water, salt, and pepper. Cook for 10 minutes with the lid on.
10. Add the bean cooking stock and cook for a further 50 minutes.
11. In the meantime, slice the bread.
12. Add the bread and the whole beans and simmer for another dozen minutes or so.
13. Heat the oven to 400°F.
14. Slice the remaining onion.
15. Pour the soup into an oven-proof dish and sprinkle with the sliced onion and a little olive oil. Bake until the onion becomes golden. Serve hot but not boiling.

◀ *Ribollita*

Risotto con le ortiche

RISOTTO WITH NETTLES* (Tuscany)

Preparation: 10 minutes
Cooking time: 20 minutes

Ingredients for 4 people:

7 ounces tender nettle leaves
½ onion
olive oil
vegetable stock
1⅔ cup arborio rice
salt
pepper
2 tablespoons butter
3 tablespoons grated Parmesan cheese

1. Wash and chop the nettle leaves.
2. Finely chop the onion and sauté in 4 tablespoons olive oil.
3. Add the nettle leaves and the rice. Salt and pepper to taste.
4. Add a ladle of stock and stir.
5. When the stock is absorbed, add another ladle and stir again. Continue in the same way until the rice is cooked (15-20 minutes).
6. When ready, remove from the heat. Add the butter and grated cheese and mix well. Serve as soon as the butter melts completely.

*Can also be made with parsley.

Risotto con le melanzane

RISOTTO WITH EGGPLANT (Various regions)

Preparation: 15 minutes
Cooking time: 40 minutes

Ingredients for 4 people:

1 pound eggplant
½ onion
4 tablespoons butter
3 tablespoons olive oil
9 ounces fresh ripe or canned tomatoes
salt
vegetable stock
1⅔ cups arborio rice
3 tablespoons grated Parmesan cheese

1. Peel and dice the eggplant.
2. Chop the onion and sauté in butter and oil.
3. When the onion begins to color, add the eggplant and salt and cook for 10 minutes.
4. In the meantime, chop the tomatoes.
5. After the first 10 minutes cooking time, add the tomatoes and cook for another 15 minutes.
6. Heat the stock.
7. Add the rice and a ladle of stock to the mixture.
8. When the stock is absorbed, add another ladle and stir again. Continue in the same way until the rice is ready (15-20 minutes).
9. When cooked, remove from the heat. Add the butter and grated cheese and mix well. Serve as soon as the butter melts.

Risotto con le seppie
RISOTTO WITH CUTTLEFISH (Tuscany)

Preparation: 20 minutes
Cooking time: 20 minutes

Ingredients for 4 people:

12 ounces cuttlefish
1 clove of garlic
2 tablespoons chopped parsley
olive oil
1 cup white wine
vegetable stock
1⅔ cup arborio rice
salt
freshly ground pepper

1. Carefully clean the cuttlefish. Remove the skin and bone. Use a knife to cut out the beak between the tentacles and the eyes. Pull the tentacles to extract the innards. Wash carefully.
2. Cut the cuttlefish (including the tentacles) into pieces.
3. Sauté the clove of garlic and 1 tablespoon parsley in 4 tablespoons olive oil.
4. Add the cuttlefish and after 5 minutes add the white wine and evaporate over high heat. Cook for another 10 minutes.
5. Heat the stock.
6. Add the rice, a ladle of boiling stock, and salt to the mixture.
7. When the stock is absorbed, add another ladleful and stir. Continue in the same way until the rice is ready (15-20 minutes).
8. Remove from the heat when cooked. Add 1 tablespoon parsley and freshly ground pepper, mix well, and serve.

▼ *Risotto con le seppie*

Stracciatella romana
EGG SOUP ROMAN-STYLE (Latium)

Preparation: 10 minutes
Cooking time: 15 minutes

Ingredients for 4 people:

4 eggs
3 tablespoons grated Parmesan
cheese
salt
nutmeg
3 cups meat stock
1 tablespoon chopped parsley

1. Beat the eggs with the cheese using a fork; add a pinch of salt and a little grated nutmeg.
2. Heat the stock.
3. When the stock comes to a boil, pour in the egg mixture and boil for 5 minutes, stirring continually with the fork.
4. When cooked, add the chopped parsley and serve.

Timballo di riso con i fegatini
RICE AND CHICKEN LIVERS TIMBALE (Latium)

Preparation: 10 minutes
Cooking time: 45 minutes

Ingredients for 4 people:

10 ounces chicken livers
½ onion
4 tablespoons butter
½ cup dry white wine
9 ounces fresh ripe or canned
tomatoes
salt
meat stock
1⅔ cup arborio rice
a little butter
3 tablespoons grated Parmesan
cheese

1. Clean the chicken livers and cut into pieces.
2. Chop the onion and sauté in the butter.
3. When the onion has colored, add the livers and wine. Evaporate the wine over high heat.
4. Add the tomatoes and salt and cook for 15 minutes.
5. Heat the stock separately.
6. Add the rice to the chicken livers with a ladle of stock and stir.
7. When the stock is absorbed, add another ladle and stir again. Continue adding stock in this way until the rice is cooked, taking care not to make the risotto too liquid. Cook for about 15 minutes and remove from the heat when cooked to a firm bite.
8. In the meantime, butter a timballo mold (you can also use a pudding mold or a simple cake dish with or without the raised central hole) and heat the oven to 400°F.
9. When the rice is ready, arrange in the mold, sprinkle with the grated cheese, and bake for 10 minutes.
10. Serve the timballo piping hot turned over onto a serving dish.

Zuppa di lenticchie
LENTIL SOUP (Latium)

Preparation: 15 minutes
Cooking time: 2 hours

Ingredients for 4 people:

9 ounces dry lentils
1 carrot, peeled
1 stalk of celery
½ onion
2 cloves of garlic
3 tablespoons olive oil
2 tablespoons butter
2 tablespoons tomato sauce
salt
pepper
a few slices of bread
1 tablespoon parsley

1. Cook the lentils over low heat in 6 cups of water for 1 hour 45 minutes.
2. Chop the carrot, celery, onion, and 1 clove of garlic.
3. Sauté these in the oil and butter.
4. Then add the tomato, a couple of tablespoons warm water, a pinch of salt and pepper, and cook for 15 minutes.
5. When the lentils are ready, blend (they are equally good whole).
6. Pour the tomato sauce over the lentils, stir, and cook for another 10 minutes.
7. Lightly toast the slices of bread in the oven and then rub with the other clove of garlic.
8. Arrange the slices of garlic bread on serving dishes. When the soup is ready, pour it over the bread. Sprinkle with chopped parsley and serve piping hot.

Zuppa di patate
POTATO SOUP (Tuscany)

Preparation: 25 minutes
Cooking time: 1 hour 10 minutes

Ingredients for 6 people:

2¼ pounds potatoes
9 ounces fresh ripe or canned tomatoes (or tomato sauce)
1 stalk of celery
1 carrot, peeled
1 onion
salt
a few slices of country bread, preferably unsalted Tuscan bread
olive oil
pepper
1 tablespoon chopped parsley
½ cup grated Parmesan cheese

1. Peel, wash, and dice the potatoes.
2. Chop the tomatoes.
3. Chop the celery, carrot, and onion.
4. Place all the vegetables in a pot, cover with 6 cups of water, add salt, and cook on low heat for 1 hour.
5. In the meantime, gently fry the slices of bread in plenty of oil or toast in the oven. Arrange on the serving dishes.
6. After an hour's cooking, blend the vegetables and then cook for another 10 minutes. Add salt and pepper as required.
7. When ready, add the parsley, grated cheese, and a little olive oil. Pour over the bread and serve piping hot.

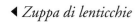
◄ *Zuppa di lenticchie*

Faraona al forno
ROAST GUINEA FOWL (Various regions)

Preparation: 20 minutes
Cooking time: 1 hour

Ingredients for 4 people:

1 guinea fowl
3 bay leaves
salt
pepper
1 cup olive oil
⅓ cup Marsala wine
2 ounces pitted green olives

1. Clean the guinea fowl.
2. Place the bay leaves inside the fowl. Add salt and pepper.
3. Heat the oven to 375°F.
4. Tie the fowl with kitchen string to keep it in shape.
5. Place the fowl in an oven-proof dish, baste with oil, and roast for 1 hour.
6. After the first 30 minutes' cooking time, baste the fowl with the Marsala wine and add the olives. As the fowl cooks, baste it occasionally with the cooking sauce.
7. Serve hot, preferably with a green salad.

Agnello con le olive alla Molisana
LAMB WITH OLIVES MOLISE-STYLE (Molise)

Preparation: 10 minutes
Cooking time: 20 minutes

Ingredients for 4 people:

a little all-purpose flour
21 ounces slices of lamb
8 tablespoons olive oil
4½ ounces black olives
dash of cayenne pepper
1 teaspoon marjoram
½ lemon
salt

1. Dip the lamb in the flour.
2. Heat the oil and fry the meat on both sides.
3. Pit and chop the olives.
4. Add the olives to the lamb, with the cayenne and marjoram, and cook on low heat.
5. Squeeze half a lemon and pour the juice over the lamb a few minutes before it is ready.
6. Remove from the heat, add salt, and serve.

Braciole d'abbacchio fritte
FRIED LAMB CHOPS (Latium)

Preparation: 15 minutes
Cooking time: 20 minutes

Ingredients for 4 people:

1¾ pounds small lamb chops
2 eggs
salt
pepper
breadcrumbs
8 tablespoons olive oil

1. Tenderize the chops.
2. Beat the eggs together with a pinch of salt and pepper using a fork.
3. Dip the chops in the egg and then in the breadcrumbs.
4. Heat the oil in a large pan. When hot, fry the chops on both sides.
5. When ready, remove from the heat and wrap a little foil around the exposed bone. Arrange on a serving plate and serve.

Abbacchio alla Romana
ROASTED-LAMB ROMAN-STYLE (Latium)

Preparation: 15 minutes
Cooking time: 1 hour 30 minutes

Ingredients for 4 people:

2¼ pounds lamb (leg, ribs, shoulder)
8 tablespoons olive oil
2 cloves of garlic
salt, pepper
2 sprigs of rosemary
2 salted anchovies
3 tablespoons white wine vinegar

1. Cut the lamb into pieces.
2. Sauté a clove of garlic in the oil. When it begins to brown, add the lamb and fry gently. Add salt and pepper.
3. Wash the sprigs of rosemary, remove the leaves and chop together with the washed and boned anchovies and a clove of garlic. Add vinegar and mix well.
4. When the lamb is cooked, add the anchovy sauce and mix. Heat for a few minutes until the vinegar evaporates. Serve hot.

▼ *Abbacchio alla Romana*

Coniglio all'Orbetellana
RABBIT ORBETELLO-STYLE (Tuscany)

Preparation: 30 minutes
Cooking time: 1 hour

Ingredients for 6 people:

1 rabbit, cut in 6-8 pieces
2 cloves of garlic
2 sprigs of rosemary
4 sage leaves
1 sprig of parsley
1 cup olive oil
½ cup white wine vinegar
salt
pepper
a few slices of country bread,
preferably unsalted Tuscan bread

1. Cut the clove of garlic in half and chop together with the rosemary, sage, and parsley.
2. Add the oil and vinegar and mix well. Salt and pepper to taste.
3. In a casserole, arrange a layer of rabbit and sprinkle with a little sauce; add a second layer and sprinkle again. Continue in this way until the ingredients are used up.
4. Cook the rabbit on low heat in a covered pot for 1 hour without stirring.
5. In the meantime, toast the slices of bread (in the oven or on a barbecue).
6. Serve the rabbit on the slices of bread.

Coniglio con le olive
RABBIT WITH OLIVES (Tuscany)

Preparation: 40 minutes
Cooking time: 1 hour 10 minutes

Ingredients for 4 people:

3 ounces *pancetta*
1 onion
1 carrot, peeled
1 stalk of celery
2 cloves of garlic
rosemary
sage
1 cup olive oil
1 rabbit, cut in 6-8 pieces
1 rabbit liver
salt
pepper
1 cup white wine
stock
7 ounces pitted black olives

1. Dice the *pancetta*.
2. Chop the onion, carrot, celery, garlic, rosemary, and sage.
3. Gently fry this mixture in the oil.
4. Add the rabbit and fry gently. Salt and pepper.
5. Pour in the wine and evaporate on high heat.
6. Then cook slowly for 1 hour, adding a little stock occasionally.
7. Wash the rabbit liver and cut into small pieces.
8. Add the diced liver 15 minutes before the rabbit is ready.
9. Remove from the heat and place the rabbit aside, keeping it warm. Chop up the cooking sauce.
10. Pour the sauce over the rabbit, add a little stock and the olives. Cook for another 5 minutes and then serve.

◀ *Coniglio all'Orbetellana*

Fettine di maiale umbre

PORK CUTLETS UMBRIAN-STYLE (Umbria)

Cooking time: 10 minutes

Ingredients for 6 people:

8 tablespoons olive oil
1¾ pound pork cutlets
2 tablespoons capers
1 small cup red wine
the juice of half a lemon
salt
pepper

1. Pour the olive oil into a pan; when it is hot, add the pork slices and cook for a few minutes on one side.
2. Turn the slices of meat and sprinkle with red wine and lemon juice.
3. Add the capers and a pinch of salt and pepper.
4. Serve hot.

Fiorentina

T-BONE STEAK FLORENTINE (Tuscany)

Cooking time: 5 minutes

Ingredients for 4 people:

2 large T-bone steaks, about 1 inch thick
salt
pepper

1. Heat the grill or the barbecue.
2. When very hot, cook the steaks.
3. Cook on one side until marked by the grill, then turn and cook on the other side.
4. The steaks should be served rare; add salt and pepper just before serving.

Florentine T-bone steaks are famous for their size and may even weigh over 2 pounds each. They should be cooked very quickly so that they are browned on the outside and rare in the middle.

Frittata con le cipolle
ONION OMELET (Abruzzo)

Preparation: 25 minutes
Cooking time: 10 minutes

Ingredients for 4 people:

2 onions
olive oil
6 eggs
1 tablespoon marjoram
salt
pepper

1. Finely slice the onions.
2. Cook the onions on low heat with 5 tablespoons olive oil and 2 tablespoons water for 15 minutes.
3. In the meantime, beat the eggs with the marjoram, a pinch of salt, and pepper.
4. Take the onions off the heat, add to the eggs, and mix well.
5. Grease a pan with a little oil and place over medium-low heat.
6. When the oil is hot, pour in the egg and onion mixture and cook on one side.
7. When the first side is cooked, turn the omelet by sliding it onto a dish or pan lid and cook on the other side. Serve hot or cold as preferred.

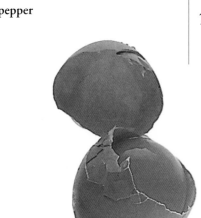

Frittata di spaghetti
SPAGHETTI FRITTERS (Various regions)

Preparation: 10 minutes
   (if you don't have left-over spaghetti, calculate an extra 20-25 minutes)
Cooking time: 10 minutes

Ingredients for 4 people:

5 ounces raw spaghetti (or about 3 cups cooked from a previous meal)
3 eggs
2 tablespoons grated Parmesan cheese
salt, pepper
nutmeg
2 tablespoons butter

1. Cook spaghetti in boiling salted water and drain.
2. Beat the eggs with the grated cheese, a pinch of salt and pepper, and a little nutmeg.
3. Mix the spaghetti and eggs.
4. Melt the butter in a pan; when hot, add the egg-spaghetti mixture and cook for a few minutes.
5. When cooked on the first side, turn by sliding onto a plate or pot lid and flipping over.
6. When ready, drain the fritter on paper towel. This dish is best served hot.

Lesso rifatto
LEFT-OVER BOILED MEAT (Tuscany)

Preparation: 15 minutes
Cooking time: 40 minutes

Ingredients for 4 people:

21 ounces left-over boiled meat;
beef, lamb, or pork
1 onion
1 carrot, peeled
1 stalk of celery
2 ounces *pancetta*
4 tablespoons olive oil
1 cup red wine
9 ounces canned peeled tomatoes
salt
pepper

1. Cut the left-over boiled meat into regular pieces.
2. Chop the onion, carrot, celery, and *pancetta*.
3. Gently fry the chopped mixture in oil.
4. Add the diced meat and fry gently for a few minutes. Add the red wine and evaporate over high heat.
5. After a few minutes, add the tomatoes, salt and pepper. Cook for 30 minutes.

Ossibuchi alla Fiorentina
OSSO BUCO FLORENTINE (Tuscany)

Preparation: 10 minutes
Cooking time: 1 hour 30 minutes

Ingredients for 6 people:

6 veal ossibuchi
a little flour
1 onion
a few sage leaves
1 clove of garlic
8 tablespoons olive oil
1 cup white wine
9 ounces canned tomato sauce
2 cups of stock
salt
pepper

1. Tenderize the ossibuchi and dip in the flour.
2. Finely slice the onion and sauté with the sage leaves and clove of garlic in the olive oil.
3. When the onion begins to blanch, add the ossibuchi and fry gently on both sides for a few minutes.
4. Add the white wine and evaporate over high heat.
5. Lower the heat and pour the tomato sauce and 2 cups of stock over the ossibuchi. Add salt and pepper and cook for 1 hour 15 minutes on low heat.

◄ *Lesso rifatto*

Pasticcio di patate
POTATO TIMBALE (Abruzzo)

Preparation: 30 minutes
Cooking time: 1 hour

Ingredients for 4-6 people:

1¾ pounds potatoes
1 small smoked mozzarella cheese
and 1 small provola cheese (or 9
ounces mixed cheeses)
butter
salt
nutmeg
2 eggs
2 cups milk
½ cup grated Parmesan cheese
a few breadcrumbs

1. Wash the potatoes and place in a large pot of water; bring to a boil; continue boiling for ten minutes.
2. In the meantime, cut the cheese into thin slices.
3. When ready, drain, peel, and slice the potatoes.
4. Butter an oven-proof dish (or a tube pan).
5. Arrange alternating layers of potatoes and cheese in the dish until all the ingredients are used; season each layer with pats of butter, salt, and a pinch of nutmeg.
6. Heat the oven to 375°F.
7. Beat the eggs with a pinch of salt, then gradually add the milk and mix well. Pour this mixture over the potatoes.
8. Sprinkle the potatoes with grated Parmesan cheese and some breadcrumbs. Bake for about 1 hour. Serve the pasticcio hot or lukewarm as preferred.

▼ *Pasticcio di patate*

Petti di pollo alle melanzane

CHICKEN BREAST WITH EGGPLANT (Various regions)

Preparation: 1 hour
Cooking time: 15 minutes

Ingredients for 4 people:

1 eggplant
salt
1 cup olive oil
4 slices of chicken breast
a little flour
1 sprig of parsley
1 clove of garlic
4 tablespoons butter
1 cup white wine

1. Peel and dice the eggplant. Sprinkle with salt and set aside for about 30 minutes to extract the bitter juice.
2. Dry the diced eggplant on a paper towel.
3. In a pan, heat the olive oil. When the oil is hot, add the diced eggplant. As soon as the pieces are golden, remove from the heat and drain on paper towels.
4. Tenderize the chicken breasts and dip in the flour.
5. Chop the parsley and the clove of garlic.
6. Melt the butter in a pan; add the chicken slices and brown on both sides.
7. Add the eggplant and the chopped garlic and parsley.
8. Pour in the wine and evaporate over medium-high heat. Lower the heat and cook until a thick sauce is made. Salt and serve the chicken.

Pollo alla diavola

GRILLED PEPPERED CHICKEN (Tuscany)

Preparation: 40 minutes; plus time to
prepare the barbecue, if used
Cooking time: 45 minutes

Ingredients for 4 people:

1 chicken
1 cup olive oil
salt
1 teaspoon freshly ground black
pepper

1. Wash and cut the chicken along the back and open out like a book.
2. Flatten out as far as possible with a tenderizing mallet (but be careful not to break the bones).
3. Mix the oil with a pinch of salt and the pepper. Baste the chicken.
4. Place the chicken in a dish, cover, and marinate for about 30 minutes, turning occasionally so that the chicken absorbs the seasoning.
5. Grease a grill or griddle well.
6. Heat the griddle or prepare red-hot barbecue charcoals.
7. Place the chicken on the grill or over the charcoals and cook for 45 minutes. If cooked on a griddle, cover and place a weight on top. Turn the chicken halfway through cooking. Serve piping hot.

◀ *Timballo di patate*

Pollo alla cacciatora in bianco

HUNTER'S CHICKEN (Tuscany)

Preparation: 15 minutes
Cooking time: 50 minutes

Ingredients for 4 people:

1 chicken cut into 6-8 pieces
a little flour
1 onion
3 tablespoons olive oil
3 tablespoons butter
5 sage leaves
1 cup white wine
salt, pepper
meat stock
2 cloves of garlic
1 sprig of rosemary
a little vinegar

1. Dip the pieces of chicken in the flour.
2. Finely slice the onion, then sauté in the oil and butter with the sage leaves.
3. Add the chicken and sauté for a few minutes.
4. Pour the wine over the chicken and evaporate over medium-high heat.
5. Add salt and pepper to the chicken, and then cook on low heat for 45 minutes. As the chicken cooks, turn the pieces occasionally and baste with a little stock so that the dish does not become too dry.
6. Chop the cloves of garlic with the rosemary.
7. When the chicken is cooked, add the chopped herbs and 2 tablespoons vinegar. Evaporate the vinegar over high heat and then serve the chicken.

Pollo alla Romana

CHICKEN ROMAN-STYLE (Latium)

Preparation: 15 minutes
Cooking time: 50 minutes

Ingredients for 4 people:

3 green bell peppers
14 ounces fresh ripe tomatoes
2 cloves of garlic
5 tablespoons olive oil
1 chicken cut into 6-8 pieces
½ cup white wine
salt
pepper
a little stock

1. Wash the peppers, remove the seeds and stringy fibers, and then cut into pieces. Chop the tomatoes.
2. Sauté the cloves of garlic in the oil. Add the pieces of chicken and fry gently.
3. After 5 minutes, remove the cloves of garlic, add the white wine, and evaporate on high heat for a few minutes.
4. Add the chopped tomatoes and peppers. Add salt and pepper and cook for 40 minutes on medium heat. If the chicken dries too much as it cooks, add a little stock. Serve hot.

◄ *Pollo alla cacciatora in bianco*

269

Pollo in fricassea

CHICKEN FRICASSEE (Tuscany)

Preparation: 15 minutes
Cooking time: 45 minutes

Ingredients for 4 people:

1 chicken cut into 6-8 pieces
a little flour
½ onion
2 tablespoons butter
3 tablespoons olive oil
a little stock
salt
pepper
1 egg
juice of half a lemon

1. Dip the chicken in the flour and shake to remove the excess.
2. Chop the onion, then sauté in the butter and oil.
3. Add the pieces of chicken, a little stock, salt, and pepper and cook for 45 minutes in a closed pot. Baste with a little stock as the chicken cooks so that it dosen't become too dry.
4. When the chicken is ready, remove from the heat.
5. Beat the egg with the lemon juice. Add this to the chicken and mix quickly so that the egg doesn't cook but forms a sauce.
6. Arrange the chicken on a serving dish and garnish with slices of lemon; serve immediately.

▼ *Pollo in fricassea*

Salsicce alla Marchigiana
SAUSAGES MARCHE-STYLE (Marches)

Preparation: 10 minutes
Cooking time: 30 minutes

Ingredients for 6 people:

2 pound Italian sausages
4 tablespoons butter
1½ tablespoons flour
½ cup dry white wine
½ cup stock

1. Prick the sausages with a fork and fry gently in a little butter.
2. Add 2-3 tablespoons water and cook for 25 minutes.
3. Remove the sausages from the pan and keep warm. Retain the cooking sauce.
4. Soften the butter without melting it completely and mix with the flour.
5. Add the wine to the cooking sauce and evaporate on high heat.
6. Mix the cooking sauce, butter/flour, and cook for a couple of minutes.
7. Return the sausages to the pan and cook everything for 2-3 minutes.
8. Add the stock and when this comes to a boil, remove from the heat and serve immediately.

Saltimbocca alla Romana
VEAL AND PROSCIUTTO ROMAN-STYLE (Latium)

Preparation: 10 minutes
Cooking time: 5-10 minutes

Ingredients for 4 people:

8 slices of prosciutto
8 sage leaves
8 slices of tenderized veal
4 tablespoons butter
½ cup dry white wine
salt

1. Place a slice of prosciutto and a sage leaf on each slice of veal and hold together with a toothpick.
2. Melt the butter in a pan and gently fry the meat on both sides.
3. Baste with the white wine and cook for a few minutes.
4. When ready, remove the meat from the pan and arrange on a serving dish. Add a couple tablespoons water to the cooking sauce, boil for a minute, and then pour over the saltimbocca; salt and serve.

Tomaxelle
MEAT ROLLS LUNI-STYLE (Toscana)

Preparation: 20 minutes
Cooking time: 20 minutes

Ingredients for 4 people:

3½ ounces ground veal
4 tablespoons butter
1 clove of garlic
2 eggs
3½ ounces grated Parmesan cheese
salt
pepper
nutmeg
8 thin slices of veal
1 onion
1 carrot, peeled
1 stalk of celery
2 ounces *pancetta*
5 tablespoons olive oil
4 sage leaves
1 sprig of rosemary
½ cup dry white wine
meat stock

1. Gently fry the ground veal in 2 tablespoons butter.
2. Cut the clove of garlic in half, and chop.
3. Mix the eggs and grated cheese in a bowl, together with the chopped garlic, fried ground veal, a pinch of salt and pepper, and a little grated nutmeg.
4. Spread the egg and ground meat mixture over the slices of veal and roll up; secure with a toothpick.
5. Finely slice the onion.
6. Chop the carrot, celery, and *pancetta*.
7. Gently fry the chopped vegetables and *pancetta* in the oil and remaining butter together with the sage leaves and rosemary.
8. Add the meat rolls ("involtini") to the fried vegetables and fry gently for a few minutes.
9. Add the wine and evaporate over high heat for a few minutes.
10. Add salt and pepper and cook for 15 minutes, stirring frequently and adding stock occasionally so that the involtini do not become too dry.
11. When ready, arrange the involtini on a serving dish, pour the cooking sauce on top, and serve.

Tortino di cipolle

ONION PIE (Various regions)

Preparation: 40 minutes; 30 minutes resting
Cooking time: 40 minutes

Ingredients for 6 people:

11 tablespoons butter
10½ ounces (about 2 cups) flour
salt
4 eggs
3¼ pounds onions
olive oil
5 ounces pitted black olives
3½ ounces gruyère cheese
4 tablespoons breadcrumbs
3 tablespoons grated Parmesan cheese
pepper

1. Dice 7 tablespoons butter and soften.
2. Heap the flour on a work-top. Add a pinch of salt, the butter, and an egg. Knead to a smooth, regular dough. Cover the dough with a cloth and leave in the refrigerator for 30 minutes.
3. In the meantime, slice the onions finely and sauté in 4 tablespoons butter and 2 tablespoons oil. Turn off the heat when they begin to brown and set aside to cool.
4. Slice the olives.
5. Cut the cheese into thin slices.
6. Beat the remaining eggs with a fork and reserve 1 tablespoon in a small bowl.
7. In a separate bowl mix the onions, a tablespoon breadcrumbs, grated cheese, the beaten eggs, salt, and pepper.
8. Heat the oven to 375°F; butter a medium-size cake pan and sprinkle with breadcrumbs.
9. Divide the dough into two parts, one larger than the other. Spread the larger piece over the base and sides of the cake pan.
10. Prick the dough with a fork and then arrange layers of cheese, onions, and olives.
11. Roll out the second piece of dough and cover the pie. Seal the edges well so that the filling cannot ooze out.
12. Brush the surface of the pie with the reserved beaten eggs and bake for 40 minutes. Serve hot.

◀ *Tomaxelle*

273

◄ *Acciughe al forno*

Acciughe al forno
FONT BAKED FRESH ANCHOVIES (Tuscany)

Preparation: 30 minutes
Cooking time: 20 minutes

Ingredients for 6 people:

3 pounds fresh anchovies
1 clove of garlic
olive oil
4 tablespoons chopped parsley
juice of 1 lemon
salt
pepper

1. Prepare the anchovies by opening in half from the belly and removing the head, innards, and the dorsal fin. Wash well and dry, taking care not to detach the two fillets.
2. Heat the oven to 400°F.
3. Chop the clove of garlic.
4. Oil an oven-proof dish and arrange the anchovies in a single layer.
5. Sprinkle with the chopped garlic and parsley, pour a little olive oil on top, the lemon juice, a pinch of salt and pepper, and bake for 20 minutes.

Baccalà alla Fiorentina
FLORENTINE CODFISH (Tuscany)

Preparation: 40 minutes
Cooking time: 20 minutes

Ingredients for 6 people:

1 onion
1 clove of garlic
5 tablespoons olive oil
25 ounces canned peeled tomatoes
salt, pepper
42 ounces softened baccalà (dried codfish)
a little flour
plenty of cooking oil for frying
5 sage leaves
1 sprig of rosemary
1½ tablespoon chopped parsley

1. Chop the onion and sauté with the garlic in the oil.
2. When the onion has browned, add the tomatoes, salt, and pepper and cook for 30 minutes.
3. In the meantime, clean the baccalà and cut into uniform pieces. Wash and dry, then dip in the flour.
4. Heat plenty of cooking oil in a pot, adding the sage leaves and rosemary.
5. When the oil is hot, remove the sage and rosemary and fry the baccalà.
6. Drain the baccalà on paper towels to remove the excess oil.
7. Mix the baccalà with the tomatoes and cook for 5-10 minutes.
8. Serve the baccalà hot, sprinkled with chopped parsley.

275

Brodetto alla Marchigiana

SEAFOOD BROTH MARCHES-STYLE (Marches)

Preparation: 45 minutes
Cooking time: 45 minutes

Ingredients for 6 people:

2¼ pound mixed seafood (the traditional recipe uses 13 kinds of fish chosen from: calamari, mullet, crayfish, shrimps, cod, baby octopus, whiting, dogfish, plaice, jumbo shrimp, scorpion fish, cuttlefish, sole, bass, and red mullet)
1 onion
1 clove of garlic
1 sprig of parsley
1 cup olive oil
17½ ounces peeled tomatoes
1 tablespoon vinegar
salt
pepper
a few slices of dense country bread

1. Prepare the fish carefully. Remove the scales, innards, heads, and tails. Cut into fillets and remove the spines.
2. Clean the seafood, removing the skin (except for the baby octopus), remove the bone, eliminate the eyes and beaks between the tentacles, detach the tentacles, and force out the innards (be careful with the ink sac of the cuttlefish); wash well.
3. Shell and clean the shellfish.
4. Finely chop the onion.
5. Chop the garlic together with the parsley.
6. Gently fry the onion in the oil.
7. Add the chopped garlic and parsley to the fried onion, together with the cuttlefish and calamari, and fry gently for a few minutes.
8. Add the tomato and vinegar and cook on low heat for 15 minutes.
9. Add the other fish, beginning with the larger ones and finishing with the cod, sole, and shellfish. Salt and pepper, cook for about 20-25 minutes.
10. In the meantime, toast or grill the slices of bread and arrange on serving plates.
11. When the "broth" is ready, pour it over the bread and serve.

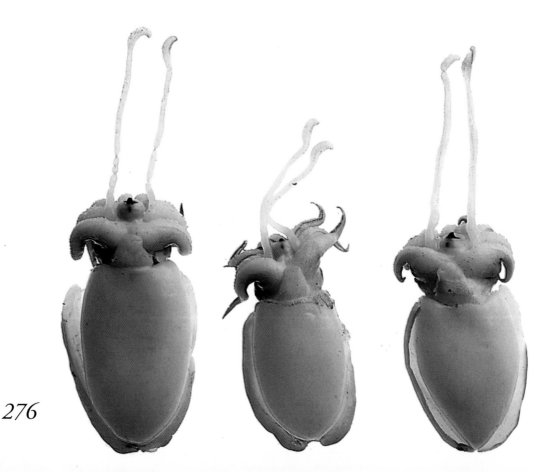

276

Calamari farciti

STUFFED SQUID (Various regions)

Preparation: 40 minutes
Cooking time: 50 minutes

Ingredients for 4 people:

8 whole, small squid
1 clove of garlic
1 sprig of parsley
1 boiled egg
1 tablespoon capers
3 anchovies
16 ounces canned peeled tomatoes
some breadcrumbs
olive oil
½ onion
salt
pepper

1. Carefully clean the squid. Remove the skin. Pull out the clear, cartilaginous bone from the sac. Remove the beak between the tentacles and the eyes. Pull on the tentacles to remove the innards. Wash well but be careful not to spoil the sacs.
2. Chop the tentacles, garlic, parsley, boiled egg, capers, and anchovies. Mix this mixture with 2 tablespoons peeled tomatoes and a few breadcrumbs.
3. Cook everything in 3 tablespoons olive oil for a few minutes.
4. Fill the squid with this mixture and close the open end with kitchen string so that the filling can't ooze out.
5. Chop half an onion and sauté in 4 tablespoons olive oil.
6. Pour in the remaining tomato and a drop of water.
7. Add the squid, salt and pepper, and cook covered, over low heat for 45 minutes.

▼ *Calamari farciti*

Frittata di cozze

OMELET WITH MUSSELS (Tuscany)

Preparation: 25 minutes
Cooking time: 10 minutes

Ingredients for 4 people:

2¼ pounds mussels
olive oil
6 eggs
4 tablespoons grated pecorino
cheese
1 tablespoon chopped parsley
salt
pepper

1. Clean and scrub the shells of the mussels with a stiff brush and remove the "beard."
2. Place the mussels in a large pan with a small amount of oil and heat for a few minutes.
3. Remove from heat when the shells open (about 15 minutes). Discard any mussels that have not opened because these may not be fresh.
4. Remove the meat from the shells.
5. Beat the eggs with the grated cheese, parsley, a pinch of salt, and pepper.
6. Pour a little olive oil into a pan and heat. When the oil is hot, pour in the beaten eggs.
7. Arrange the mussels quickly over the top of the omelet with the thickest part downward. When this is done, the omelet is ready to turn.
8. Turn the omelet by sliding it onto a plate and flipping it. Cook on the other side for a few minutes. Serve piping hot.

Fettine di palombo con i piselli

SHARK STEAKS WITH PEAS (Latium)

Preparation: 10 minutes
Cooking time: 25 minutes

Ingredients for 4 people:

1 clove of garlic
1 sprig of parsley
4 tablespoons olive oil
10½ ounces shelled peas
2 tablespoons tomato sauce
1½ pounds shark steaks
salt
pepper

1. Chop the garlic with the parsley.
2. Sauté the chopped mixture in 4 tablespoons oil.
3. Add the peas, tomato sauce, and a cup of lukewarm water. Cook with the lid on for 10 minutes.
4. Add the fish, salt, and pepper and cook for a further 15 minutes. Turn the fish halfway through. Serve hot.

◀ *Frittata di cozze*

Fettine di palombo con i pinoli
SHARK STEAKS WITH PINE NUTS (Tuscany)

Preparation: 10 minutes
Cooking time: 20 minutes

Ingredients for 4 people:

1½ pounds shark steaks
3 tablespoons pine nuts
olive oil
1 clove of garlic
1 tablespoon chopped parsley
1 cup white wine
salt
pepper

1. Chop the pine nuts and toast them in a tablespoon of oil.
2. Gently fry the garlic and parsley in a cup of oil.
3. Add the shark steaks and fry for 5 minutes on each side.
4. Pour in the wine and evaporate over medium-high heat for 5 minutes. Salt and pepper.
5. Add the pine nuts and heat for another 5 minutes. Serve piping hot.

▼ *Fettine di palombo con i pinoli*

Filetti di sogliola alla mugnaia
FRIED FILLETS OF SOLE (Various regions)

Preparation: 10 minutes
Cooking time: 15 minutes

Ingredients for 4 people:

8 sole fillets
a little flour
4 tablespoons butter
juice of 1 lemon
salt
1½ tablespoon chopped parsley

1. Wash and dry the fillets of sole and dip in the flour.
2. Heat the butter in a large pan and then add the fillets and fry on both sides (cook over very low heat for a total of about 15 minutes).
3. Halfway through, add the lemon juice, salt, and sprinkle with parsley. Serve piping hot.

Filetti di sogliola al vino bianco
FILLETS OF SOLE IN WHITE WINE (Various regions)

Preparation: 15 minutes
Cooking time: about 15 minutes

Ingredients for 4 people:

5 tablespoons butter
8 sole fillets
2½ cups white wine
juice of one lemon
salt, pepper
½ cup flour
2 egg yolks

1. Melt 2 tablespoons butter in a large pan.
2. Add the fillets of fish. Pour in the wine and lemon juice, add salt and pepper, and cook for 15 minutes with the lid on.
3. In the meantime, mix the remaining butter with the flour.
4. When the fish fillets are ready, remove from the heat and arrange on a serving dish.
5. Add the butter and flour to the cooking sauce; add the egg yolks and stir very well.
6. Pour this sauce over the fish and serve immediately.

Moscardini affogati
MARINATED BABY OCTOPUS (Latium)

Preparation: 20 minutes
Cooking time: 25 minutes

Ingredients for 4 people:

1½ pounds baby octopus
1 cup olive oil
1 cup wine vinegar
salt, pepper
juice of 1 lemon

1. Use a sharp knife to clean the baby octopus, removing the eyes and the beak between the tentacles. Cut the larger ones in half. Wash well. Heat oven to 375°F.
2. Place the baby octopus in a pan, add the oil, vinegar, a pinch of salt, and pepper. Mix well and cook for 20-25 minutes.
3. When ready, add the lemon juice and serve immediately.

Naselli agli aromi
WHITING WITH HERBS (Various regions)

Preparation: 15 minutes; time needed to thaw frozen whiting
Cooking time: 30 minutes

Ingredients for 4 people:

2 whiting, 17½ ounces each (fresh or frozen)
4 sage leaves
6 leaves of basil
sprig of parsley
2 sprigs of rosemary
1 clove of garlic
breadcrumbs
olive oil
½ cup white wine
salt, pepper

1. If you wish to cook fresh whiting, clean well (frozen fish is generally already cleaned). Remove the scales, innards, and skin (to do this, cut around the head and then grasp the skin with a cloth and pull). If using frozen whiting, thaw.
2. Heat the oven to 400°F.
3. Chop the sage, basil, parsley, and rosemary with the clove of garlic.
4. Mix the breadcrumbs with these chopped ingredients.
5. Oil an oven-proof dish.
6. Sprinkle a little oil over the fish and place in the oven dish.
7. Pour the wine over the fish and add salt and pepper; sprinkle with the chopped herbs. Bake for 30 minutes. Baste the fish occasionally as it cooks with the sauce. Serve hot.

Orate in rosso
JOHN DORY IN RED SAUCE (Various regions)

Preparation: 20 minutes
Cooking time: 20-25 minutes

Ingredients for 4 people:

4 John Dory (about 9 ounces each)
3 ripe tomatoes
½ onion
olive oil
1 clove of garlic
1 cup white wine
stock
salt
1 tablespoon chopped parsley

1. Clean the fish. Remove the scales and innards and wash well.
2. Remove the skin and core of the tomatoes and then cut into slices. Remove the seeds.
3. Finely chop the onion.
4. Sauté the onion and whole clove of garlic in oil in a pan large enough to hold all the dory in a single layer. As soon as the onion begins to blanch, add the slices of tomato, wine, a ladle of stock, and a pinch of salt. Simmer for a few minutes.
5. Add the fish and cook over medium heat for 20-25 minutes, turning them halfway through. Add a little stock if they become too dry while cooking.
6. When ready, sprinkle with chopped parsley and serve immediately.

Polpo ai peperoni

OCTOPUS WITH BELL PEPPERS (Tuscany)

Preparation: 30 minutes
Cooking time: 40 minutes

Ingredients for 4 people:

salt
1 bay leaf
1½ onions
1 stalk of celery
1 carrot, peeled
1 octopus (about 28 ounces)
1 red bell pepper
1 green bell pepper
2 fresh ripe tomatoes
1 clove of garlic
4 tablespoons olive oil
½ cup vinegar
pepper

1. Bring a pot of salted water to a boil with the bay leaf, 1 onion, celery, and the carrot.
2. Prepare the octopus. Turn the sac inside out and remove the innards. Remove the beak and the eyes using a knife. Pull off the skin and wash well.
3. Clean the peppers, removing the white fibers and seeds inside; cut into strips.
4. Wash and dice the tomatoes.
5. Chop the garlic with the remaining half onion. Sauté these chopped ingredients in 4 tablespoons olive oil, add the peppers and tomatoes, and cook for 20 minutes.
6. When the water comes to a boil, slowly immerse the octopus and cook for 35 minutes.
7. Drain the octopus and cut into pieces.
8. Add the octopus to the pepper and tomato sauce. Add the vinegar and evaporate over high heat. After 5 minutes, remove from the heat, add pepper, and serve.

▼ *Polpo ai peperoni*

Scampi in guazzetto
STEWED JUMBO SHRIMP (Tuscany)

Preparation: 10 minutes
Cooking time: 20 minutes

Ingredients for 6 people:

18 jumbo shrimp, shelled
2 cloves of garlic
1 sprig of parsley
1 red chili pepper
1 cup olive oil
1 cup white wine
salt

1. Wash and drain the shrimp.
2. Chop the garlic with the parsley.
3. Sauté these chopped ingredients with the chili pepper in the oil.
4. As soon as the garlic begins to brown, remove it and add the shrimp; sauté in the oil for 5 minutes, stirring and turning.
5. Add the wine and evaporate over high heat.
6. Lower the heat and cook for 10 minutes.

Scorfano saporito
SEASONED BLOWFISH (Various regions)

Preparation: 15 minutes
Cooking time: 40 minutes

Ingredients for 4 people:

1 blowfish, about 2¼ pounds
(or the same amount of smaller fish)
olive oil
salt
pepper
8 anchovy fillets
1 cup white wine

1. Carefully clean the blowfish, taking care to avoid pricking yourself with the spines, as this is rather painful. Remove the scales, fins, and innards.
2. Heat the oven to 400°F.
3. Baste the fish with oil and add salt and pepper.
4. Oil an oven-proof dish and place the fish inside. Bake for 20 minutes.
5. In the meantime, heat ½ cup oil and the anchovies. Crush the anchovies with a fork and cook until they become a paste.
6. Add the wine and evaporate over high heat. Mix well and form a sauce.
7. After the first 20 minutes cooking time, add the anchovy sauce to the fish and cook for another 20 minutes. Serve hot.

◄ *Scampi in guazzetto*

285

Tranci di tonno ai ferri
GRILLED TUNA (Various regions)

Preparation: 10 minutes; time to prepare the charcoal
Cooking time: 20 minutes

Ingredients for 4 people:

4 slices of fresh tuna, about 7 ounces each
olive oil
½ lemon
1½ tablespoons of chopped parsley
salt
pepper

1. If you wish to barbecue the tuna, prepare the charcoal. You can also cook the tuna on a kitchen griddle.
2. Baste the tuna slices with plenty of olive oil.
3. When the charcoal is ready or the griddle is very hot, cook the tuna for about 20 minutes, turning halfway through.
4. As the fish cooks, baste with oil so that it doesn't become too dry.
5. Prepare a sauce with oil, lemon, parsley, salt, and pepper.
6. When the tuna is cooked, arrange the slices on a serving dish and moisten with the sauce. Garnish with lemon quarters and serve hot.

Pesce spada al pomodoro
SWORDFISH WITH TOMATO (Various regions)

Preparation: 10 minutes
Cooking time: 30 minutes

Ingredients for 4 people:

1 clove of garlic
1 sprig of parsley
olive oil
7 ounces canned peeled tomatoes
2 tablespoons capers
3 ounces pitted black olives
4 slices of swordfish, about 7 ounces each
salt
pepper

1. Chop the garlic with the parsley.
2. Sauté these in 4 tablespoons oil.
3. Add the tomatoes, capers, and olives and cook for 10 minutes.
4. Add the fish, salt, and pepper; cook for 20 minutes. Serve hot.

Carciofi fritti
FRIED ARTICHOKES (Tuscany)

Preparation: 15 minutes
Cooking time: frying time

Ingredients for 4 people:

4 artichokes
juice of ½ a lemon
2 eggs
1 cup flour
olive oil
salt

1. Remove the tougher outer leaves of the artichokes but leave the stalk attached.
2. Cut the artichokes into quarters and soak in water and lemon juice so that they do not turn black.
3. Beat 2 eggs with a pinch of salt.
4. Drain the artichokes and dry well.
5. Place the artichokes in a paper bag with flour and shake to dust in flour thoroughly.
6. Dip the artichokes in the beaten egg.
7. Heat plenty of oil in a pan.
8. When the oil is hot, add the artichoke quarters one at a time.
9. Turn when cooked on one side.
10. When cooked, drain on paper towels. Serve hot on a serving dish garnished with lemon quarters.

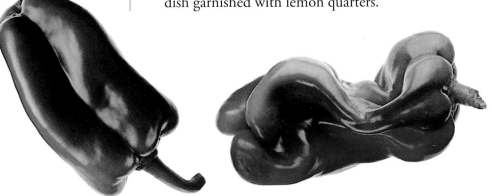

Gurguglione
STEWED MIXED VEGETABLES (Tuscany)

Preparation: 25 minutes
Cooking time: 40 minutes

Ingredients for 4 people:

5 zucchini
2 green bell peppers
2 large eggplant
1 large white onion
1 pound fresh ripe tomatoes
1 tablespoon chopped parsley
1 tablespoon chopped basil
salt
pepper
1 cup olive oil

1. Top and tail the zucchini, wash and cut into thick slices.
2. Clean the peppers, remove the seeds and the stringy fibers inside; cut into strips.
3. Wash and dice the eggplant.
4. Peel the onion and slice.
5. Skin and core the tomatoes and then cut into slices.
6. Place all the vegetables in a large pan; add the chopped parsley and basil, a pinch of salt and pepper, oil, and cook for 40 minutes on medium heat.

Frigò di Seravezza

FRIED POTATOES AND ONIONS (Tuscany)

Preparation: 25 minutes
Cooking time: 50 minutes

Ingredients for 4 people:

1 pound potatoes
1 pound red onions
1 pound fresh ripe tomatoes
¾ cup olive oil
1 clove of garlic
1 red chili pepper
salt
pepper
1 tablespoon chopped parsley

1. Peel the potatoes and cut into slices.
2. Peel the onions and cut into slices.
3. Wash the tomatoes, core, and cut into slices.
4. Heat the oil with the garlic and chili pepper. Remove the garlic as soon as it begins to brown.
5. Add the onion and potatoes and cook for 15 minutes.
6. Remove the chili pepper and add the tomatoes, salt, and pepper; cook for another 40 minutes.
7. When ready, sprinkle with the chopped parsley and serve piping hot.

Insalata ricca

RICH SALAD (Various regions)

Preparation: 25 minutes

Ingredients for 4 people:

1 bunch of green lettuce
1 yellow bell pepper
1 carrot
1 bunch of arugula
6 white mushrooms
2 tomatoes
3 boiled eggs
1 tablespoon capers
salt, pepper
wine vinegar
olive oil

1. Carefully wash and dry the lettuce.
2. Clean the pepper, remove the seeds and the stringy fibers inside; cut into strips.
3. Peel the carrot and then cut into strips.
4. Carefully wash the arugula.
5. Wash and slice the mushrooms.
6. Wash and slice the tomatoes.
7. Cut the boiled eggs into quarters.
8. Mix all these ingredients in a single salad bowl or prepare individual plates.
9. Season with salt, pepper, vinegar, and oil. Mix well and serve.

Melanzane al funghetto
DICED EGGPLANT (Various regions)

Preparation: 20 minutes
Cooking time: 25 minutes

Ingredients for 4 people:

4 eggplant
2 cloves of garlic
5 tablespoons olive oil
2 tablespoons chopped parsley
salt

1. Wash the eggplant, cut into quarters, and scoop out the seeds in the middle.
2. Rinse and dice the eggplant.
3. Chop the clove of garlic.
4. Heat the eggplant with the oil, chopped garlic, and parsley.
5. Cook for 25 minutes, stirring occasionally; add a little water as required if the sauce becomes too dry. Add salt when cooked.

Padella di patate, zucchine e cipolle
POTATOES, ZUCCHINI, AND ONIONS SAUTÉ (Tuscany)

Preparation: 25 minutes
Cooking time: about 50 minutes

Ingredients for 6 people:

3 potatoes
3 red onions
6 zucchini
olive oil
salt
pepper

1. Peel the potatoes and cut into slices.
2. Peel the onions and cut into slices.
3. Top and tail the zucchini, wash, and slice.
4. Place all the vegetables in a pan. Add plenty of oil, salt, and pepper and cook over high heat for 10 minutes.
5. Lower the heat, cover, and cook until all the vegetables are ready, stirring frequently.

Peperoni in agrodolce
SWEET AND SOUR BELL PEPPERS (Various regions)

Preparation: 15 minutes
Cooking time: 30 minutes

Ingredients for 4 people:

1 red bell pepper
1 yellow bell pepper
1 green bell pepper
5 tablespoons olive oil
a pinch of salt
3 tablespoons white wine vinegar
a pinch of sugar

1. Clean the peppers, remove the seeds and the stringy fibers inside; cut into pieces.
2. Add the pieces to a pan with the olive oil and salt; sauté for 5 minutes.
3. Add vinegar and a pinch of sugar. Mix well and cook for 25 minutes (if the peppers become too dry as they cook, add a few drops of water).

Peperoni con olive e capperi
BELL PEPPERS WITH OLIVES AND CAPERS (Tuscany)

Preparation: 20 minutes
Cooking time: 40 minutes

Ingredients for 4 people:

1 red bell pepper
1 yellow bell pepper
1 green bell pepper
10 black olives
olive oil
salt
1 tablespoon capers

1. Clean the peppers, remove the seeds and the stringy fibers inside; cut into pieces.
2. Pit and chop the olives.
3. Place the peppers in a pan with oil and cook for 20 minutes.
4. Add the capers and black olives and cook for a further 20 minutes, stirring frequently (if the peppers become too dry as they cook, add a few drops of water).

Peperoni ripieni di riso
PEPPERS STUFFED WITH RICE (Latium)

Preparation: 40 minutes
Cooking time: 30 minutes

Ingredients for 4 people:

4 bell peppers, any color
½ onion
4 tablespoons olive oil
tomato
salt
½ cup rice
1 clove of garlic
6 tablespoons butter
3½ ounces tuna in oil
1 anchovy in oil
2 tablespoons chopped parsley
1 egg

1. Wash the peppers and cut off the top. Remove the seeds and stringy fibers inside.
2. Finely chop the onion and sauté in oil.
3. Add the crushed tomato and cook for 10 minutes.
4. Heat plenty of salted water; when it comes to a boil, add the rice and cook for 15 minutes.
5. Chop the garlic.
6. Melt 4 tablespoons butter in a small pot and add the garlic, tuna, and anchovy. Mix well and break up the tuna and anchovy.
7. Drain the rice and place in a bowl with the tuna, parsley, and egg; mix well.
8. Heat the oven to 375°F.
9. Grease an oven-proof dish with a little butter.
10. Stuff the peppers with the rice mixture and arrange in the dish.
11. Place a pat of butter on each pepper, add the tomato, and bake for 30 minutes. Serve hot or cold as preferred.

◄ *Peperoni con olive e capperi*

Pinzimonio
VEGETABLES CRUDITÉE (Tuscany)

Preparation: 40 minutes

Ingredients for 4 people:

8 radishes
2 bunches of radicchio
2 fennel bulbs
3 carrots, peeled
1 red bell pepper
1 yellow bell pepper
8 stalks of celery
1 bunch of green lettuce
¾ cup olive oil
4 tablespoons vinegar
salt, pepper

1. Carefully wash all the vegetables (but don't top the radishes).
2. Cut the radishes, radicchio, and fennel into quarters.
3. Cut the carrots, peppers, and celery into large strips.
4. Split the larger leaves of lettuce in half.
5. Carefully arrange the vegetables in a large salad bowl.
6. Prepare a small bowl for each diner, adding as follows: 3 tablespoons olive oil, 1 tablespoon vinegar, a pinch of salt, and pepper; mix well.
7. Serve everything. Each diner will select pieces of vegetables and dip them in the individual bowl of dressing.

Spinaci alla Fiorentina
FLORENTINE SPINACH (Tuscany)

Preparation: 45 minutes
Cooking time: 25 minutes

Ingredients for 4 people:

2¼ pounds fresh spinach or 9 ounces frozen spinach
2 tablespoons heavy cream
salt
pepper
4 tablespoons grated Parmesan cheese

for the white sauce:
1 ounce butter
1 ounce flour
1 cup cold milk
salt

1. Carefully wash the spinach.
2. Boil some water. When it comes to a boil, add the spinach and cook for 10 minutes.
3. Prepare the white sauce as explained in the recipe on page 35.
4. When ready, strain and squeeze the spinach, mix with the white sauce and cream; add salt and pepper.
5. Heat the oven to 400°F and butter an oven-proof dish.
6. Place the spinach in the dish, sprinkle with the grated cheese, and bake for 15 minutes.

Piselli alla pancetta
PEAS WITH *PANCETTA* (Tuscany)

Preparation: 5 minutes
Cooking time: 15-20 minutes

Ingredients for 4 people:

1 clove of garlic
21 ounces fresh shelled peas
8 tablespoons olive oil
1½ tablespoon chopped parsley
salt
pepper
2 ounces *pancetta* (single slice)

1. Cut the clove of garlic in half.
2. Put the peas in a pan, add the oil, garlic, salt, pepper, parsley, and a little water and cook for 15-20 minutes.
3. Cut the *pancetta* into thin strips and add to the peas when partially cooked.

▼ *Piselli alla pancetta*

Pomodori farciti
STUFFED TOMATOES (Various regions)

Preparation: 20 minutes

Ingredients for 4 people:

4 fresh ripe tomatoes
3 ounces pitted black olives
2 tablespoons capers
3 ounces tuna
4 tablespoons mayonnaise (see the recipe on page 76)

1. Wash the tomatoes, cut in half, and scoop out the insides.
2. Roughly chop the olives with the capers and tuna.
3. Mix this with the mayonnaise.
4. Stuff the tomatoes with this mixture. Arrange on a serving plate (garnish with lettuce and whole olives as preferred). Serve cold.

Zucchine ripiene
STUFFED ZUCCHINI (Marches)

Preparation: 20 minutes
Cooking time: 40 minutes

Ingredients for 4 people:

4 zucchini
2 tablespoons chopped parsley
2 tablespoons breadcrumbs
salt
pepper
olive oil

1. Wash, top, and tail the zucchini. Cut in half lengthwise.
2. Scoop out the zucchini and reserve the pulp.
3. Chop the pulp.
4. Mix this pulp with the parsley and breadcrumbs. Add salt and pepper.
5. Heat the oven to 350°F.
6. Oil an oven-proof dish.
7. Fill the zucchini with the mixture and arrange in the dish. Bake for 40 minutes.

Biscotti all'arancia

ORANGE BISCOTTI (Various regions)

*Preparation: 15 minutes; 2 hours
    rising*
Cooking time: 15 minutes

Ingredients for 6 people:

10 tablespoons butter
¾ cup sugar
2 egg yolks
grated orange peel
orange juice
**10½ ounces (about 2 cups) sifted
flour**
2 teaspoons baking powder
a pinch of salt
a little butter
a little flour

1. Beat the butter to a creamy consistency.
2. Add the sugar, one egg yolk, the grated orange peel, and the orange juice.
3. Add the flour, baking powder, and a pinch of salt. Knead to a smooth and uniform consistency. Set aside to rise for 2 hours.
4. Roll out the dough very thinly. Cut out the biscotti with cookie cutters.
5. Heat the oven to 350°F.
6. Butter and flour a baking sheet or use parchment paper.
7. Arrange the biscotti on the sheet.
8. Beat the remaining egg yolk and brush it on the surface of the biscotti.
9. Bake for 15 minutes.

▼ *Biscotti all'arancia*

Biscotti alla marmellata

Jam cookies (Various regions)

Preparation: 20 minutes;
2 hours rising
Cooking time: 15 minutes

Ingredients for 6 people:

14 tablespoons butter
¾ cup sugar
3 eggs
3 tablespoons liqueur (marsala or rum)
grated peel of half a lemon
10½ ounces (about 2 cups) sifted flour
a pinch of salt
a little butter
a little flour
3½ ounces apricot jam

1. Beat the butter to a creamy consistency.
2. Add the sugar, eggs, liqueur, and grated lemon peel. Mix well.
3. Add sifted flour and a pinch of salt. Knead to a smooth, uniform dough. Set aside to rise for 2 hours.
4. Heat the oven to 350°F.
5. Butter and flour a baking sheet or use parchment paper.
6. Prepare balls of dough about the size of walnuts, squash a little with a glass, and arrange on the baking sheet.
7. Use the tip of a finger to make a little hollow in the top and then add a tablespoon of jam.
8. Bake for 15 minutes.

Brigidini

Aniseed cookies (Tuscany)

Preparation: 15 minutes; 2 hours
rising
Cooking time: 15 minutes

Ingredients for 6 people:
3 eggs
⅔ cup sugar
10½ ounces (about 2 cups) sifted flour
salt
1 tablespoon aniseed

1. Beat the eggs together with the sugar.
2. Add sifted flour, a pinch of salt, and the aniseed. Knead carefully to prepare a smooth, uniform dough. Set aside to rise for 2 hours.
3. Heat the oven to 350°F.
4. Butter and flour a baking sheet or use parchment paper.
5. Prepare balls of dough about the size of walnuts, squash a little with a glass and arrange on the oven tray.
6. Bake for 15 minutes.

Berlingozzo

MEDIEVAL BUTTER CAKE (Tuscany)

Preparation: 20 minutes
Cooking time: 40 minutes

Ingredients for 4 people:

6 tablespoons butter
4 eggs
1 cup sugar
14 ounces (about 3½ cups) sifted flour
½ cup milk
2 teaspoons baking powder
salt
grated lemon peel
a little butter
a little flour
¼ cup powdered sugar

1. Dice and melt the butter.
2. Beat two whole eggs and two egg yolks in a bowl with the sugar.
3. Add the sifted flour and mix well.
4. Add the butter, milk, baking powder, a pinch of salt, and the grated lemon peel. Mix well to a smooth, uniform dough.
5. Heat the oven to 350°F.
6. Butter and flour a medium-size cake pan.
7. Pour the mixture into the cake pan and bake for 40 minutes.
8. When cooked, take out of the oven and sprinkle with powdered sugar.

This is an extremely old Tuscan recipe; it was already well-known in the 1400s.

Biscotti di Prato

PRATO BISCOTTI (Tuscany)

Preparation: 20 minutes
Cooking time: 25 minutes

Ingredients for 6 people:

3½ ounces shelled and peeled almonds
3 whole eggs and 1 egg yolk
1 cup sugar
10½ ounces (about 2 cups) flour
a pinch of salt
2 teaspoons baking powder
a little butter
a little flour

1. Chop the almonds into large pieces.
2. Beat the eggs with the sugar to a foamy cream.
3. Add the flour, a pinch of salt, baking powder, and the chopped almonds and knead well.
4. Heat the oven to 350°F.
5. Butter and flour a baking sheet or cover with parchment paper.
6. Shape the dough into rolls about 2 inches wide and 1 inch high, arrange on the baking sheet, and bake for 15 minutes.
7. Cut the cylinders somewhat diagonally into pieces about 1 inch wide.
8. Bake for another 8-10 minutes.

These biscotti keep for a long time in an air-tight container. They are best enjoyed dipped in wine.

◄ *Berlingozzo*

Castagnaccio
CHESTNUT FLOUR TART (Tuscany)

Preparation: 20 minutes; 1 hour rising
Cooking time: 40 minutes

Ingredients for 6 people:

10½ ounces (about 2 cups) chestnut flour
4 tablespoons olive oil
2 tablespoons sugar
salt
⅔ cup raisins
½ cup pine nuts
1 sprig of rosemary
5 chopped walnuts

▼ *Castagnaccio*

1. Slowly dissolve the chestnut flour in 1½ cups of water, taking care not to form lumps.
2. Add a tablespoon olive oil, the sugar, and a pinch of salt, and set aside to rise for 1 hour.
3. Soften the raisins in lukewarm water.
4. Heat the oven to 350°F.
5. Grease a large cake pan with 2 tablespoons olive oil.
6. Pour the mixture into the pan.
7. Sprinkle the surface with pine nuts, rosemary, well-drained raisins, chopped walnuts, and a tablespoon olive oil. Bake for 40 minutes. Can be enjoyed hot or cold.

Ciambella con le pere

SWEET ROLL WITH PEARS (Various regions)

Preparation: 40 minutes
Cooking time: 1 hour

Ingredients for 6 people:

¾ pound fresh pears
½ cup white wine
⅔ cup sugar
5 tablespoons butter
2 eggs, separated
½ cup milk
grated peel of half a lemon
1¾ cup sifted flour
a pinch of salt
2 teaspoons baking powder
a little butter
a little flour
¼ cup powdered sugar

1. Wash, peel, core, and dice the pears.
2. Cook the pears for 15 minutes in the wine with 1 tablespoon sugar. Set aside to cool.
3. Beat the butter to a creamy consistency.
4. Add the remaining sugar and mix well.
5. Add the egg yolks, milk, grated lemon peel, sifted flour, a pinch of salt, and baking powder. Mix well.
6. Whisk the egg whites until firm but not dry and then fold with the rest of the ingredients. Add the pears.
7. Heat the oven to 350°F.
8. Butter and flour a tube pan and pour in the mixture.
9. Bake for one hour. Serve the ciambella sprinkled with powdered sugar.

Croccanti di arachidi e cioccolato

PEANUT AND CHOCOLATE SLICES (Various regions)

Preparation: 30 minutes
Cooking time: 30 minutes

Ingredients for 6 people:

6 ounces semi-sweet chocolate
6 tablespoons butter
½ cup shelled peanuts
2 eggs
⅔ cup sugar
1 cup sifted flour
a pinch of salt
a little butter
a little flour

1. Finely chop the chocolate.
2. Melt the chocolate with the butter in a double-boiler.
3. In the meantime, chop the peanuts.
4. Set aside the chocolate to cool.
5. Beat the eggs and mix with the chocolate.
6. Add the peanuts, sugar, sifted flour, and a pinch of salt.
7. Heat the oven to 350°F.
8. Butter and flour a baking sheet or cover with parchment paper.
9. Spread the mixture over the baking sheet to a thickness of about 1/5 inch.
10. Bake for 30 minutes.
11. Cool and cut into shapes as preferred.

Crema al caffè
COFFEE CREAM (Various regions)

Preparation: 30 minutes
Cooking time: 50 minutes

Ingredients for 6 people:

3 whole eggs and 3 egg yolks
⅔ cup sugar
1 vanilla bean, split
3 cups milk
2 tablespoons instant coffee
butter
6-12 coffee beans

1. Beat the eggs and egg yolks with the sugar to a foamy cream.
2. Heat the vanilla bean in the milk. Bring to a boil. Mix well.
3. Take the milk off the heat and add the instant coffee. Remove the vanilla bean. Add all the eggs, stirring continually.
4. Butter six custard or soufflé cups and pour in the coffee cream.
5. Heat the oven to 350°F.
6. Place the cups in a large roasting pan, and add enough hot water to come halfway up the sides of the cups. Bake for about 50 minutes.
7. When ready, cool thoroughly. To serve the cream, tip the molds over onto a dessert plate and garnish with coffee beans.

Fragole al limone
STRAWBERRIES WITH LEMON (Various regions)

Preparation: 10 minutes; 1 resting

Ingredients for 6 people:

1½ pounds fresh strawberries
juice of 2 lemons
⅔ cup sugar

1. Carefully wash the strawberries and pull out the core.
2. Cut into pieces and place in a bowl.
3. Pour the lemon juice and sugar over the strawberries and mix well.
4. Set aside for 1 hour. Mix well again before serving.

This strawberry dessert can also be served with scoops of ice cream or whipped cream.

Ciambellone o schiacciata di Pasqua
EASTER ROLL CAKE (Tuscany)

Preparation: 20 minutes
Cooking time: 40 minutes

Ingredients for 6-8 people:

6 tablespoons butter
4 eggs
1⅓ cups sugar
1 pound (about 3¼ cups) flour
1 cup milk
⅓ cup rum
grated lemon peel
2 teaspoons baking powder
salt
a little butter
a little flour

1. Melt the butter.
2. In the meantime, beat the eggs with the sugar until they are almost white (at least 10 minutes).
3. Add the flour, melted butter, baking powder, milk, rum, grated lemon peel, and a pinch of salt and mix well with a wooden spoon.
4. Heat the oven to 375°F.
5. Butter and flour a medium-size tube pan.
6. Pour the mixture into the pan and bake for 40 minutes.

▼ *Ciambellone o schiacciata di Pasqua*

Frullato di fragole
STRAWBERRY FRAPPÉ (Various regions)

Preparation: 10 minutes

Ingredients for 4 people:

½ pound fresh strawberries
2 cups milk
1 cup heavy cream
3 tablespoons sugar
2 tablespoons chopped ice

1. Wash the strawberries, remove the core, and chop into pieces.
2. Place the strawberries in the blender and add the milk, cream, sugar, and chopped ice. Blend everything for a couple of minutes. Serve immediately.

Maritozzi
DOUGHNUTS ROMAN-STYLE (Latium)

Preparation: 10 hours
Cooking time: 15 minutes

Ingredients for 6 people:

2 teaspoons active dry yeast
12 ounces (about 2⅓ cups) flour
a pinch of salt
2 eggs
4 tablespoons olive oil
⅔ cup raisins
1½ ounce candied lime
½ cup pine nuts
¼ cup sugar

1. Dissolve the yeast in a little lukewarm water.
2. Knead ½ cup flour with the yeast and a pinch of salt. Let the dough rise in a warm place, covered with a cloth, for 2 hours.
3. To this dough, add ¾ cup flour, a pinch of salt, 1 egg, and a tablespoon olive oil. Knead well and set aside to rise again in a warm place, covered with a cloth, for 2 hours.
4. In the meantime, soften the raisins in lukewarm water.
5. Cut the candied lime into pieces and chop the pine nuts into large pieces.
6. Add to this dough the remaining flour, 2 tablespoons olive oil, sugar, an egg, a pinch of salt, the chopped candied lime, pine nuts, the well-drained raisins, and a little lukewarm water.
7. Grease a baking sheet or cover with parchment paper.
8. Shape oval buns from the dough and arrange on the baking sheet. Set aside to rise for a further 5 hours.
9. Heat the oven to 350°F.
10. Bake for 15 minutes.
11. Serve the maritozzi cold and enjoy with a fine white wine.

◄ *Frullato di fragole*

Panpepato
DRIED FRUIT CAKE (Umbria)

Preparation: 30 minutes
Cooking time: 30 minutes

Ingredients for 6 people:

¼ cup raisins
¼ cup walnuts
¼ cup shelled hazelnuts
¼ cup shelled and peeled almonds
1 ounce semi-sweet chocolate
¼ cup honey
1 ounce mixed candied fruits, diced
a pinch of cinnamon
a pinch of nutmeg
a pinch of salt
a pinch of pepper
¼ cup sifted flour
olive oil

1. Soften the raisins in lukewarm water.
2. Chop the walnuts, hazelnuts, and almonds.
3. Grate the chocolate.
4. Dissolve two-thirds of the honey in 2 tablespoons hot water, then add the chopped dry fruit, chocolate, well-drained raisins, the candied fruit, a pinch of cinnamon, nutmeg, salt, and pepper.
5. Add the sifted flour and knead well.
6. Heat the oven to 350°F.
7. Grease a baking sheet or cover with parchment paper.
8. Make six buns from the dough and place on the the baking sheet.
9. Brush with the remaining honey and then bake for 30 minutes.

Variants of this bread-cake are also prepared in Abruzzo (Teramo) and Tuscany (Siena).

Pizza dolce ai canditi
SWEET PIZZA WITH CANDIED FRUIT (Latium)

Preparation: 1 hour; 12 hours rising
Cooking time: 30 minutes

Ingredients for 6 people:

2 teaspoons active dry yeast
10½ ounces (about 2 cups) flour
6 tablespoons butter, softened
⅓ cup sugar
5 eggs
1 ounce candied orange peel, diced
1 ounce candied lime, diced
a pinch of cinnamon
a pinch of salt
a little butter
a little flour

1. Dissolve the yeast in a little lukewarm water.
2. Prepare the bread dough: knead the flour with the yeast and a little water, then set aside to rise for 2 hours.
3. Knead the bread dough with the butter, sugar, 4 eggs, the candied fruit, a pinch of cinnamon, and a pinch of salt.
4. Butter and flour a medium cake pan and spread out the dough inside. Leave the dough covered with a cloth in a warm place for 12 hours.
5. When the dough has risen, heat the oven to 375°F.
6. Beat the remaining egg and baste over the "pizza." Bake for 30 minutes.

Torta al caffè e al cioccolato
MOCHA CAKE (Various regions)

Preparation: 20 minutes
Cooking time: 50 minutes

Ingredients for 6 people:

4 tablespoons butter
2 ounces semi-sweet chocolate
2 eggs
⅔ cup sugar
2 cups sifted flour
2 teaspoons baking powder
a pinch of salt
¼ cup espresso coffee
a little butter
a little flour
¼ cup powdered sugar

1. Melt the butter and cool.
2. Grate the chocolate.
3. Beat the eggs with the sugar to make a foamy cream.
4. Add the butter, sifted flour, baking powder, grated chocolate, a pinch of salt, and the coffee.
5. Heat the oven to 375°F.
6. Butter and flour a medium-size cake pan.
7. Add the mixture and bake for about 50 minutes.
8. Serve the cake sprinkled with powdered sugar.

Torta all'ananas
PINEAPPLE UPSIDE-DOWN CAKE (Various regions)

Preparation: 30 minutes
Cooking time: 45 minutes

Ingredients for 6 people:

8 tablespoons butter
½ cup sugar
3 eggs, separated
½ cup sifted flour
½ cup potato starch
2 teaspoons baking powder
a pinch of salt
a little butter
3 tablespoons sugar
7 slices of pineapple in syrup

1. Soften the butter without melting it completely. Set aside to cool.
2. Beat the butter with the sugar and egg yolks to make a foamy cream.
3. Add the sifted flour, potato starch, and baking powder to this mixture, together with a pinch of salt.
4. Whisk the egg whites until stiff but not dry and mix carefully with the other ingredients.
5. Heat the oven to 325°F.
6. Butter a medium-size cake pan.
7. Melt 3 tablespooons sugar with 3 tablespoons water and pour into the cake pan so that it completely covers the base.
8. Arrange the pineapple slices on the base of the cake dish on top of the sugar.
9. Pour the mixture into the cake pan and bake for 40-45 minutes.
10. When baked, turn the cake over onto a serving dish so that the pineapple slices are on top.

Gattò aretino

JELLY ROLL AREZZO-STYLE (Tuscany)

Preparation: 40 minutes
Cooking time: 30 minutes

Ingredients for 6-8 people:

3 tablespoons butter
¼ cup sugar
6½ cups milk
½ cup sifted flour
1½ teaspoons baking powder
(about ⅓ oz)
4 eggs, separated
a pinch of salt
⅓ cup of Alchermes (or other
dessert liqueur)
¼ cup powdered sugar

for the cream:
2 egg yolks
¼ cup sugar
⅛ cup flour
¼ cup unsweetened cocoa powder
1 cup milk

1. Prepare the base as follows. Melt the butter, sugar, and half the milk on low heat and set aside to cool.
2. Add the flour, baking powder, egg yolks, a pinch of salt and stir well.
3. Add the remaining milk and stir to avoid forming lumps.
4. Whisk the egg whites until stiff but not dry and fold into the mixture.
5. Heat the oven to 350°F.
6. Place a sheet of parchment paper over a jelly roll pan.
7. Pour the mixture onto the paper and carefully smooth off the surface.
8. Bake for 25-30 minutes.
9. In the meantime, prepare the chocolate cream filling as follows: beat the egg yolks together with the sugar in a bowl. Add the flour and cocoa. Mix well.
10. Bring the milk to a boil.
11. Place the mixture on low heat and slowly add the boiling milk, stirring continually with a whisk. When the cream is ready, remove from the heat immediately.
12. When the pastry base is ready, take it out of the oven.
13. Moisten the pastry with the liqueur, then cover completely with the chocolate cream.
14. With the aid of the paper, roll up the pastry. Serve sprinkled with powdered sugar.

Torta di riso alla Senese

RICE CAKE SIENA-STYLE (Tuscany)

Preparation: 1 hour
Cooking time: 30 minutes

Ingredients for 6 people:
¼ cup raisins
2½ cups milk
⅔ cup sugar
1 cup rice
3 tablespoons butter
2 eggs
2½ ounces mixed candied fruits,
diced
¼ cup pine nuts, roughly chopped
grated peel of half a lemon
1 teaspoon vanilla extract
a little butter and a little flour

1. Soften the raisins in lukewarm water.
2. Heat the milk and sugar together. When it comes to a boil, add the rice. Cook the rice until it has absorbed all the milk, stirring frequently.
3. Take the rice off the heat and add the butter. Mix well. Allow to cool.
4. When the rice is cold, add the eggs, candied fruit, pine nuts, well-drained raisins, grated lemon peel, and vanilla.
5. Heat the oven to 375°F.
6. Butter and flour a medium-size cake pan, pour in the mixture, and bake for 30 minutes. Let the cake cool before serving.

Mediterranean area

Caprese
CAPRESE SALAD (Campania)

Preparation: 10 minutes

Ingredients for 4 people:

2 medium fresh ripe tomatoes
2 fresh mozzarella cheeses
a little olive oil
salt
pepper
a pinch of dried marjoram
a few leaves of basil

1. Wash and dry the tomatoes; then cut them into thick slices. Cut the mozzarella cheese into the same thick slices as the tomatoes.
2. Arrange the slices of tomato and cheese on a serving plate.
3. Dress with oil, salt, a little pepper, and marjoram. Garnish with a few leaves of basil.

Crostini foggiani
CROSTINI FOGGIA-STYLE (Puglia)

Preparation: 10 minutes
Cooking time: about 10 minutes

Ingredients for 4 people:

a little olive oil
4 slices of country bread
4 anchovy fillets
a little parsley
2 medium fresh ripe tomatoes
7 ounces fresh mozzarella
salt

1. Heat the oven to 350°F.
2. Heat a little oil in a skillet and gently fry the slices of bread; then arrange them in an oven-proof dish.
3. Cut the anchovies into very small pieces and chop the parsley; cut the tomatoes and the cheese into thin slices.
4. Arrange the anchovies, the tomatoes, the parsley, and cheese on the pieces of bread. Salt, and bake in the oven until the cheese completely melts. Serve immediately.

Cacio alla Sarda

"Cacio" cheese sardinian-style (Sardinia)

Preparation: 10 minutes
Cooking time: a few minutes

Ingredients for 4 people:

14 ounces of "caciocavallo" cheese
2 teaspoons sugar
2 teaspoons vinegar
1 clove of garlic
a little olive oil

1. Cut the cheese into thin slices. Dissolve the sugar in the vinegar.
2. Sauté the clove of garlic in a little oil in a pan. When the garlic begins to brown, remove it from the pan and add the cheese slices.
3. Gently fry the cheese and sprinkle with the sugar-vinegar. Serve immediately.

Crostoni alla Napoletana

Crostini neapolitan-style (Campania)

Preparation: 25 minutes

Ingredients for 4 people:

2 eggs
12 black olives
4 ounces sardines in oil
8 anchovy fillets
2 cloves of garlic
salt
⅓ cup olive oil
4 large slices of crusty bread

1. Place the eggs in a pot with cold water. When the water boils, simmer the eggs for 6-7 minutes; set aside to cool.
2. In the meantime, pit the olives and bone the sardines. Chop together the sardines, olives, anchovies, and garlic.
3. When cool, chop the eggs and add to the other ingredients. Salt and blend, adding the olive oil a little at a time.
4. Toast the bread in the oven or a toaster. Spread a little of the mixture over each slice and serve.

Insalata appetitosa
SAVORY SALAD (Calabria)

Preparation: 45 minutes

Ingredients for 6 people:

4 small potatoes
salt
¼ pound thin green beans
4 eggs
4 medium fresh ripe tomatoes
2 yellow or green bell peppers
16 ounces tuna in olive oil
3½ ounces black olives
6 anchovy fillets
½ cup olive oil

1. Wash the potatoes and boil in a pot of salted water. Boil the beans in another pot.
2. Hard boil the eggs in another pot.
3. Wash the tomatoes and cut into quarters. Wash the peppers, open them, remove the seeds, and cut into thin strips. Shell the hard-boiled eggs and cut into quarters.
4. When ready, drain the beans and dry thoroughly.
5. When the potatoes are ready, peel and cut into thick slices.
6. Break up the tuna fish in a bowl. Add the olives, egg, tomatoes, pepper, potatoes, and beans. Garnish with the anchovies.
7. Dissolve the salt in the oil and pour over the salad. Best enjoyed cold.

◀ *Insalata appetitosa*

Insalata napoletana
NEAPOLITAN SALAD (Campania)

Preparation: 15 minutes

Ingredients for 4 people:

4 medium fresh ripe tomatoes
2 cloves of garlic
6-8 leaves of basil
8 green olives
4 anchovy fillets
2 slices of dense country bread
salt
pepper
⅓ cup olive oil

1. Wash the tomatoes, dry them, and cut into thin slices; arrange in a bowl.
2. Finely chop the garlic and basil; pit the olives and chop; cut the anchovies into very small pieces. Add these ingredients to the tomatoes.
3. Toast the bread; dice and add to the tomatoes.
4. Add salt and pepper as preferred; season with olive oil and serve.

315

Polpi conditi
SEASONED OCTOPUS (Campania)

Preparation: about 30 minutes
Cooking time: 1 hour

Ingredients for 6 people:

2 octopus, about 1¾ pound each
5 cloves of garlic
1 cup olive oil
1 bay leaf
salt
a pinch of cayenne pepper
2 sprigs of parsley
1 sprig of rosemary

1. Clean the octopus, removing the eyes, beak, and innards; remove the skin by making incisions with a sharp knife.
2. Tenderize the octopus (beat them against a wooden carving board), then wash under running water.
3. Cut the garlic in half and chop finely. Place the garlic with half the olive oil in a terra cotta baking dish and add the bay leaf.
4. Place the octopus in the pot, cover, and cook on very low heat until ready (about 1 hour).
5. When the octopus is tender, remove the bay leaf, drain, and season with the remaining oil, salt, cayenne, and whole leaves of parsley and rosemary. Mix and serve.

Prosciutto e melone
PROSCIUTTO AND MELON (Various regions)

Preparation: 10 minutes

Ingredients for 4 people:

1 medium size ripe melon
(honeydew or canteloupe)
8 slices of prosciutto

1. Cut the melon in half and scoop out the seeds. Cut the melon into 8 slices and then remove the hard outer skin.
2. Wrap the slices of prosciutto around each piece of melon. Arrange the slices on a platter and serve.

Focaccia al rosmarino
FOCACCIA WITH ROSEMARY (Various regions)

Preparation: 10 minutes
Cooking time: 45-50 minutes

Ingredients for 1 focaccia:

10½ ounces bread dough
(see page 217)
a little olive oil
1 sprig of rosmary
coarse salt

1. Heat the oven to 375°F. Lightly grease a baking sheet with oil and roll out the dough over it to a thickness of about ½ inch.
2. Arrange the rosemary leaves evenly over the dough. Sprinkle with a little coarse salt. Season with a little olive oil.
3. Place in the oven and cook for 45-50 minutes, until the dough browns slightly. Serve immediately.

Focaccia alle olive
FOCACCIA WITH OLIVES (Sicily)

Preparation: 10 minutes
Cooking time: 45 minutes

Ingredients for 1 focaccia:

a little olive oil
10½ ounces bread dough
(see page 217)
3½ ounces black olives

1. Heat the oven to 375°F. Lightly grease a pizza pan with oil and roll out the dough over it to a thickness of about ½ inch.
2. Arrange the olives, pressing them lightly down into the dough with your fingers. Season with a little oil and bake for about 45 minutes. Serve hot.

Pizza Margherita
PIZZA "MARGHERITA" (Campania)

Preparation: 10 minutes
Cooking time: 15-20 minutes

Ingredients for the pizza:

7 ounces bread dough (see page 217)
a little olive oil
½ cup chopped fresh tomatoes
3½ ounces mozzarella cheese
a pinch of marjoram or rosemary

1. Heat the oven to 425°F. Roll out the leavened dough to form a disk.
2. Lightly grease a pizza pan or baking sheet with oil and arrange the dough.
3. Spread the tomatoes evenly over the dough. Cut the mozzarella into thin slices and arrange over the tomatoes.
4. Cook the pizza in the hot oven for about 15 minutes.

The pizza Margherita is the basis for all other pizzas. You can garnish with ham or other delicatessen meats, cooked or raw vegetables, various kinds of cheese, sea food (without cheese). Use your imagination!

Calzone
CALZONE (Campania)

Preparation: about 10 minutes
Cooking time: 15-20 minutes

Ingredients for 1 pizza:

7 ounces bread dough (see page 217)
2½ ounces mozzarella cheese
2 ounces boiled ham
½ cup chopped fresh tomatoes
3½ ounces cottage cheese
1 spoonful of grated pecorino cheese
a pinch of marjoram

1. Heat the oven to 425°F. Roll out the dough into a disk. Dice the mozzarella and break the slices of ham into smaller pieces by hand.
2. Arrange all the ingredients on one half of the disk of dough: first the tomato, then the pieces of ricotta, the ham, mozzarella, and pecorino cheese. Sprinkle with marjoram.
3. Fold the other half of the dough over the ingredients and press down well on the edges. Lightly grease a baking sheet with oil and place the calzone on it. Place in the oven and cook for about 15-20 minutes.

◀ *Pizza margherita.*

319

Fusilli mediterranei

FUSILLI MEDITERRANEAN-STYLE (Puglia)

Preparation: 10 minutes; 30 minutes for the eggplant
Cooking time: 25 minutes

Ingredients for 4 people:

1 large eggplant
a sprig of parsley
1 clove of garlic
2 anchovy fillets
⅓ cup olive oil
7 ounces canned chopped tomatoes
a pinch of cayenne pepper
salt
1 pound fusilli
2 tablespoons of capers

1. Dice the eggplant and leave in a bowl of cold water for 30 minutes.
2. After this time, bring plenty of water to a boil. In the meantime, wash and chop the parsley. Also chop the garlic. Cut the anchovies into small pieces.
3. Gently fry the garlic and anchovies in the oil. Add the tomatoes, diced eggplant, parsley and cayenne pepper. Salt, and cook on medium heat for about 15 minutes.
4. When the water comes to a boil, add salt and the fusilli; cook to a firm bite.
5. Add the capers to the sauce, mix, and cook for a few more minutes.
6. Drain the pasta, flavor with the sauce, and serve immediately.

Fusilli ai broccoli

FUSILLI WITH BROCCOLI (Puglia)

Preparation: 10 minutes
Cooking time: 35 minutes

Ingredients for 4 people:

2¼ pounds broccoli
salt
1 pound fusilli
olive oil
1 clove of garlic
¾ cup breadcrumbs
a pinch of cayenne pepper

1. Wash the broccoli; remove the leaves and the tougher outer parts; cut into pieces.
2. Boil the broccoli in plenty of salted water. When tender, drain well (but keep the cooking water) and place in a bowl.
3. Bring the cooking water back to a boil. Add the pasta and cook to a firm bite.
4. In the meantime, pour a little olive oil into a non-stick pan and sauté the clove of garlic.
5. Remove the garlic when it begins to brown. Then add the breadcrumbs and cayenne pepper. Brown the breadcrumbs, stirring frequently so that they do not burn.
6. Drain the pasta and add to the bowl of broccoli. Season with a little olive oil and the breadcumbs. Serve immediately.

◄ Fusilli mediterranei

Cavatieddi con la rucola

HOMEMADE PASTA WITH ARUGULA (Puglia)

Preparation: about 1 hour
Cooking time: 40 minutes

Ingredients for 4 people:

for the pasta:
1 part durum wheat flour
(7 ounces)
2 parts white flour (3½ ounces)
salt

for the sauce:
½ small onion
1 clove of garlic
3 tablespoons olive oil
7 ounces canned crushed tomatoes
½ pound arugula
salt
½ cup grated pecorino cheese

1. Prepare the dough as explained in the recipe on page 10.
2. Break the dough into pieces and roll out on a work-top to form cylinders about 12 inches long and about ½ inch in diameter. Before beginning to prepare the cavatieddi from the first roll, cover the others with a cloth so that the dough does not become too dry.
3. Cut the cylinders into pieces of about 1 inch. As you cut the pieces, draw the pieces of dough lightly over the work-top with the tip of the knife to form shells (the typical shape of cavatieddi).
4. Set aside the cavatieddi to dry uncovered.
5. In the meantime, bring salted water to a boil in a pot.
6. Chop the onion. Sauté the garlic and onion with the oil.
7. When the garlic begins to brown, remove it and add the crushed tomatoes. Cook for about 15 minutes, stirring occasionally.
8. Carefully wash the arugula and blanch in boiling salted water.
9. When the arugula is almost ready, add the cavatieddi and cook to a firm bite. Then drain the pasta with the vegetables.
10. Season with the tomato sauce and pecorino cheese. Mix well and serve immediately.

322

Culingiones
HOMEMADE FILLED PASTA (Sardinia)

Preparation: about 1½ hours
Cooking time: few minutes

Ingredients for 4 people:

for the pasta:
14 ounces (about 3 cups) flour
4 eggs
salt

for the filling:
½ pound spinach
salt
14 ounces pecorino cheese
⅛ cup flour
2 eggs
a pinch of nutmeg
pepper

for the sauce:
2 tablespoons butter
14 ounces cannned chopped
tomatoes
salt
½ cup grated pecorino cheese

1. Prepare the egg pasta following the recipe on page 10. Set aside to rise.
2. Carefully wash the spinach and boil in a little salted water. Grate the pecorino cheese.
3. When the spinach is ready, drain and squeeze; chop finely and place in a bowl.
4. Add the pecorino cheese, flour, eggs, and nutmeg to the spinach; add a little salt and pepper. Mix well.
5. Roll out the pasta to about 1/4 inch thick and cut into 2 inch squares.
6. Place a little filling on each square; fold over, pressing down firmly on the edges to seal. Arrange the culingiones on a cloth and set aside to dry.
7. Bring plenty of water to a boil in a pot.
8. Melt the butter in a pan; add the crushed tomatoes and a pinch of salt. Cook on medium heat for about 15 minutes, stirring occasionally.
9. When the water comes to a boil, add salt, add the culingiones and cook. Drain well and arrange on a serving platter.
10. Flavor with the tomato sauce and grated pecorino cheese. Serve immediately.

Gnocchetti al tonno
SMALL GNOCCHI WITH TUNA (Sardinia)

Preparation: 5 minutes
Cooking time: 35 minutes

Ingredients for 4 people:

3½ ounces pickled vegetables
2 medium fresh ripe tomatoes
1 scallion
5 ounces tuna in olive oil
sprig of parsley
⅓ cup olive oil
salt
14 ounces small gnocchi

1. Bring plenty of water to a boil.
2. Rinse the pickled vegetables under running water. Drain well and cut into large pieces.
3. Wash the tomatoes and cut into quarters; finely chop the scallion; break up the tuna with a fork; chop the parsley.
4. Heat the oil in a pan and immediately add the pickled vegetables, tuna, tomato, scallion, and parsley.
5. Salt, mix, and cook on medium heat for 15-20 minutes, stirring occasionally.
6. Salt the boiling water, add the pasta, and cook as required. When cooked to a firm bite, drain, season with the sauce, and serve.

Lasagnette con fave e patate
EGG PASTA WITH FAVA BEANS AND POTATOES (Basilicata)

Preparation: 5 minutes
Cooking time: 40 minutes

Ingredients for 4 people:

2 medium size potatoes
10½ ounces fresh fava beans
salt
2 cloves of garlic
3 tablespoons of olive oil
2 tablespoons butter
a pinch of cayenne pepper
14 ounces wide egg noodles
(lasagnette)

1. Peel the potatoes, wash, and dice. Boil the beans and potatoes.
2. Bring plenty of water to a boil to cook the pasta.
3. Chop the cloves of garlic and sauté for a few minutes in a pan with oil, butter and cayenne pepper.
4. A few minutes before the beans and potatoes are ready, salt the water of the pasta, add the noodles, and cook.
5. Drain the pasta and vegetables at the same time. Flavor with the sauce and serve immediately.

Maccheroni ai peperoni
MACARONI WITH BELL PEPPERS (Puglia)

Preparation: 15 minutes
Cooking time: 30 minutes

Ingredients for 4 people:

¾ pound bell peppers
1 medium size onion
⅓ cup olive oil
salt
pepper
½ pound fresh ripe tomatoes
a good handful of parsley
1 clove of garlic
14 ounces macaroni
3 tablespoons grated pecorino cheese

1. Wash and dry the peppers. Turn them quickly over a gas flame to slightly scald the outer skin (hold them on a fork), or place under a broiler.
2. Dip the peppers in cold water and rub well to remove the skin. Cut in half, remove the seeds, and cut into strips. Roughly chop the onion.
3. Heat the oil in a pan; add the peppers and onion, salt and pepper. Cook for 5 minutes on high heat, stirring constantly. Then remove the peppers from the pan and place on a dish.
4. Bring the water for the pasta to a boil.
5. Wash and dry the tomatoes; cut into pieces and place them into the pan where the peppers were cooked.
6. Chop the parsley and garlic together. Add to the chopped tomatoes; salt and cook on medium heat.
7. When the water comes to a boil, add salt and the macaroni, cook as required.
8. A few minutes before the pasta is ready, return the peppers to the tomatoes. Mix well and cook on low heat.
9. Drain the macaroni when cooked to a firm bite; flavor with the vegetable sauce, sprinkle with pecorino cheese, and serve immediately.

◄ *Lasagnette con fave e patate*

Maccheroni alla Calabrese
MACARONI CALABRIAN-STYLE (Calabria)

Preparation: 5 minutes
Cooking time: 30 minutes

Ingredients for 4 people:

salt
1 pound macaroni
3 ounces thick slice of smoked *pancetta*
1 large onion
1 tablespoon olive oil
pinch of cayenne pepper
pepper
¾ cup grated pecorino cheese

1. Bring plenty of water to a boil. Add salt and the macaroni and cook to a firm bite.
2. Dice the *pancetta* and chop the onion. Gently fry the *pancetta* in a pan with the oil. Add the onion and cayenne pepper and mix well. Add a little salt and pepper and fry gently for a few minutes.
3. When the pasta is ready, drain and flavor immediately with the pecorino, mixing well so that the cheese melts. Add the sauce, mix, and serve immediately.

Maccheroni del pastore
SHEPHERD'S MACARONI (Sardinia)

Preparation: 5 minutes
Cooking time: 30 minutes

Ingredients for 4 people:

6 tablespoons butter, softened
salt
1 pound macaroni
7 ounces fresh ricotta cheese
pinch of cayenne pepper
½ cup ounces green olives

1. Bring plenty of water to a boil in a pot to cook the pasta. Add salt and the macaroni and cook to a firm bite.
2. Place the ricotta cheese in a bowl; add four tablespoons of the water in which the pasta is cooking, and mix.
3. Add the butter, a little salt, and the cayenne pepper and mix well. Pit the olives, chop into large pieces, and mix gently with the other ingredients.
4. Drain the macaroni, flavor with the ricotta sauce, and serve immediately.

Maccheroni vegetariani
VEGETARIAN MACARONI (Various regions)

Preparation: 5 minutes
Cooking time: 30 minutes

Ingredients for 6 people:

1 carrot, peeled
2 zucchini
3 stalks of celery
1 medium size onion
2 cloves of garlic
5 tablespoon of olive oil
pinch of cayenne pepper
6 peeled tomatoes
1 vegetable bouillon cube
salt
21 ounces macaroni
3 tablespoons grated Parmisan cheese

1. Wash the carrot, zucchini, and celery; cut into pieces. Slice the onion.
2. Sauté the garlic and onion in the oil in a pan. When the garlic browns, remove it from the pan.
3. Add the chopped vegetables and cayenne pepper. Cook on medium heat for about 5 minutes, stirring occasionally.
4. In the meantime, bring plenty of water to a boil.
5. Heat 6 cups of water. Chop the tomatoes and add to the vegetables. Crumble the vegetable bouillon cube into the hot water. Add salt if necessary. Cover and cook on low heat for about 20 minutes.
6. When the water comes to a boil, add salt and the macaroni and cook as required.
7. Drain the pasta and flavor with the vegetable sauce. Add the Parmesan cheese, mix, and serve immediately.

Pasta alla Siciliana
PASTA SICILIAN-STYLE (Sicily)

Preparation: 5 minutes
Cooking time: 35 minutes

Ingredients for 6 people:

two sprigs of parsley
2 eggs
6 tablespoons grated pecorino cheese
salt
21 ounces penne or macaroni
6 tablespoons olive oil
1 clove of garlic
1 chili pepper

1. Bring plenty of water to a boil to cook the pasta.
2. Wash and chop the parsley. Break the eggs into a bowl, add salt, pecorino cheese, and parsley. Mix well.
3. When the water comes to a boil, add salt and the pasta; cook to a firm bite.
4. In the meantime, in a pan large enough to contain all the pasta, sauté the garlic and chili pepper in the oil. When the garlic begins to brown, remove it; also remove the chili pepper.
5. Drain the pasta, pour into the pot, and mix. Pour the egg and pecorino cheese mixture over the pasta and mix well until the egg mixture becomes firm. Remove from the heat and serve immediately.

Malloreddus

SARDINIAN GNOCCHI (Sardinia)

Preparation: 5 minutes
Cooking time: 35 minutes

Ingredients for 6 people:

1 medium size onion
3 tablespoons olive oil
1 clove of garlic
5 ounces Italian sausage
4 basil leaves
14 ounces canned chopped tomatoes
salt, pepper
21 ounces gnocchi
¼ cup grated pecorino cheese

1. Bring plenty of water to a boil.
2. Chop the onion and sauté in a pan with the oil and garlic. Break the sausage into pieces and add to the pan; add the basil and stir.
3. Remove the garlic and add the tomatoes, salt, and pepper; cook for about 30 minutes.
4. When the water comes to a boil, add salt and the pasta and cook to a firm bite.
5. Drain the gnocchi and flavor with the sauce. Sprinkle with cheese, mix, and serve immediately.

Penne alla ricotta

PENNE WITH RICOTTA CHEESE (Sicily)

Preparation: 5 minutes
Cooking time: 25 minutes

Ingredients for 6 people:

salt
21 ounces penne
7 ounces ricotta cheese
pepper
½ cup grated pecorino or
Parmesan cheese

1. Bring plenty of water to a boil. When it comes to a boil, add salt and the pasta; cook as desired.
2. Place the ricotta in a bowl; add 3-4 tablespoons of the water in which the pasta is cooking. Add a little salt and pepper and mix well to form a cream.
3. Drain the penne and flavor with the sauce. Sprinkle with grated cheese and serve immediately.

◄ *Malloreddus*

Penne al forno alla pizzaiola
BAKED PENNE PIZZAIOLA (Campania)

Preparation: 10 minutes
Cooking time: 45 minutes

Ingredients for 4 people:

salt
1 pound penne
4 anchovy fillets
sprig of parsley
½ pound mozzarella cheese
9 ounces canned crushed tomatoes
1 tablespoon of capers
a pinch of dry marjoram
a little olive oil
3 tablespoons grated Parmesan cheese

1. Bring plenty of water to a boil. When it comes to a boil, add salt and the pasta; cook to a firm bite. In the meantime, heat the oven to 425°F.
2. Chop the anchovy fillets; wash and chop the parsley; dice the mozzarella.
3. Place the crushed tomatoes in a bowl and add salt. Add the mozzarella, the anchovies, capers, parsley, marjoram, and 3 tablespoons oil. Mix well.
4. Drain the penne cooked to a firm bite and place in an oven-proof dish. Add the tomato sauce and the other ingredients; mix.
5. Sprinkle with Parmesan cheese and bake for about 15 minutes. Serve immediately.

Spaghetti ai frutti di mare
SPAGHETTI WITH SEAFOOD (Various regions)

Preparation: 30 minutes
Cooking time: 25 minutes

Ingredients for 6 people:

14 ounces mussels
14 ounces small clams
½ cup olive oil
5 ounces cleaned squid
5 ounces shrimp
sprig of parsley
1 clove of garlic
pinch of cayenne pepper
10½ ounces tomato sauce
1½ pounds spaghetti
salt

1. Clean the mussels and clams and scrub with a hard brush; remove the "beard" and wash carefully.
2. Arrange in a casserole with 4 tablespoons water and 1 tablespoon oil. Cover and cook over high heat.
3. When the heat causes the shells to open, remove the meat and discard the shells.
4. Wash the squid well; shell the shrimp. In the meantime, finely chop the parsley.
5. Bring plenty of water to a boil to cook the pasta.
6. Gently fry the garlic in the oil; when it begins to brown, remove it. Add the seafood and tomato sauce to the pan and sprinkle with parsley and cayenne pepper; add a little salt. Mix well and cook on medium heat for 15-20 minutes.
7. As the sauce cooks, salt the boiling water and cook the spaghetti. Drain, flavor with the sauce, and serve immediately.

Spaghetti alla Catanese
SPAGHETTI CATANESE-STYLE (Sicily)

*Preparation: 5 minutes; 30 minutes
for the eggplant*
Cooking time: 25 minutes

Ingredients for 4 people:

2 medium size eggplants
salt
plenty of cooking oil for frying
some flour
1 pound spaghetti
6 tablespoons butter
4 tablespoons grated Parmesan
cheese
pinch of cayenne pepper

1. Wash the eggplant, cut into wedges, and salt; set aside for about 30 minutes to extract the juice.
2. After about 20 minutes, bring plenty of water to a boil to cook the pasta.
3. Heat plenty of oil in a pan. Carefully dry the eggplant, dip in the flour, and fry in hot oil. Drain on paper towels.
4. When the water comes to a boil, add salt and the pasta; cook to a firm bite.
5. Drain the pasta and flavor with the butter, cheese, and cayenne pepper; mix well. Add the eggplant wedges and serve immediately.

Spaghetti alla puttanesca
SPAGHETTI WITH PUTTANESCA SAUCE (Campania)

Preparation: 10 minutes
Cooking time: 25 minutes

Ingredients for 4 people:

7 ounces black olives
1 tablespoon of capers
4 anchovy fillets
2 cloves of garlic
4 tablespoons butter
⅓ cup olive oil
9 ounces canned crushed tomatoes
salt
1 pound spaghetti

1. Bring plenty of water to a boil.
2. In the meantime, pit the olives and chop with the capers and anchovy fillets. Chop the garlic.
3. Melt the butter in a pan with the oil. Add the chopped mixture and fry gently for a couple of minutes. Add the crushed tomatoes, salt, and cook for about 15 minutes, stirring occasionally.
4. When the water comes to a boil, salt, and cook the spaghetti to a firm bite.
5. Drain the spaghetti, flavor with the sauce, mix well, and serve.

Spaghetti al pomodoro e basilico
SPAGHETTI WITH TOMATOES AND BASIL (Sicily)

Preparation: 10 minutes
Cooking time: 25 minutes

Ingredients for 4 people:

1 pound fresh ripe tomatoes
2 sprigs of basil
1 clove of garlic
salt
pepper
1 pound spaghetti
⅓ cup olive oil
3 tablespoons grated pecorino or
Parmesan cheese

1. Bring plenty of water to a boil to cook the pasta.
2. Wash, dry, and chop the tomatoes. Wash the basil leaves and chop finely. Place the tomatoes in a casserole; add the basil and garlic, salt and pepper, and cook on low heat, stirring poccasionally.
3. When the water comes to a boil, add salt and the spaghetti and cook to a firm bite.
4. About 5 minutes before the pasta is ready, add the oil to the sauce. Mix well and cook on low heat.
5. Drain the spaghetti and flavor with the sauce; sprinkle with cheese and serve immediately.

Spaghetti alla Turiddu
SPAGHETTI WITH ANCHOVY SAUCE (Sicily)

Preparation: 10 minutes
Cooking time: 25 minutes

Ingredients for 6 people:

3½ ounces small black olives
4 anchovy fillets
half a red chili pepper
2 cloves of garlic
⅓ cup olive oil
14 ounces canned crushed tomatoes
salt
21 ounces spaghetti
a good pinch of marjoram
4 tablespoons grated Parmesan
cheese

1. Bring plenty of water to a boil to cook the pasta.
2. Pit the olives and chop; chop the anchovies; finely chop the chili pepper.
3. Gently fry the garlic in the olive oil in a small casserole; remove the garlic when it begins to brown.
4. Add the crushed tomatoes, the olives, anchovies, and red chili pepper. Salt; mix well, and cook for about 20 minutes on medium heat.
5. When the water comes to a boil, add salt and the spaghetti; cook to a firm bite. Then drain the pasta and mix with the sauce. Sprinkle with marjoram and grated Parmesan cheese, mix, and serve immediately.

◄ *Spaghetti al pomodoro e basilico*

Spaghetti alle zucchine
SPAGHETTI WITH ZUCCHINI (Sicily)

Preparation: 15 minutes
Cooking time: 25 minutes

Ingredients for 4 people:

8 small zucchini
½ cup olive oil
1 clove of garlic
salt
10 basil leaves
1 pound spaghetti
2 eggs
freshly ground pepper

1. Wash and dry the zucchini; top and tail and cut into thin slices.
2. Gently fry the garlic with the oil in a non-stick pan for a few minutes. Then add the zucchini; salt, cover, and cook on low heat, stirring occasionally.
3. Bring plenty of water to a boil to cook the pasta.
4. When the zucchini are ready (very soft), add the basil, breaking the leaves into pieces by hand.
5. When the water comes to a boil, add salt and the spaghetti and cook as required.
6. Break the eggs into a bowl, add salt, and beat with a fork.
7. When ready, drain the pasta, add the beaten eggs and stir. Then add the zucchini and pepper to taste. Mix well and serve immediately.

Spaghetti alle cozze
SPAGHETTI WITH MUSSELS (Puglia)

Preparation: 25 minutes
Cooking time: 25 minutes

Ingredients for 6 people:

1¾ pounds mussels
1 good handful of parsley
1 clove of garlic
⅓ cup olive oil
10½ ounces canned crushed tomatoes
a pinch of cayenne pepper
salt
pepper
21 ounces spaghetti

1. Clean and scrub the mussel shells; remove the "beard." Use a knife to open the shells; remove the meat and wash well to remove all residue.
2. Bring plenty of water to a boil.
3. Chop the parsley and garlic and sauté in a pan with the oil for a few minutes.
4. Add the crushed tomatoes and mussels; add the cayenne pepper. Salt and pepper to taste; cook for about 15 minutes on medium heat, stirring occasionally.
5. When the water comes to a boil, add salt and the spaghetti and cook until firm to the bite; drain, combine with the sauce, and mix. Serve immediately.

Spaghetti alle vongole
SPAGHETTI WITH CLAMS (Campania)

Preparation: 30 minutes
Cooking time: 30 minutes

Ingredients for 4 people:

21 ounces large clams
⅓ cup olive oil
2 cloves of garlic
7 ounces canned crushed tomatoes
salt
pepper
1 pound spaghetti
sprig of parsley

1. Wash the clams thoroughly under running water, scrub the shells with a stiff brush, and remove the "beard."
2. Pour a tablespoon of olive oil into a pan and add the clams. Cook on medium-high heat to open the shells.
3. Then drain the clams, collecting the water in a bowl. Remove the meat and discard the shells.
4. Gently fry the crushed garlic with the oil in a pan.
5. When the garlic begins to brown, add the cooking water (strain through a fine mesh or a piece of cloth).
6. Add the crushed tomatoes, salt and pepper; cook for about 25 minutes on medium heat.
7. In the meantime, boil the water in a pot. When the water comes to a boil, and the salt and spaghetti and cook to a firm bite.
8. Five minutes before the pasta is ready, add the clams to the tomato sauce, mix, and cook on low heat.
9. Chop the parsley. Drain the pasta, mix with the sauce, sprinkle with parsley, and serve immediately.

Pasta alle cime di rapa
PASTA WITH TURNIP GREENS (Puglia)

Preparation: 5 minutes
Cooking time: 40 minutes

Ingredients for 6 people:

1 pound turnip greens
salt
21 ounces pasta (orecchiette, penne,
or fusilli)
1 cup olive oil
2 cloves of garlic
2 anchovy fillets
4 tablespoons grated pecorino or
Parmesan cheese
freshly ground pepper

1. Bring plenty of water to a boil in a pot. Clean and wash the turnip greens carefully.
2. When the water comes to a boil, add salt and the pasta. After 5-10 minutes, add the turnip greens to the same pot. Boil the pasta and vegetables together.
3. In the meantime, pour the oil into a non-stick pan and gently fry the garlic.
4. Chop the anchovy fillets. When the garlic begins to color, remove from the pan and add the anchovies.
5. When the pasta is ready, drain together with the turnip greens.
6. Dress the pasta with the oil and anchovies. Add the grated cheese and a little freshly ground pepper. Mix well and serve immediately.

◀ *Pasta alle cime di rapa*

337

Timballo di maccheroni

MACARONI TIMBALE (Campania)

Preparation: 30 minutes; 30 minutes resting
Cooking time: 45 minutes

Ingredients for 6 people:

for the timbale:
10½ ounces (about 2 cups) flour
10 tablespoons butter
1 egg
salt

for the filling:
2 large eggplants
plenty of olive oil
salt
10½ ounces macaroni
1 clove of garlic
7 ounces canned crushed tomatoes
5-6 basil leaves
¾ cup Parmesan cheese

1. Heat the oven to 350°F.
2. Prepare the timballo: knead the flour with the butter, egg, a pinch of salt, and a few tablespoons of water on a work-top. Try to achieve a uniform dough without kneading the ingredients excessively. Leave the dough to rise for 30 minutes.
3. Roll out the dough to about 1/10 inch in thickness. Grease a round oven-proof dish with butter and arrange the dough over the base.
4. Trim the excess and knead again; roll out into a disk that will cover the dish.
5. Bake the oven dish; make sure that the timballo doesn't burn but remains light in color.
6. Boil a pot of water.
7. Prepare the filling. Cut the eggplant into strips and fry in a pan with plenty of oil. Drain the eggplant on paper towels.
8. When the water comes to a boil, add salt and the macaroni; cook to a firm bite.
9. Heat 3 tablespoons oil in a pan and sauté the garlic until it browns. Add the crushed tomatoes and the basil. Salt, and cook for about 10 minutes.
10. Drain the macaroni; season with the tomato sauce and Parmesan cheese. Arrange a third of this mixture over the timballo, cover with half the eggplant; add another layer of macaroni, another of vegetables, and then finish off with the remaining macaroni.
11. Cover the timballo with the circle of dough and place in the hot oven for a few minutes. Serve immediately.

Zite al pomodoro e tonno

ZITI WITH TOMATOES AND TUNA (Sicily)

Preparation: 5 minutes
Cooking time: 35 minutes

Ingredients for 4 people:

half a medium onion
1 clove of garlic
2 anchovy fillets
⅓ cup olive oil
7 ounces chopped tomatoes
salt
14 ounces ziti (or other types of pasta)
3 ounces tuna in olive oil
pepper

1. Chop the onion with the garlic and the anchovy fillets. Heat the oil in a pan and add the onion, garlic, and anchovies; cook on medium heat for about 5 minutes.
2. In the meantime, boil plenty of water in a pot.
3. Add the crushed tomatoes to the pan, salt, and mix well. Cover and cook for 10 minutes.
4. When the water comes to a boil, add salt and cook the pasta.
5. Break the tuna into pieces and add to the sauce together with a pinch of salt. Mix well and cook for another 10 minutes.
6. Drain the ziti, mix with the sauce and serve immediately.

Zite con le melanzane

ZITI WITH EGGPLANT (Sicilia)

Preparation: 10 minutes; 1 hour for the eggplants
Cooking time: 30 minutes; frying time

Ingredients for 4 people:

3 thin, long eggplants
salt
plenty of cooking oil for frying
1 clove of garlic
⅓ cup olive oil
7 ounces chopped tomatoes
4-5 basil leaves
pinch of ground chili pepper
14 ounces ziti
1 ounce grated Parmesan cheese

1. Wash the eggplants and cut into pieces about ½ inch thick by 2 inches long. Arrange on a large dish and sprinkle with salt (to make them less bitter); set aside for about 1 hour.
2. Rinse the eggplant well and dry. Heat plenty of oil in a large pan. When the oil is hot, fry the eggplant a few at a time. Drain on paper towels.
3. In the meantime, bring a pot of water to a boil to cook the pasta.
4. Chop the garlic finely and fry gently with the oil in a pan. Add the crushed tomatoes, the lightly chopped basil, chili pepper, and a little salt. Mix and cook for 15-20 minutes on medium heat.
5. When the water comes to a boil, add salt and the ziti and cook as required.
6. Then drain the pasta and flavor with the tomato and eggplant sauce. Sprinkle with Parmesan cheese, mix, and serve immediately.

Minestra di cavolo

CABBAGE SOUP (Calabria)

Preparation: 5 minutes; frying time
Cooking time: 20 minutes

Ingredients for 4 people:

1 medium size savoy cabbage
salt
⅓ pound crusty bread
⅓ cup olive oil
3 cups meat stock
3 tablespoons grated pecorino cheese

1. Remove the tougher outer leaves of the cabbage and wash well. Separate the leaves and boil in water.
2. Boil the stock in a pot.
3. Dice the bread. Heat the oil in a non-stick pan and gently fry the bread. When the bread browns, remove from the pan and drain on paper towels.
4. When the cabbage is ready, drain well. Chop and add to the hot stock and cook for a few minutes.
5. Arrange the bread croutons on serving dishes; pour the soup over the top, sprinkle with pecorino cheese, and serve immediately.

Minestra di fave

FAVA BEAN SOUP (Puglia)

Preparation: 12 hours resting
Cooking time: 3-4 hours

Ingredients for 6 people:

21 ounces dry fava beans
salt
⅓ cup olive oil

1. Wash the beans and place them in the cooking pot. Add 6 cups of cold water and set aside for about 12 hours.
2. Salt the beans and cook over very low heat for 3-4 hours with the lid slightly ajar. Stir occasionally so that the beans do not stick to the base of the pot.
3. When the beans have cooked to a creamy consistency, flavor with olive oil, mix and serve immediately.

The ideal way to cook this dish is in a terra cotta casserole.

Minestrone alla Napoletana
MINESTRONE NEAPOLITAN-STYLE (Campania)

Preparation: 10 minutes
Cooking time: 1 hour 10 minutes

Ingredients for 4 people:

1 ounce Parma ham
½ onion
2 tablespoons butter
7 ounces canned chopped tomatoes
2 medium size potatoes
2 medium size zucchini
1 stalk of celery
1 yellow bell pepper
salt
pepper
8-10 basil leaves
sprig of parsley
2 tablespoons grated Parmesan
cheese

1. Chop the ham and onion and fry gently in a casserole with the butter and a sprig of parsley. Add the tomatoes, mix, and cook for 10 minutes on medium heat.
2. Wash the vegetables and peel the potatoes. Dice the potatoes and the zucchini; chop the celery. Remove the seeds from the bell pepper and cut into strips.
3. Add the celery to the casserole; then add about 3 cups of water, salt, and pepper; cook for about 30 minutes.
4. Chop the basil and parsley and add to the casserole. Add the other vegetables; mix and cook for another 30 minutes.
5. When the soup is ready, flavor with cheese and serve.

Insalata di riso
RICE SALAD (Various regions)

Preparation: 25 minutes
Cooking time: 20 minutes

Ingredients for 4 people:

salt
1⅓ cups rice
2 eggs
5 ounces gruyère cheese
¼ pound ham (one thick slice)
2 small frankfurter sausages
5 ounces tuna in olive oil
4 ounces pickled vegetables in oil
7 tablespoons olive oil

1. Boil plenty of water in a pot. When it comes to a boil, add salt and the rice and cook as required.
2. In the meantime, hard boil the eggs. Dice the cheese and ham and place in a large salad bowl.
3. Cut the sausages into slices; break up the tuna with a fork; drain the oil from the pickles. Add these ingredients to the salad bowl.
4. When the eggs have hard boiled, cool in cold water, shell, and chop into large pieces. Add to the other ingredients.
5. When the rice is ready, cool the cooking pot under cold running water. Drain and add rice to the salad bowl. Season with oil and mix well. Serve cold.

◀ *Insalata di riso*

Riso alle vongole
RICE WITH CLAMS (Campania)

Preparation: 20 minutes
Cooking time: about 30 minutes

Ingredients for 4 people:

14 ounces littleneck clams
3 cups stock
1 bell pepper
⅓ cup olive oil
1 clove of garlic
1⅔ cups rice
salt
sprig of parsley

1. Clean the clams and scrub with a hard brush. Split the shells with a sharp knife and remove the clams.
2. Boil the stock in a pot. Wash the pepper; remove the seeds and cut into strips.
3. Cook the pepper in the oil in a casserole over medium heat for 5 minutes. Chop the garlic and add to the casserole.
4. When the garlic browns, add the rice and the clams; fry gently for 1 minute. Chop the parsley and add to the other ingredients.
5. Cover with the stock and cook over medium-high heat until the rice is ready (about 20 minutes). Serve immediately.

Riso con le patate
RICE WITH POTATOES (Calabria)

Preparation: 15 minutes
Cooking time: about 35 minutes

Ingredients for 4 people:

1 medium onion
sprig of parsley
1 pound potatoes
3 tablespoons olive oil
3½ ounces canned chopped tomatoes
salt
1⅔ cups rice
3 tablespoons grated pecorino cheese

1. Boil plenty of water in a pot.
2. Finely chop the onion; chop the parsley. Peel the potatoes, wash and dice.
3. Sauté the onion in a casserole with the oil; add the tomatoes and the parsley; add salt and mix.
4. Add 2 cups of cold water; when it comes to a boil, add the potatoes. Cook on low heat, stirring occasionally.
5. When the other pot of water comes to a boil, add salt and the rice. Cook to a firm bite.
6. When the potatoes are ready, mix with the rice and sprinkle with pecorino cheese; mix well and cook for a couple of minutes. Serve immediately.

344

Risotto all'agnello
RISOTTO WITH LAMB (Sardinia)

Preparation: 10 minutes
Cooking time: 1 hour

Ingredients for 4 people:

1 pound shoulder of lamb
2 ounces slice of smoked *pancetta*
½ cup olive oil
½ glass dry white wine
salt
pepper
4 cups stock
¾ pound zucchini
sprig of parsley
1 small onion
1 clove of garlic
1⅔ cups arborio rice
2 tablespoons butter
2 tablespoons grated Parmesan cheese

1. Dice the meat and the *pancetta*. Gently fry the *pancetta* in half the oil in a casserole; then add the pieces of lamb.
2. Gently fry the meat; then add the wine, salt, and pepper and stir. Cover and cook on low heat for about 30 minutes.
3. Boil the stock.
4. In the meantime, wash the zucchini and slice. Wash the parsley and chop finely. Add these two ingredients to the meat and cook for another 10 minutes.
5. Chop the onion and garlic. Heat the oil in another casserole and sauté the garlic and onion for a few minutes.
6. Add the rice to the garlic and onion; fry gently for 1 minute. Then add the meat and zucchini and mix well.
7. Add a little stock to the rice and mix with a wooden spoon until it is absorbed. Continue adding stock and mixing until the rice is ready (about 20 minutes).
8. When the rice is cooked, add the butter, the sprig of parsley, and the grated Parmesan cheese. Mix and serve immediately.

Risotto alla Sarda
RISOTTO SARDINIAN-STYLE (Sardinia)

Preparation: 10 minutes
Cooking time: about 45 minutes

Ingredients for 4 people:

about 5 cups stock
½ small onion
¼ cup olive oil
7 ounces ground pork
7 ounces canned crushed tomatoes
pinch of saffron
salt
pepper
1⅔ cups arborio rice
2 tablespoons grated pecorino cheese

1. Boil the water in a pot.
2. As the water comes to a boil, finely chop the onion and sauté with the oil in a casserole.
3. Add the meat and cook over medium-high heat, stirring continually.
4. Add the crushed tomatoes, saffron, salt, and pepper and mix well. Cook over medium heat.
5. When the meat is ready, add the rice. Add the hot stock a little at a time, stirring continually until the rice is cooked (about 20 minutes).
6. Sprinkle with pecorino and serve immediately.

Risotto alla Siciliana
RISOTTO SICILIAN-STYLE (Sicily)

Preparation: 15 minutes
Cooking time: about 40 minutes

Ingredients for 4 people:

4 artichokes
1 small onion
2 cloves of garlic
4 anchovy fillets
⅓ cup olive oil
salt
pepper
1⅔ cups arborio rice
2 tablespoons grated pecorino cheese
1 tablespoon of chopped parsley

1. Wash the artichokes. Remove the tougher outer leaves and the tips; cut into thin strips. Chop the onion and garlic. Cut the anchovies into large pieces.
2. Gently fry the chopped garlic, onion, and anchovies in oil in a casserole.
3. Add the artichokes, salt, and pepper and stir. Cover the casserole and cook over low heat for about 15 minutes.
4. In the meantime, boil 3 cups of water in a pot.
5. Add the rice to the casserole and fry gently with the artichokes for 1-2 minutes. Add a ladle of boiling water and stir until it is absorbed.
6. Continue adding water and stirring until the rice is ready (about 20 minutes). Then sprinkle with pecorino cheese and parsley. Mix and serve.

Suppa quatta
BREAD AND CHEESE SOUP (Sardinia)

Preparation: 25 minutes
Cooking time: 20 minutes

Ingredients for 6 people:

1 pound fresh "cacio" cheese
1 pound crusty bread
1 cup grated pecorino cheese
4 cups stock

1. Heat the oven to 350°F. Cut the cheese into thin slices.
2. Cover an oven-proof dish with a layer of bread and then add a layer of cheese slices; sprinkle with grated pecorino cheese.
3. Add another layer of bread, then cheese, and so on until the ingredients are used, finishing with a layer of cheese.
4. Then add the stock so that it almost covers the last layer of bread.
5. Cook in the oven for 20 minutes. Serve immediately.

This "suppa" (soup) has very humble origins; it was often the main meal of poor families in Gallura.

◀ *Risotto alla Siciliana*

Tiella di riso pugliese
RICE PUGLIESE-STYLE (Puglia)

Preparation: 30 minutes
Cooking time: 25-30 minutes

Ingredients for 6 people:

1 pound seafood
a sprig of parsley
1 clove of garlic
2 medium onions
salt
1 pound small ripe tomatoes
1 pound potatoes
2 cups rice
2 tablespoons grated pecorino cheese
⅓ cup olive oil

1. Heat the oven to 350°F.
2. Wash the seafood very carefully. Scrub the shells well and open them with a sharp knife; remove the meat and throw the shells away.
3. Finely chop the parsley and garlic. Slice the onions. Chop the tomatoes. Peel the potatoes and cut into thin slices.
4. Arrange a layer of onions in an oven-proof dish; sprinkle with salt and half the chopped garlic and parsley.
5. Add half the tomatoes and cover with the potato slices.
6. Wash the rice and arrange on top of the potatoes; cover with the seafood. Add the remaining chopped garlic and parsley, tomatoes, sliced potatoes, and salt to taste.
7. Sprinkle with pecorino cheese; add the oil and 3 cups cold water.
8. Place the dish in the oven and cook until the rice is ready (when the liquid is completely absorbed). Serve immediately.

This is also an ideal summer dish: set the rice aside for a little while after taking it out of the oven and serve lukewarm.

Zuppa estiva di zucchine
SUMMER ZUCCHINI SOUP (Campania)

Preparation: 15 minutes
Cooking time: 30-40 minutes

Ingredients for 4 people:

2¼ pounds zucchini
3 tablespoons butter
2½ tablespoons olive oil
salt
pepper
4 slices of dense country bread
two sprigs of parsley
10 basil leaves
3 tablespoons grated Parmesan cheese

1. Wash, top and tail the zucchini, and cut into round slices.
2. Sauté the zucchini for 5 minutes in a casserole with the butter, sprig of parsley, and oil.
3. Add 5 cups of water, salt, and pepper. Cover and cook for 30-40 minutes over medium heat.
4. Toast the slices of bread and dice. Chop the parsley and basil.
5. When the soup is ready, add the chopped parsley and basil; sprinkle with grated cheese and pour the soup over the bread.

Zuppa di finocchi

FENNEL SOUP (Calabria)

Preparation: 20 minutes
Cooking time: about 20 minutes

Ingredients for 6 people:

6 medium fennel bulbs
1 clove of garlic
a sprig of parsley
⅓ cup olive oil
salt
6 slices of country bread

1. Wash the fennel, remove the tough outer leaves, and cut into slices.
2. Chop the garlic and parsley; arrange in a casserole with the oil.
3. Add the fennel slices and 5 cups of cold water. Add salt and bring to a boil.
4. When the water comes to a boil, lower the heat and simmer.
5. In the meantime, toast the slices of bread (in a toaster or in the oven) and place in a soup bowl.
6. When the soup is ready, pour over the bread. Serve immediately.

Zuppa di pesce
FISH SOUP (Various regions)

Preparation: about 30 minutes
Cooking time: 20 minutes

Ingredients for 4 people:

about 4 pounds of various fish
(scorpion fish, red mullet, squid,
shrimp, mussels, clams)
2 cloves of garlic
⅓ cup olive oil
pinch of cayenne pepper
10½ ounces fresh ripe tomatoes
4 slices of country bread
a sprig of parsley
salt

1. Prepare the fish, removing the scales, heads, tails, and innards; wash well under running water.
2. Finely chop the garlic and fry gently in a casserole with the oil and cayenne pepper.
3. Chop the tomatoes and add to the casserole. Add the fish, beginning with the squid and ending with the shellfish.
4. Add 2 cups of water and salt. Cover the casserole and cook for about 20 minutes.
5. In the meantime, toast the slices of bread. Chop the parsley.
6. Place a slice of bread in each serving dish and, when the soup is ready, pour it over the bread. Sprinkle with chopped parsley and serve.

Zuppa di vongole
CLAM SOUP (Campania)

Preparation: 25 minutes
Cooking time: about 15 minutes

Ingredients for 4 people:

4½ pounds clams
½ cup olive oil
½ cup dry white wine
1 clove of garlic
sprig of parsley
4 medium ripe tomatoes
salt
pepper
4 slices of country bread

1. Clean the clams and scrub the shells.
2. Place the clams in a casserole with 2 tablespoons oil, 4 tablespoons water, and a little wine. Cover and cook over medium-high heat.
3. When the heat causes the clams to open, remove the meat from the shells. Strain the cooking liquid through a cloth.
4. Chop the garlic and parsley and sauté in a casserole with the remaining oil. Add the rest of the white wine and cook until it evaporates almost completely.
5. Blend the tomatoes and add to the casserole. Add the liquid used to cook the clams; add salt and pepper and cook for about 10 minutes on medium heat. In the meantime, toast the slices of bread.
6. Add the clams, leave them to flavor for a few minutes, and serve each portion with a slice of toasted bread.

◀ *Zuppa di pesce*

Bistecche al rosmarino

STEAK SEASONED WITH ROSEMARY (Various regions)

Preparation: 5 minutes
Cooking time: 35 minutes

Ingredients for 4 people:

14 ounces beef steak
some flour
1 pat of butter
⅓ cup olive oil
1 clove of garlic
a pinch of rosemary
salt
pepper
1 cup stock
a little dry white wine

1. Tenderize the slices of meat and dip in the flour.
2. Heat the butter and oil in a pan; then add the slices of meat.
3. Cook the steaks over low heat for 5 minutes; then turn and cook for another 5 minutes.
4. Chop the garlic with the rosemary and spread over the steaks. Add salt and pepper.
5. Then pour the stock over the meat and cook on medium heat for about 20 minutes.
6. Before taking the pan off the heat, baste the steaks with a little wine and raise the heat to evaporate. Serve immediately.

Bistecche alla Napoletana

NEAPOLITAN STEAK (Campania)

Preparation: 10 minutes
Cooking time: 10 minutes

Ingredients for 4 people:

3½ ounces cured ham
½ small onion
2½ tablespoons olive oil
8 beef steaks (about 21 ounces)
salt
pepper
7 ounces canned chopped tomatoes

1. Chop the ham finely together with the onion.
2. Gently fry these in the oil in a non-stick pan.
3. Place the steaks in the pan and cook over medium-high heat. Add salt and pepper.
4. Add the chopped tomatoes; check the salt and cook for about 10 minutes on medium heat, turning the steaks.
5. If necessary, you can add a little salted water as the steaks cook. Serve the steaks immediately when ready.

This dish is often served with mushrooms.

Bistecche alla pizzaiola
STEAK PIZZAIOLA (Campania)

Preparation: a few minutes
Cooking time: 15 minutes

Ingredients for 4 people:

⅓ cup olive oil
4 beef steaks
salt
pepper
1 clove of garlic
9 ounces canned chopped tomatoes
1 teaspoon marjoram

1. Heat 2 tablespoons olive oil in a pan; arrange the steaks in the pan and fry over medium-high heat for a couple of minutes.
2. Remove the steaks and arrange on a plate; add salt and pepper and keep warm.
3. Chop the garlic. Add 2 tablespoons olive oil to the pan and sauté the garlic until it begins to brown.
4. Add the chopped tomatoes and marjoram, salt, and pepper. Mix well and cook for 10 minutes on medium heat.
5. Place the steaks in the pan and leave to flavor for a few minutes. Serve immediately.

Bistecche alle acciughe
STEAK WITH ANCHOVIES (Puglia)

Preparation: 10 minutes
Cooking time: 20 minutes

Ingredients for 4 people:

1 ounce anchovy fillets
6 tablespoons butter
4 beef steaks
salt
pepper
3½ ounces green olives

1. Chop the anchovy fillets finely and mix them well with 4 tablespoons butter to make a paste.
2. Melt the remaining butter in a pan; arrange the steaks and sauté for a few minutes.
3. Add salt and pepper to the steaks and cook for another ten minutes or so on moderate heat. Pit the olives.
4. When the steaks are ready, remove them from the pan, arrange them on a plate, and keep hot.
5. Add the pitted olives and the butter and anchovy paste to the pan and cook on medium heat for 5 minutes.
6. Return the steaks to the pan and flavor for one minute. Serve immediately.

Agnello alla Sarda
LAMB SARDINIAN-STYLE (Sardinia)

Preparation: 15 minutes
Cooking time: 1 hour

Ingredients for 6 people:

1¾ pounds potatoes
2¼ pounds lamb (breast and cutlets)
10-12 juniper berries
salt
pepper
1 sprig of rosemary
3 cloves of garlic
⅓ cup olive oil

1. Peel the potatoes, wash and cut them into pieces, and place in a large oven-proof dish.
2. Cut the lamb into regular pieces and place on top of the potatoes. Sprinkle the juniper berries on top. Add salt and pepper.
3. Chop the rosemary finely together with the garlic and then spread over the lamb. Add the oil and a cup of water.
4. Cover and cook for about one hour. Serve hot.

Agnello con funghi
LAMB WITH MUSHROOMS (Basilicata)

Preparation: 25 minutes
Cooking time: 1 hour

Ingredients for 4 people:

21 ounces Portobello or other mushrooms
2¼ pounds lamb
a generous pinch of red pepper flakes
salt
a little olive oil

1. Heat the oven to 325°F.
2. Wash the mushrooms carefully and set aside to dry.
3. Cut the lamb into pieces and place in casserole; then add the mushrooms.
4. Sprinkle with pepper flakes and salt; add the oil and cook in the oven for about an hour.
5. Baste the lamb occasionally with the roasting sauce.

◀ *Agnello alla sarda*

Agnello Pasquale
EASTER LAMB (Campania)

Preparation: 30 minutes
Cooking time: 1 hour

Ingredients for 4 people:

6 tablespoons butter
⅓ cup olive oil
2 bay leaves
2 sprigs of rosemary
5 or 6 sage leaves
2¾ pounds boneless lamb
½ pound small onions
1 pound new potatoes (small)
salt
pepper

1. Heat the oven to 300°F.
2. Place the butter, oil, bay leaves, rosemary, and sage in a roasting pan.
3. Cut the lamb into pieces and place in the dish; add the small onions evenly.
4. Peel the potatoes and place them in the same dish. Add salt and pepper.
5. Place in the oven and cook for an hour, stirring and basting occasionally.

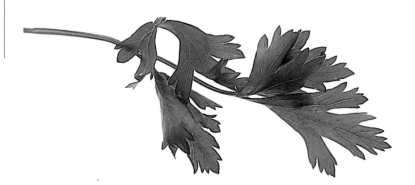

Capretto o agnello alla Pugliese
GOAT OR LAMB PUGLIA-STYLE (Puglia)

Preparation: 45 minutes
Cooking time: 1 hour 30 minutes

Ingredients for 4 people:

2 handfuls of parsley
2 cloves of garlic
¾ cup grated pecorino cheese
2¼ pounds potatoes
2¼ pounds leg of goat (or lamb)
4 tablespoons butter
some breadcrumbs
salt
pepper
a little olive oil

1. Heat the oven to 350°F.
2. Clean and chop the parsley together with the cloves of garlic; mix half of this with ½ cup pecorino cheese.
3. Peel the potatoes and cut into slices about ½ inch thick.
4. Make cuts into the leg of goat or lamb. Fill these cuts with the mixture of parsley, garlic, and pecorino cheese.
5. Grease an oven-proof dish with 2 tablespoons butter; cover the base with the sliced potatoes.
6. Sprinkle breadcrumbs over the potatoes and then add pats of the remaining butter. Add salt and pepper.
7. Arrange the leg of meat on top of the potatoes; sprinkle with the remaining parsley. Add salt and pepper.
8. Pour a little oil over the meat and potatoes. Place in the oven and roast for about one and a half hours.
9. After 45 minutes, turn the meat over and baste with salt and a little oil.

356

Braciole alla Siciliana

BEEF ROLLS SICILIAN-STYLE (Sicily)

Preparation: 25 minutes
Cooking time: 1 hour

Ingredients for 4 people:

⅓ cup raisins
1 clove of garlic
2 ounces lard
4 slices of beef
salt
pepper
4 slices of cooked ham
4 slices provolone cheese
1 small onion
2 tablespoons olive oil
2 tablespoons butter
¼ cup pine nuts
1 sprig of mixed herbs: basil,
marjoram, and parsley
⅓ cup white wine
5 ounces tomato sauce

1. Soak the raisins in lukewarm water. Chop the garlic with the lard.
2. Place the sliced beef on a work-top and sprinkle with salt and pepper. Place a slice of ham and cheese on each slice of beef. Roll up the beef and tie with kitchen string.
3. Chop the onion and sauté with the oil and butter.
4. Then add the steaks. Sprinkle with the garlic mixture, drained raisins, and pine nuts.
5. Add salt and pepper; add the mixed herbs. Pour a little wine over the meat and cook until it almost evaporates entirely.
6. Add the tomato sauce and cover with just enough hot water to cover the meat completely. Add salt.
7. Cover and cook for about one hour. Thicken the sauce as required before serving.

Bistecche all'aglio
GRILLED STEAK WITH GARLIC (Puglia)

Preparation: 1 hour
Cooking time: 15-20 minutes

Ingredients for 6 people:

2 handfuls of parsley
3 cloves of garlic
⅓ cup olive oil
salt
freshly ground pepper
6 beef steaks (with bone) about
1 inch thick

1. Chop the parsley together with the garlic. Pour the oil into a bowl and add the mixture, and salt and pepper. Mix well.
2. Arrange the steaks separately in a roasting pan. Pour the seasoned oil over the meat and marinate for about 1 hour, turning the steaks occasionally.
3. Heat a griddle. When it is hot, cook the steaks on both sides, basting the meat with the remaining oil. Serve immediately.

Cosciotto d'agnello alla Calabrese
LAMB CHOPS CALABRIAN-STYLE (Calabria)

Preparation: 15 minutes
Cooking time: 15 minutes

Ingredients for 4 people:

1 cup olive oil
1½ pounds lamb chops
1 small onion
2 sprigs of parsley
14 ounces canned peeled tomatoes
2 bell peppers
3½ ounces green olives
salt

1. Pour half the oil into a pan and heat. When it is hot, gently fry the chops.
2. Chop the onion finely; wash the parsley and break into pieces; slice the tomatoes; wash the peppers, cut them open, remove the seeds, and then cut into small pieces.
3. Pour the remaining oil into a pan and gently fry the vegetables (including the whole olives). Salt and cook on medium heat for about 10 minutes
4. Then add the chops to the vegetables. Salt lightly. Leave to flavor for a few minutes and serve piping hot.

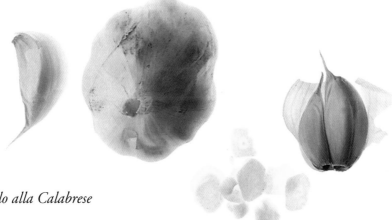

◄ *Cosciotto d'agnello alla Calabrese*

Costolette di vitello e basilico

VEAL CUTLETS WITH BASIL (Sicily)

Preparation: a few minutes
Cooking time: approx. 20 minutes

Ingredients for 4 people:

4 tablespoons butter
4 veal cutlets
salt
pepper
½ cup dry white wine
10-15 leaves of fresh basil
5-6 tablespoons stock

1. Melt half the butter in a pan and gently fry the cutlets for a few minutes on medium-high heat. Add salt and pepper.
2. Lower the heat and continue cooking the cutlets, turning occasionally.
3. When the cutlets are ready, remove them from the pan, arrange on a plate, and keep warm.
4. Pour the wine and cooking juice into the pan; evaporate almost completely.
5. Chop the basil and add to the pan; pour in the broth and thicken on low heat.
6. Add the remaining butter and melt. Arrange the cutlets in the pan and cook for a few moments. Serve immediately.

Costolette di vitello alla Palermitana

VEAL CUTLETS PALERMO-STYLE (Sicily)

Preparation: 15 minutes; 1 hour for marinating
Cooking time: 10-15 minutes

Ingredients for 4 people:

4 veal cutlets
⅓ cup vinegar
a sprig of parsley
2 cloves of garlic
¾ cup grated pecorino cheese
1 egg
salt, pepper
¾ cup breadcrumbs
½ cup olive oil

1. Tenderize the meat a little, then arrange the cutlets in a large pan and sprinkle with vinegar. Marinate for one hour.
2. Wash and chop the parsley together with the garlic. Mix this and the pecorino cheese in a bowl.
3. Remove the meat from the marinade, drain, and dry with a clean cloth.
4. Break an egg into a bowl and beat with a fork. Dip the cutlets in the egg one at a time. Add salt and pepper.
5. Sprinkle the cutlets with the chopped parsley and garlic mixed with pecorino. Then dip them in the breadcrumbs.
6. Heat the oil in a non-stick pan. Add the cutlets and brown both sides on rather high heat. Serve immediately.

360

Sarmoriglio

ROAST MEAT CALABRIAN-STYLE (Calabria)

Preparation: 5 minutes
Cooking time: 10 minutes

Ingredients for 4 people:

1 clove of garlic
1 tablespoon olive oil
a pinch of majoram
salt
4 slices of roast meat (21 ounces)
1 sprig of fresh marjoram

1. Chop the garlic finely. Mix the oil, 2 tablespoons water, crumbled marjoram, garlic, and a pinch of salt in a bowl. Mix well with a fork.
2. Heat a griddle. Cook the slices of meat on both sides.
3. As the meat cooks, baste continually with the sprig of fresh marjoram dipped in the sauce. Serve immediately.

This "roast" sauce—called sarmoriglio—can also be used to flavor grilled fish.

Gallina col mirto

FOWL WITH OREGANO (Sardegna)

Preparation: 5 minutes; 24 hours resting
Cooking time: about 2 hours

Ingredients for 6 people:

salt
1 onion
1 carrot, peeled
1 stalk celery
a sprig of parsley
1 large fowl (chicken, capon, or large game bird)
plenty of fresh oregano srings

1. Heat plenty of salted water. Add the onion, carrot, celery, and parsley.
2. When the water comes to a boil, place the fowl in the pot. Cover and simmer.
3. In the meantime, arrange the oregano on a plate.
4. When the fowl is tender, remove from the pot, drain, and place on top of the oregano. Cover with more oregano so that it can absorb the flavor.
5. Set the fowl aside for 24 hours. Serve cold.

▼ *Oregano*

Frittata ai peperoni
OMELET WITH BELL PEPPERS (Calabria)

Preparation: 10 minutes
Cooking time: about 20 minutes

Ingredients for 4 people:

1 red bell pepper
3 tablespoons butter
6 eggs
salt
2 tablespoons grated Parmesan
cheese

1. Cut the pepper in half; remove the seeds and the white flesh. Cut into strips.
2. Melt the butter in a pan. Add the strips of pepper and cook on low heat for about 20 minutes, stirring occasionally.
3. In the meantime, break the eggs into a bowl and add salt and the grated cheese. Mix briskly to blend well.
4. Pour all the mixture into pan where the peppers are cooking. Cook for 2 minutes, then turn the omelet and cook for another minute. Serve immediately.

Impanadas
SMALL MEAT TIMBALES (Sardegna)

Preparation: 30 minutes; 24 hours
for marinating
Cooking time: 50 minutes

Ingredients for 8 people:

a sprig of parsley
1 clove of garlic
2 sun-dried tomatoes
1¾ pounds boneless lamb in small
dices
½ pound boneless pork in small
dices
a pinch of saffron
salt
pepper
a little olive oil

for the pasta:
1 pound (about 3 cups) durum
wheat flour
3 tablespoons olive oil
salt

1. Chop the parsley, the garlic, and the sun-dried tomatoes together.
2. Place the diced meats in a bowl; add the chopped vegetables, saffron, salt, and pepper. Mix well.
3. Cover the bowl and marinate in the refrigerator for about 24 hours.
4. Heat the oven to 350°F.
5. Arrange the flour on a work-top; add the oil and salted water. Knead until a uniform dough is made.
6. Grease a round oven-proof dish. Roll out two-thirds of the dough and arrange in the dish. Fill with the marinated meats.
7. Roll out the remaining dough to form a disk the same size as the dish. Cover the meat with this dough.
8. Bake for about 50 minutes.

Impanadas are small timballi. To make preparation easier, a single timballo is often prepared, as in this recipe.

◀ *Frittata ai peperoni*

Involtini con carciofi
BEEF ROLLS WITH ARTICHOKES (Sicily)

Preparation: 10 minutes
Cooking time: 25 minutes

Ingredients for 4 people:

2 tender artichokes
salt
1½ ounces cooked ham
4 tablespoons butter
8 slices of beef (approx. 1 pound)
a little flour
½ medium-size onion
a little olive oil
⅓ cup white wine

1. Wash the artichokes. Boil some salted water in a small pot.
2. When the water comes to a boil, blanch the artichokes. Drain and cool.
3. Chop the ham and place in a bowl; mix with half the butter to form a kind of creamy paste.
4. Cut the artichokes into quarters. Spread a little ham "mousse" over each slice of meat. Add a quartered artichoke.
5. Roll up the slices of meat and tie with kitchen string. Dip these in the flour.
6. Chop the onion and sauté in a pan with a little oil and the remaining butter.
7. Fry the involtini over medium-high heat; pour in the wine and cook on medium heat. Serve immediately.

Pollo ai peperoni
CHICKEN WITH BELL PEPPERS (Calabria)

Preparation: 15 minutes
Cooking time: 45 minutes

Ingredients for 4 people:

1 whole chicken
    (about 2½-3 pounds)
1 sprig of rosemary
1 sage leaf
1 bay leaf
2 cloves of garlic
freshly ground pepper
salt
⅓ cup olive oil
1 red bell pepper
1 yellow bell pepper
2-3 basil leaves
a little broth

1. Heat the oven to 375°F. Wash and dry the chicken and clean the inside.
2. Place the rosemary, sage, bay leaf, and a clove of garlic inside the chicken. Add a little freshly ground pepper and salt.
3. Tie up the chicken, baste with a little oil, and arrange it in an oven-proof dish. Place the dish in the oven and cook for about 45 minutes, basting with oil as required.
4. Cut the bell peppers in half and remove the seeds; wash well and cut into irregular pieces.
5. Fry a clove of garlic in a pan with 4 tablespoons of oil. When the garlic begins to color, remove it and add the peppers.
6. Add the basil and 3-4 tablespoons stock. Add salt and cook on medium heat for about 15 minutes.
7. Take the chicken out of the oven and cut into 4 portions. Combine the chicken portions and the peppers and allow to flavor for a few minutes. Serve immediately.

Pollo con funghi e patate

CHICKEN WITH MUSHROOMS AND POTATOES (Basilicata)

Preparation: 20 minutes
Cooking time: 1 hour

Ingredients for 4 people:

1 whole chicken (about 3 pounds)
⅓ cup olive oil
1 medium onion
⅓ cup dry white wine
7 ounces canned chopped tomatoes
a sprig of parsley
6 basil leaves
salt
pepper
½ pound fresh mushrooms
¾ pound potatoes
1 clove of garlic

1. Wash and cut the chicken into pieces and fry gently in a pan with 2 tablespoons oil. Slice the onion and add to the chicken.
2. When the onion browns, sprinkle with wine and evaporate. Add the chopped tomatoes and stir.
3. Chop the parsley and the basil; mix with the chicken. Add salt and pepper and cook on medium heat for about one hour.
4. In the meantime, carefully clean the mushrooms. Cut in half. Peel the potatoes and cut into thin slices.
5. Sauté the garlic in a casserole with the remaining oil; when the garlic browns, remove it and begin cooking the mushrooms and potatoes. Add salt, stir, and cook for about 30 minutes on medium heat.
6. When ready, place the chicken on a serving dish. Arrange the mushrooms and potatoes around the chicken and serve.

Spiedini

KEBABS (Various regions)

Preparation: 30 minutes
Cooking time: 30 minutes

Ingredients for 4 people:

9 ounces veal
5 ounces lean turkey
5 ounces salami sausage
3½ ounces bacon
1 yellow bell pepper
a little olive oil
salt
pepper

1. Dice the veal, turkey, and sausage. Cut the bacon into squares.
2. Wash the bell pepper, cut in half, and remove the seeds; cut into squares the same size as the meat.
3. Prepare 8 spiedini: arrange pieces of veal, bacon, turkey, and pepper on a wooden skewer.
4. Heat a large grill. Baste the spiedini in the oil and cook for 10 minutes, turning occasionally.
5. Lower the heat and cook for another 20 minutes. Salt and pepper. Serve hot.

Mozzarella ai ferri

GRILLED MOZZARELLA CHEESE (Campania)

Preparation: a few minutes
Cooking time: 5 minutes

Ingredients for 4 people:

1½ pounds mozzarella
salt

1. Heat a griddle. Cut the cheese into slices about ½ inch thick.
2. When the griddle is scalding hot, arrange the cheese slices and grill on both sides to a golden crust. Serve immediately.

Mozzarella in carrozza

FRIED MOZZARELLA SANDWICHES (Campania)

Preparation: 15-20 minutes
Cooking time: frying time

Ingredients for 4 people:

7 ounces fresh mozzarella cheese
8 slices of sandwich bread
2 eggs
salt
1 cup milk
a little flour
plenty of oil for frying

1. Slice the mozzarella cheese and arrange on 4 slices of bread. Cover with the other 4 slices of bread and skewer with a toothpick.
2. Beat an egg together with a little salt in a bowl.
3. Sprinkle the filled sandwich bread with a little milk and then dip in the flour. Dip both sides of the sandwiches in the beaten egg for a few seconds.
4. Heat the oil in a pan; add the sandwiches and brown on both sides.
5. Drain on paper towels and serve immediately.

◀ *Mozzarella*
  in carrozza

367

Scaloppine ai capperi
VEAL CUTLETS WITH CAPERS (Puglia)

Preparation: 10 minutes
Cooking time: 10-15 minutes

Ingredients for 4 people:

8 slices of veal or beef
(about 21 ounces)
salt
pepper
a pinch of nutmeg
a little flour
4 tablespoons butter
a little olive oil
a sprig of parsley
2 tablespoons capers
5 tablespoons stock

1. Add salt and pepper to the slices of meat and sprinkle with nutmeg; dust with flour. Chop the parsley.
2. Melt the butter in a pan with a little oil and gently fry the cutlets.
3. Add the parsley, the capers, and the stock. Cook on medium heat for 10-15 minutes. Serve immediately.

Scaloppine al Marsala
VEAL CUTLETS IN MARSALA WINE (Sicily)

Preparation: 10 minutes
Cooking time: 15 minutes

Ingredients for 4 people:

1 ounce ground bacon
2½ tablespoons olive oil
1 clove of garlic
1 pound lean veal slices
salt
pepper
1 tablespoon flour
2 tablespoons butter
½ cup dry Marsala wine

1. Warm the oven.
2. Gently fry the bacon with the oil and a clove of garlic in a pan.
3. When the garlic begins to brown, remove it and then add the slices of meat. Add salt and pepper and cook for a few minutes, turning the meat occasionally.
4. Take the pan off the heat and arrange the slices of meat in a serving dish. Turn off the oven and place the dish inside.
5. Mix the flour and butter and return the pan to the heat; pour in the Marsala wine and the butter-flour paste. Cook for a few minutes, mixing well.
6. Pour this sauce over the cutlets and serve immediately.

Scaloppine alle olive
CUTLETS WITH OLIVES (Sicily)

Preparation: 10 minutes
Cooking time: 10 minutes

Ingredients for 4 people:

1 clove of garlic
4 tablespoons butter
1 pound slices lean veal
a little flour
5 ounces canned chopped tomatoes
3½ ounces pitted black olives
a pinch of cayenne pepper
salt

1. Finely chop the garlic, place in a pan with the butter, and sauté.
2. When the butter is hot, place the sliced veal in the pan and sear on both sides over medium-high heat.
3. Sprinkle the meat with a little flour on both sides.
4. Add the chopped tomatoes to the pan and mix well.
5. Cut the olives into pieces and add to the pan; then add the cayenne and salt. Cook for 10 minutes, stirring occasionally.

Vitello alla Sarda
SARDINIAN VEAL (Sardinia)

Preparation: 10 minutes
Cooking time: 1 hour 30 minutes

Ingredients for 4 people:

a little flour
1 cut of lean veal (about 21 ounces)
1 onion
1 carrot, peeled
a sprig of parsley
⅓ cup olive oil
1 clove of garlic
1 tablespoon capers
½ cup dry white wine
1 slice of lemon
salt

1. Dip the meat lightly in the flour. Chop the onion, carrot, and parsley.
2. Fry the meat gently in a pan with oil for a few minutes. Then add the chopped vegetables, the garlic, capers, wine, and the peeled slice of lemon.
3. Add salt and cover tightly (place a sheet of parchment paper between the pan and the lid). Cook for about one and a half hours.
4. Remove the sliced meat and pour the cooking sauce over it. Serve immediately.

Acciughe con il finocchio
ANCHOVIES WITH DILL (Sicily)

Preparation: 20 minutes
Cooking time: 10-15 minutes

Ingredients for 4 people:

12 large fresh anchovies
2 cloves of garlic
⅓ cup olive oil
salt
pepper
1 tablespoon of dill seeds
dash of dry white wine

1. Clean the anchovies, removing the scales and innards, and wash well.
2. Gently fry the garlic in a large pan with the oil. When the garlic begins to brown, remove it and add the fish in a single layer.
3. Sprinkle the anchovies with salt, pepper, and dill seeds. Sprinkle with wine and cook for 10-15 minutes, turning frequently. Serve immediately.

Fritto misto di mare
MIXED FRIED SEAFOOD (Various regions)

Preparation: about 30 minutes
Cooking time: frying time

Ingredients for 6 people:

14 ounces crayfish tails
14 ounces small shrimp
14 ounces large shrimp
14 ounces small squid
3 tablespoons flour
plenty of oil for frying
1 lemon in quarters
salt

1. Remove the shells as required and wash repeatedly in cold salted water.
2. Clean the squid, remove the skin and the transparent, cartilaginous bone. Remove the beak between the eyes with a knife and then the eyes.
3. Dry everything well and dip in the flour.
4. Heat plenty of oil in a pan.
5. Fry the larger pieces of fish on moderate heat. Turn frequently so that they brown all over. Drain on paper towels.
6. Fry the smaller pieces on medium-high heat; drain on paper towels.
7. Arrange the mixed fried seafood on a serving dish and garnish with the lemon quarters. Serve immediately.

◄ *Acciughe con il finocchio*

371

Aragosta al forno
BAKED LOBSTER (Sardinia)

Preparation: 10 minutes
Cooking time: 20-30 minutes

Ingredients for 4 people:

a sprig of parsley
1 lobster (about 2¼ pounds)
⅓ cup olive oil
2 tablespoons breadcrumbs
1 lemon
salt

1. Heat the oven to 350°F. Chop the parsley.
2. Cut the lobster lengthwise and remove the tail from the shell.
3. Place the lobster in an oven-proof dish; season with oil and sprinkle with parsley and breadcrumbs. Pour over the lemon juice and salt.
4. Cook in the hot oven for 20-30 minutes (depending on the size of the lobster).
5. When the tail is cooked, cut the lobster into pieces and serve immediately.

Aragosta lessa
BOILED LOBSTER (Sardinia)

Preparation: 20 minutes; 2 hours resting
Cooking time: 25 minutes

Ingredients for 4 people:

1 live lobster (about 2¼ pounds)
⅓ cup olive oil
1 lemon
a pinch of salt

1. Boil plenty of salted water in a pot.
2. Tie up the lobster and cook for 25 minutes in the boiling water, inserting it head first.
3. After it cools, cut the lobster into pieces and keep the liquid formed inside.
4. Prepare a sauce by mixing this liquid with the oil, lemon juice, and salt.
5. Season the lobster with this sauce; set aside for a couple of hours and serve.

Merluzzo in salsa d'acciughe

COD IN ANCHOVY SAUCE (Sicily)

Preparation: about 20 minutes
Cooking time: frying time

Ingredients for 4 people:

8 anchovy fillets
2 eggs
salt
4 cod fillets (about 1½ pounds)
a little flour
¾ cup breadcrumbs
plenty of olive oil

1. Finely chop the anchovies and place in a small pan with a little oil. Cook over very low heat for 10-15 minutes, until they dissolve.
2. Beat the eggs in a bowl and add salt. Dip the fish fillets in the flour and then in the eggs. Then dip in the breadcrumbs.
3. Heat plenty of oil in a large pan. When the oil begins to smoke, fry the cod pieces.
4. Fry until golden on both sides. Drain on paper towels. Serve with the anchovy sauce.

Pepata di cozze

PEPPERED MUSSELS (Campania)

Preparation: 20 minutes
Cooking time: about 20 minutes

Ingredients for 4 people:

60 fresh mussels
sprig of parsley
freshly ground pepper
1 lemon

1. Clean the mussels and scrub with a hard brush; remove the "beard" and wash well again. Heat 4-5 tablespoons water in a casserole.
2. When the heat causes the shells to open, remove the meat from the shells.
3. Strain the cooking water through a clean cloth and pour into a pot.
4. Chop the parsley. Place the mussels in the pot; add the parsley, a little pepper, and the lemon juice.
5. Cook for another 5 minutes and serve immediately.

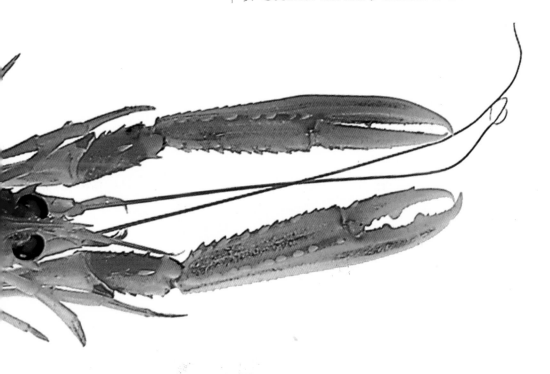

◀ *Calamari ripieni*

Calamari ripieni
STUFFED SQUID (Sardinia)

Preparation: 30 minutes
Cooking time: 45 minutes

Ingredients for 4 people:

8 medium-size squid
2 sprigs of parsley
2 cloves of garlic
8-10 small rosemary leaves
1 egg yolk
salt
pepper
⅓ cup olive oil
½ cup dry white wine
1 sliced lemon

1. Clean the squid and remove the skin and the cartilage inside along the entire length of the body. Use a knife or your fingers to remove the beak and the eyes.
2. Wash in cold water until the squid are white. Separate the heads and the tentacles from the body.
3. Chop the tentacles and the head together with parsley, garlic, and rosemary.
4. Place this mixture in a bowl; add the egg yolk, salt, pepper, and 2 tablespoons oil; mix well.
5. Fill each squid with this mixture. Close with a toothpick so that the filling cannot ooze out.
6. Heat the remaining oil in a pan and sauté the squid. Sprinkle with the white wine and evaporate almost entirely.
7. Cover and cook on low heat for about 45 minutes. Serve garnished with slices of lemon.

Pesce al forno
BAKED FISH (Puglia)

Preparation: 15-20 minutes
Cooking time: 20 minutes

Ingredients for 4 people:

5 ounces olives in brine
2 pounds cleaned and scaled whole
fish (John Dory or red
mullet)
a little olive oil
a little vinegar
salt

1. Heat the oven to 300°F. Pit the olives and cut into pieces.
2. Rinse the fish well and salt the inside.
3. Pour a little oil into a baking pan and arrange the fish inside. Sprinkle with a little vinegar and salt lightly.
4. Add the chopped olives and place in the oven. Cook for about 20 minutes.

Pesce spada al limone
SWORDFISH WITH LEMON (Sicily)

Preparation: 15 minutes.
Cooking time: 15-20 minutes

Ingredients for 4 people:

4 slices of swordfish (about 1½
pounds)
4 lemons
salt, pepper
sprig of parsley
4 sage leaves
2 cloves of garlic
some marjoram

1. Heat the oven to 375°F. Wash and dry the fish. Wash the lemon carefully and slice thinly.
2. Arrange the lemon on 4 large pieces of parchment paper or foil. Salt and pepper the slices of fish, and arrange each on the paper/foil to cover the lemon.
3. Chop the parsley with the sage and the garlic. Sprinkle this over the fish. Sprinkle with a pinch of marjoram.
4. Wrap up the paper/foil, place on a baking sheet and bake for 15-20 minutes; serve.

Pesce spada impanato
BREADED SWORDFISH (Sicily)

Preparation: 10 minutes.
Cooking time: about 10 minutes

Ingredients for 4 people:

2 eggs
salt, pepper
4 slices of swordfish
(about 1½ pounds)
⅓ cup breadcrumbs
plenty of oil for frying
1 lemon

1. Break the eggs into a bowl, add a pinch of salt and a little pepper, and beat with a fork.
2. Dip the fish slices into the egg and then into the breadcrumbs.
3. Heat the oil in a pan and, when it begins to smoke, add the breaded fish slices.
4. Fry until golden on both sides, turning occasionally. Drain on paper towels, sprinkle with the lemon juice, and serve immediately.

Sarde alla Napoletana
NEAPOLITAN SARDINES (Campania)

minutes.
Cooking time: 20 minutes

Ingredients for 4 people:
1 pound whole fresh sardines,
cleaned and scaled
1 clove of garlic
1 sprig of parsley
3 medium fresh ripe tomatoes
½ cup olive oil
salt, pepper
a good pinch of marjoram

1. Heat the oven to 350°F.
2. Rinse the sardines. Chop the garlic with the parsley. Cut the tomatoes into pieces.
3. Pour the oil into a baking pan and arrange the fish inside. Sprinkle with salt, pepper, and marjoram.
4. Arrange the pieces of tomato and the chopped garlic-parsley over the fish.
5. Place in the oven and cook for about 20 minutes.

Sgombri alla griglia
GRILLED MACKEREL (Calabria)

Preparation: 20 minutes
Cooking time: 20 minutes

Ingredients for 4 people:

about 1 pound mackerel fillets
a little olive oil
sprig of parsley
3 tablespoons anchovy paste
2 tablespoons butter
the juice of a lemon
salt

1. Heat a griddle. Baste mackerel with a little oil and place on the griddle. Cook for 20 minutes, turning after 10 minutes.
2. Chop the parsley. Mix the anchovy paste in a bowl with the butter using a wooden spoon. Add the parsley and the lemon juice.
3. When the mackerel is ready, arrange on a serving dish; add salt and pepper as preferred. Arrange the anchovy sauce over each piece of fish and serve immediately.

Seppioline alle olive
BABY CUTTLEFISH WITH OLIVES (Calabria)

Preparation: 10 minutes.
Cooking time: about 40 minutes

Ingredients for 4 people:

1 pound cleaned baby cuttlefish
some flour
2 cloves of garlic
⅓ cup olive oil
salt
pepper
⅓ cup dry white wine
1 large onion
12 green olives
2 pickled gherkins
sprig of parsley

1. Clean the cuttlefish, removing the skin and the hard, white bone. Use a knife to remove the beak between the eyes and then the eyes themselves. Wash the cuttlefish well and dry. Dip in a little flour.
2. Sauté the garlic with 4 tablespoons oil in a pan; when the garlic browns, remove it and gently fry the cuttlefish for a few minutes. Salt and pepper.
3. Add the wine, allow it to evaporate, and continue cooking over medium heat.
4. Slice the onion thinly and sauté in a pan with 2 tablepoons oil over low heat. After a few minutes, add the onions to the cuttlefish.
5. Pit the olives and chop together with the gherkins; add this mixture to the cuttlefish and stir gently.
6. A few minutes before the dish is ready, chop the parsley. When ready, sprinkle the chopped parsley over the cuttlefish and serve immediately.

Spiedini di gamberi
SHRIMP KEBABS (Various regions)

Preparation: 10 minutes
Cooking time: 15 minutes

Ingredients for 4 people:

32 large shrimp, shelled
2 cloves of garlic
½ cup olive oil
4 tablespoons butter
1 tablespoon flour
1 pat of butter
⅓ cup dry sparkling wine
sprig of parsley
half a lemon
salt

1. Wash the shrimp and skewer (4 per skewer).
2. Finely chop the garlic and sauté in a pan with the oil and butter.
3. Place the skewers in a pan and cook over medium-high heat for 3-4 minutes, turning occasionally.
4. Remove the skewers from the pan, arrange on a plate, and cover to keep warm.
5. In the meantime, mix the flour well with the butter.
6. Add this to the cooking pan, dilute with the sparkling wine, and cook until rather thick.
7. Chop the parsley and add to the sauce with the lemon juice. Salt and mix well.
8. Pour the sauce over the shrimp and serve immediately.

◀ *Seppioline alle olive*

Spiedini di pesce
SEAFOOD KEBABS (Various regions)

Preparation: 15 minutes.
Cooking time: about 15 minutes

Ingredients for 4 people:

16 large shrimp
8 medium cleaned squid
1 clove of garlic
sprig of parsley
2 tablespoons olive oil
2 tablespoons breadcrumbs
salt
pepper
1 lemon

1. Clean and shell the shrimp. Wash all the seafood very well.
2. Finely chop the garlic and the parsley; place in a bowl with the oil and breadcrumbs. Salt, pepper, and stir.
3. Skewer the seafood, alternating shrimp and squid. Sprinkle the skewers with the chopped mixture.
4. Heat a grill; when very hot, cook the kebabs until the fish is golden.
5. Serve the spiedini hot, squeezing the lemon over them.

Stoccafisso alla Calabrese
CALABRIAN CODFISH (Calabria)

Preparation: 20 minutes
Cooking time: 1 hour and 10 minutes

Ingredients for 4 people:

1 onion
a sprig of parsley
⅓ cup olive oil
1 tablespoon tomato sauce
1½ pounds codfish fillets
1¼ pounds potatoes
a sprig of basil
salt
pepper
3½ ounces black olives

1. Chop the onion and parsley finely; place in a casserole. Add the oil and the tomato sauce and cook over medium heat.
2. Heat a ladle of water and add to the sauce; continue cooking over low heat.
3. Cut the codfish into pieces. Peel the potatoes and slice thinly.
4. Place the fish and potatoes in the casserole together with the basil (remove this before serving). Salt and pepper.
5. Cover the casserole and cook for 50 minutes.
6. Drain the olives and add to the casserole. Cook for another 10 minutes. Serve immediately.

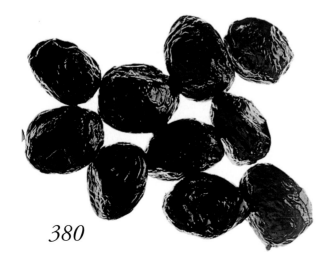

380

Tonno alla Mediterranea

TUNA MEDITERRANEAN (Sicily)

Preparation: 10 minutes
Cooking time: 40 minutes

Ingredients for 4 people:

3 ounces green or black olives
10 basil leaves
3 tablespoons olive oil
½ pound fresh ripe tomatoes
4 slices of fresh tuna
(about 1¼ pounds)
2 tablespoons breadcrumbs
2 tablespoons capers
salt
pepper

1. Heat the oven to 325°F.
2. Pit and chop the olives; cut the basil into large pieces. Pour the oil into a baking pan. Chop the tomatoes.
3. Dip the tuna in the breadcrumbs and arrange in the pan. Sprinkle the basil on top, together with the olives, capers, and tomatoes.
4. Salt, pepper, and sprinkle with a little oil. Bake for about 40 minutes. Serve immediately.

Tonno lessato

BOILED TUNA (Calabria)

Preparation: 15 minutes
Cooking time: 1 hour

Ingredients for 4 people:

1 carrot, peeled
1 medium-size onion
1 stalk of celery
2 bay leaves
salt
1 fresh tuna steak
(about 1½ pounds)
freshly ground pepper
2 cloves of garlic
3 tablespoons parsley
⅓ cup olive oil

1. Wash the vegetables well and arrange in a pot with 6 cups of salted water. Bring to a boil and simmer for 40 minutes.
2. Place whole tuna steak in a casserole.
3. Strain the stock, cool a little, and add to the tuna. Salt and pepper.
4. Cook on low heat until the tuna is ready (about 20 minutes).
5. Remove the tuna and cut into slices.
6. Chop the garlic and the parsley; mix with oil and arrange this sauce over the fish. Serve immediately.

Fave alla Calabrese
CALABRIAN FAVA BEANS (Calabria)

Preparation: about 15 minutes
Cooking time: 40 minutes

Ingredients for 6 people:

salt
2¼ pounds whole fava beans
2 cloves of garlic
¼ cup olive oil
5-6 mint leaves
4 tablespoons breadcrumbs
2 tablespoons vinegar

1. Boil the salted water. Top and tail the beans.
2. When the water comes to a boil, add the beans and cook for about 15 minutes; then drain and dry.
3. Chop the garlic and sauté in a pan with oil for a few minutes. Add the beans and cook on medium-high heat for 5 minutes.
4. Then chop the mint and sprinkle it and the breadcrumbs over the beans. Continue cooking for a further 10-15 minutes.
5. A few minutes before the beans are ready, sprinkle with vinegar, stir, and evaporate. Serve immediately.

Caponata
STEWED MIXED VEGETABLES (Sicily)

Preparation: 1 hour
Cooking time: 30 minutes

Ingredients for 4 people:

1 pound eggplant
salt
½ pound onions
2 stalks celery
3½ ounces green olives
½ pound fresh ripe tomatoes
⅓ cup olive oil
1 tablespoon sugar
½ cup vinegar
½ pound zucchini
2 tablespoons capers

1. Wash the vegetables well. Dice the eggplant into 1-inch cubes. Place in a bowl and sprinkle with plenty of coarse salt. Mix and set aside for about 1 hour to eliminate the bitter juices.
2. In the meantime, slice the onion, chop the celery, olives, and tomatoes.
3. Sauté the onion slices in a pan with 2 tablespoons oil. When the onion browns, add the celery and olives; last, add the tomatoes and salt. Mix, cover, and cook over medium heat for about 10 minutes.
4. Dissolve the sugar in the vinegar and pour into the pan. Add the capers and mix well. Cook on medium heat for 15 minutes.
5. Rinse the eggplant well and dry on paper towels. Cut the zucchini into round slices. Heat the remaining oil in a non-stick pan.
6. When the oil is hot, fry the eggplant and zucchini. Drain these vegetables on paper towels and place in a bowl.
7. Add the cooked vegetables and tomatoes to the bowl; mix well and cool. Serve when the caponata is lukewarm.

◀ *Fave alla Calabrese*

Cime di rapa stufate

BRAISED TURNIP GREENS (Puglia)

Preparation: 15 minutes
Cooking time: about 20 minutes

Ingredients for 4 people:

3½ pounds turnip greens
2 onions
salt
pepper
½ cup olive oil

1. Remove the tough and stringy parts of the turnip greens; wash carefully. Slice the onion.
2. Place the turnip greens in a casserole with 2 cups of water and the sliced onion; add salt and pepper.
3. Cover the casserole and cook for about ten minutes, stirring occasionally.
4. Add the oil and continue cooking over a medium-high heat.
5. Just before taking the turnip greens off the heat, stir to thicken the juices.

Turnip greens are an ideal accompaniment to boiled, roast, and grilled meats.

Crocchette di patate

POTATO CROQUETTES (Various regions)

Preparation: about 45 minutes
Cooking time: frying time

Ingredients for 4 people:

1 pound potatoes
salt
1 ounce boiled ham
sprig of parsley
1½ ounces "caciocavallo" cheese
2 tablespoons butter
2 eggs, separated
pepper
½ cup breadcrumbs
plenty of oil for frying

1. Wash the potatoes thoroughly and place in a pot with salted water. Bring to a boil and cook.
2. Chop the ham, parsley, and cheese.
3. When the potatoes are ready, peel and mash them; place in a casserole.
4. Add the butter and mix until it melts; add 2 egg yolks (keep the whites in a bowl) and stir briskly. Add salt and pepper; cook on low heat for a few minutes.
5. Add the chopped ham, parsley, and cheese to the mashed potatoes; mix well.
6. Mold the mixture into rolls about 1 inch high by 2 inches long. Dip in the beaten egg white and then in the breadcrumbs.
7. Heat the oil in a non-stick pan and gently fry the croquettes. When they are golden, drain on paper towels. Serve immediately.

Melanzane alla Calabrese

EGGPLANT CALABRIAN-STYLE (Calabria)

Preparation: 10 minutes; 30 minutes resting
Cooking time: 10-20 minutes

Ingredients for 4 people:

2 large eggplants
10-12 mint leaves
1 clove of garlic
salt
⅓ cup olive oil
1 tablespoon vinegar

1. Wash the eggplant and cut into slices or cubes and set aside in cold water for about 30 minutes.
2. Boil water, add the eggplant, and cook until ready (about 10-20 minutes, depending on the size of the pieces).
3. Chop the mint and garlic. When the eggplant is ready, drain and season with salt, oil, vinegar, mint, and garlic. Serve immediately.

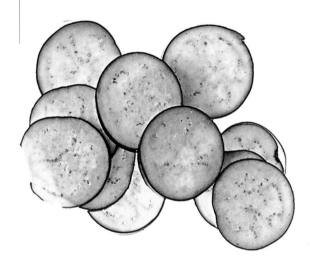

Melanzane alla Siciliana

EGGPLANT SICILIAN-STYLE (Sicily)

Preparation: 10 minutes; 1 hour for the eggplant
Cooking time: frying time; 10-15 minutes

Ingredients for 4 people:

4 medium-size eggplants
salt
2 eggs
a little flour
plenty of oil for frying
½ pound mozzarella cheese
pinch of marjoram

1. Wash the eggplant and cut into thin slices. Sprinkle with salt to eliminate the bitter juice and set aside for about an hour.
2. Heat the oven to 350°F.
3. Beat the eggs in a bowl and add a little salt. Drain and dry the eggplant. Dip in the flour and then in the beaten eggs.
4. Fry the eggplant a few at a time in a pan with plenty of oil. When they are golden, drain on paper towels.
5. Cut the mozzarella into slices. Arrange half the eggplant slices in an oven dish; arrange the mozzarella slices on top and sprinkle with marjoram.
6. Cover with the remaining eggplant and bake for 10-15 minutes. Serve immediately.

Melanzane alla griglia
GRILLED EGGPLANT (Various regions)

Preparation: 5 minutes; 30 minutes resting
Cooking time: about 20 minutes

Ingredients for 4 people:

2 large eggplants
salt
1 clove of garlic
sprig of parsley
¼ cup olive oil

1. Wash the eggplant and cut into thin slices. Sprinkle with salt to eliminate the bitter juice and set aside for about 30 minutes.
2. Finely chop the garlic and parsley; place in a bowl with oil and salt. Mix well.
3. Heat a grill. Drain and dry the eggplant, and grill on both sides.
4. Arrange the eggplant on a serving dish and baste with the oil sauce. Best served cold.

Melanzane ripiene
STUFFED EGGPLANT (Various regions)

Preparation: about 30 minutes
Cooking time: 30 minutes

Ingredients for 4 people:

salt
4 medium-size eggplants
1 yellow bell pepper
1 clove of garlic
sprig parsley
4 anchovy fillets
1 tablespoon capers
2½ tablespoons olive oil
12 black olives
2 tablespoons breadcrumbs

1. Heat a little salted water in a pot. When it comes to a boil, cook the eggplant for 5 minutes. Drain and cool.
2. Heat the oven to 350°F. In the meantime, wash the bell pepper, remove the seeds, and cut into pieces.
3. Cut the eggplant in half lengthwise. Scoop out the flesh, leaving an edge about ½ inch thick.
4. Chop the scooped eggplant with the pepper, garlic, parsley, anchovies, and capers. Gently fry this chopped mixture with the oil in a small pot for a few minutes.
5. Pit the olives and cut into pieces; add this to the pot. Add salt, mix well, and remove from the heat.
6. Arrange the eggplant halves in an oven-proof dish and fill with the mixture; sprinkle with breadcrumbs and bake for about 30 minutes. Serve hot.

◀ *Melanzane alla griglia*

Patate al pomodoro
POTATOES WITH TOMATOES (Campania)

Preparation: 15 minutes
Cooking time: 40 minutes

Ingredients for 4 people:

1½ pounds potatoes
1 medium-size onion
2 tablespoons butter
⅓ cup olive oil
10½ ounces canned chopped tomatoes
salt

1. Peel the potatoes, wash, and cut into quarters. Chop the onion finely.
2. Heat the butter and oil in a pan and gently fry the onions for a few minutes.
3. Dry the potatoes and add to the onions. Add the tomatoes and half a cup of water; salt and mix.
4. Cover and cook on low heat until the potatoes are ready (add a few tablespoons of water if necessary as they cook). Serve hot.

Patate ai capperi
POTATOES WITH CAPERS (Puglia)

Preparation: 5 minutes
Cooking time: about 40 minutes

Ingredients for 4 people:

5 medium-size potatoes
salt
sprig parsley
½ clove of garlic
2 tablespoons capers
⅓ cup olive oil

1. Wash the potatoes and boil whole in salted water.
2. When the potatoes are ready, drain, peel, and dice. Place in a salad bowl.
3. Chop the parsely with the garlic and capers. Sprinkle the potatoes with this mixture; season with oil and salt. Mix and serve.

Patate profumate
SEASONED POTATOES (Puglia)

Preparation: 15 minutes
Cooking time: 20 minutes

Ingredients for 4 people:

1½ pounds potatoes
8-10 sage leaves
5-6 rosemary leaves
4 tablespoons butter
⅓ cup olive oil
1 clove of garlic
salt
pepper

1. Peel the potatoes, wash, dry, and dice. Chop the sage and rosemary finely.
2. Gently fry the garlic with butter and oil in a pan. When it begins to brown, remove and add the potatoes.
3. Cover with the chopped sage and rosemary; add salt and pepper and mix well. Cover and cook on medium-high heat until tender and browned.

Peperoni alla Calabrese
BELL PEPPERS CALABRIAN-STYLE (Calabria)

Preparation: 10 minutes.
Cooking time: 15 minutes

Ingredients for 4 people:

1¾ pounds bell peppers
⅓ cup olive oil
1 tablespoon capers
3 tablespoons grated pecorino cheese
pinch of marjoram
2 tablespoons breadcrumbs
salt

1. Cut the peppers in half and remove the seeds; wash and cut into rather large pieces.
2. Heat the oil and add the peppers when hot. Cook for 5 minutes over medium-high heat, stirring.
3. Arrange the capers, pecorino cheese, and marjoram over the peppers; sprinkle with breadcrumbs and salt. Mix well and cook for another 10 minutes on medium heat. Serve immediately.

389

Peperoni ripieni
STUFFED BELL PEPPERS (Puglia)

Preparation: 15 minutes
Cooking time: 45 minutes

Ingredients for 4 people:

4 bell peppers (red or yellow)
6 anchovy fillets
1 tablespoon capers
1½ ounces pitted olives
sprig of parsley
1 clove of garlic
⅓ cup breadcrumbs
1 tablespoon grated pecorino
cheese
some oil
salt

1. Heat the oven to 350°F. Wash and dry the peppers; cut off the top (the part with the stem) and place aside. Remove the seeds.
2. Chop together the anchovies, capers, olives, parsley, and garlic. Place these in a bowl and add the breadcrumbs, pecorino cheese, and 2 tablespoons olive oil. Salt and mix.
3. Stuff the peppers with this mixture and then cover with the top part. Arrange in an oiled oven-proof dish and bake for about 45 minutes. Serve hot.

Pomodori alla Siciliana
TOMATOES SICILIAN-STYLE (Sicily)

Preparation: 30 minutes
Cooking time: 30 minutes

Ingredients for 4 people:

8 tomatoes
1 small onion
sprig of parsley
6 anchovy fillets
2½ tablespoons olive oil
16 black olives
8-10 basil leaves
1 tablespoon capers
2 tablespoons breadcrumbs
salt
pepper

1. Slice the tops off the tomatoes, remove the seeds and juice. Remove the pulp and reserve it.
2. Finely chop the onion and parsley; cut the anchovies into pieces. Sauté the onion in oil in a pan; when it begins to color, add the anchovies and the parsley. Cook on low heat for 5 minutes.
3. Pit and chop the olives; chop the basil. Add the tomato pulp to a bowl with the olives, capers, basil, and breadcrumbs. Salt, pepper, and mix. Cook for 10-15 minutes.
4. Heat the oven to 350°F.
5. Arrange the hollow tomatoes in an oiled oven-proof dish. Stuff with the mixture and bake for 30 minutes. Serve hot.

◀ Peperoni ripieni

391

Arancini di riso

Rice balls (Sicily)

Preparation: 20 minutes
Cooking time: 30 minutes; frying time

Ingredients for 6-8 people:

4 cups milk
salt
1⅓ cups rice
2 ounces candied cherries
2 ounces candied orange, diced
1 tablespoon rum
1 lemon
½ cup superfine sugar
3 eggs
plenty of oil for frying
2 teaspoons baking powder
¼ cup powdered sugar

1. Heat the milk in a pot, adding a pinch of salt. When the milk is hot, add the rice and cook for about 30 minutes over low heat, stirring occasionally.
2. In the meantime, place the candied fruit in a bowl, sprinkle with rum and set aside. Wash the lemon and grate the rind.
3. When the rice is cooked, remove from the heat. Add the superfine sugar, the grated lemon rind, two eggs, and 1 egg yolk a little at a time.
4. Cool a little and then add the baking powder, mixing well. Then add the candied fruit. If the mixture is too soft, add a little flour.
5. Wet your hands and mold the mixture into 3-inch balls.
6. Heat the frying oil in a pot; when it is very hot, deep-fry the rice balls a few at a time.
7. When the rice balls are golden all over, drain and turn in the powdered sugar. Best served hot.

Biancomangiare

Blancmange (Sicily)

Preparation: 20 minutes; 1 hour resting
Cooking time: 10 minutes

Ingredients for 4-6 people:

1 cup peeled almonds
1 cup milk
1 cup sugar
1 cup cornstarch
1 lemon
1 stick of cinnamon

1. Chop the almonds finely to form a kind of flour and place this in a clean linen cloth.
2. Pour 3 cups of cold water into a bowl. Keeping the cloth closed like a sack, immerse in the water.
3. Shake the "sack" and leave in the water until it becomes completely flavored with the almonds and turns white. Remove and discard the almonds.
4. Pour the almond milk into a cooking pot. Mix well and add the milk, sugar, cornstarch, lemon rind (cut spirally), and the cinnamon.
5. Cook on low heat until the cream becomes thick.
6. Remove the lemon rind and the cinnamon, pour the blancmange into small serving dishes, and cool. Serve cold.

◀ Arancini di riso

Cannoli alla Siciliana

SICILIAN CANNOLI (Sicily)

Preparation: 50 minutes; 1 hour resting
Cooking time: frying time

Ingredients for 6 people:

10½ ounces (about 2 cups) flour
1 cup granulated sugar
½ cup dry white Marsala wine
salt
16 ounces fresh ricotta cheese
2 tablespoons pistachio nuts
2 ounces candied fruit, diced
a little butter
plenty of cooking oil for frying
⅓ cup powdered sugar

1. Heap the flour on a work-top and make a hollow in the top; add ¼ cup granulated sugar, Marsala, and a pinch of salt. Knead well.
2. When the dough is well-kneaded, wrap it in a clean cloth and set aside to rise for about 1 hour.
3. Prepare the filling: mix the ricotta cheese with the remaining granulated sugar. Roughly chop the pistachio nuts. Add the candied fruit and the pistachio nuts to the bowl and mix. Keep in the refrigerator.
4. Roll out the dough to about 1/10 inch thick and cut out 4-inch squares.
5. Butter the special metal cake tubes used to make the cannoli (4x4.5). Wrap the pastry squares diagonally around the tubes.
6. Heat the oil in a pan and, when it smokes, fry the pastry tubes over medium heat and then drain on paper towels when ready.
7. Slide the pastry off the tubes and cool.
8. Fill a large-tipped pastry bag with the ricotta cheese mixture and fill the cannoli. Sprinkle with powdered sugar and serve.

Cassata Siciliana

SICILIAN CASSATA (Sicily)

Preparation: 30 minutes; the time to make the sponge cake(Pan di Spagna); 2 hours resting
Cooking time: -

Ingredients for 6 people:

1 Pan di Spagna (sponge cake, see page 194)
12 ounces fresh ricotta cheese
1⅔ cup powdered sugar
2 ounces milk chocolate
5 ounces candied fruit, diced
1 cup orange liqueur

1. Prepare the spongecake and set aside to cool.
2. Place the ricotta in a bowl, add the sugar, and work well. Cut the chocolate into pieces and add to the bowl together with the candied fruit. Mix well.
3. Cut the sponge cake into parallel vertical slices and soak in the liqueur.
4. Cover the base and sides of a cake mold with the sponge cake slices, keeping a few to cover.
5. Fill the mold with the ricotta mixture and then cover with the last slices of sponge cake. Leave in the refrigerator for about 2 hours.

394

Coviglie al cioccolato

CHOCOLATE CUSTARD (Campania)

Preparation: 30 minutes; 1 hour resting
Cooking time: 10 minutes

Ingredients for 4 people:

⅔ cup sugar
½ cup unsweetened cocoa
¼ cup flour
2 cups milk
2 tablespoons butter
1¾ cup heavy cream
2 ounces candied cherries

1. Place the sugar, cocoa, and flour in a pan and mix well. Add the milk a little at a time and blend well with the other ingredients.
2. Heat the pan on medium heat and bring to a boil, stirring continually. Then add the butter and mix well.
3. Leave the custard to cool, stirring occasionally so that it doesn't form a skin.
4. Whip 1¼ cups cream and add to the chocolate custard a little at a time, mixing gently so that it remains whipped.
5. Pour the custard into serving goblets and place in the refrigerator for at least 1 hour. When serving, whip the rest of the cream and garnish the goblets, adding a few candied cherries to each one.

Dolci alla pasta di mandorle

ALMOND PASTRIES (Sicily)

Preparation: 25 minutes
Cooking time: 10 minutes

Ingredients for 4 people:

1 cup peeled almonds
½ cup sugar
orange or lemon flavoring
3 egg whites
a little butter
a little flour
¼ cup powdered sugar

1. Heat the oven to 375°F.
2. Put the almonds and sugar in a mortar and work with the pestle into a pulp.
3. Add the flavoring and 2 tablespoons water; mix well.
4. Whisk the egg whites until stiff but not dry, and fold into the other ingredients.
5. Butter and flour small cookie molds; pour in the almond paste and bake for about 10 minutes. Cool and serve.

Crostata di frutta

FRUIT TART (Various regions)

Preparation: 45 minutes
Cooking time: 15-20 minutes

Ingredients for 6 people:

for the shortcake:
8 ounces (about 5¾ cups) flour
½ cup sugar
7 tablespoons butter
2 egg yolks
1 teaspoon baking powder
1 pinch of salt

for the filling:
1 pound mixed fresh fruit and nuts
(pineapple, grapes, peaches,
apricots, strawberries, hazelnuts,
walnuts, etc.)
5 ounces peach or apricot jam

1. Heat the oven to 350°F. Prepare the shortcake following the recipe on page 105.
2. Butter and flour a medium cake pan and roll out the pastry (having left it to rise). Prick with a fork and bake for 15-20 minutes.
3. When the pastry is golden, remove from the oven and cool. In the meantime, cut the fruit into slices (except the grapes).
4. Spread 3½ ounces of jam over the cake and then arrange the slices of fruit in a regular pattern.
5. Pour the remaining jam into a small pan; add 1 tablespoon water, heat gently, and stir to mix the ingredients. Pour this all over the fruit. Keep in the refrigerator until served.

Gelato alla vaniglia

VANILLA ICE CREAM (Various regions)

Preparation: 25 minutes; 2 hours to chill
Cooking time: about 15 minutes

Ingredients for 6 people:

1½ cups milk
1¼ cups heavy cream
1 teaspoon vanilla extract
6 egg yolks
¾ cup powdered sugar

1. Bring the milk to a boil in a small pan. Remove from the heat and add the cream and vanilla; mix and set aside for about 10 minutes.
2. Whisk the yolks in a casserole with the sugar to form a cream.
3. Gradually add the contents of the pan to the egg and sugar cream, stirring continually.
4. Place the casserole on very low heat and thicken, stirring continually but never boiling.
5. Remove from the heat and cool, stirring frequently. Pour the cream into a container and leave in the refrigerator for about 2 hours.
6. Freeze in an ice-cream maker, according to manufacturer's instructions.

◄ *Crostata di frutta*

397

Granita al caffè
COFFEE GRANITA (Various regions)

Preparation: 20 minutes; 2 hours to chill
Cooking time: 5 minutes

Ingredients for 4 people:

⅔ cup superfine sugar
1 cup espresso coffee
1 cup heavy cream
2 tablespoons vanilla sugar

1. Place the sugar in a casserole with 2 cups of water and bring to a boil.
2. Take the syrup off the heat and add the coffee, mixing well. Cool and then place in the freezer for at least 2 hours, mixing every 30 minutes.
3. To serve, chop up the chilled mixture and whip the cream with the vanilla-flavored sugar. Arrange the granita in 4 cups and decorate with whipped cream. Serve immediately.

Macedonia con gelato
FRUIT SALAD WITH ICE CREAM (Various regions)

Preparation: about 30 minutes

Ingredients for 4 people:

1 small melon
4 kiwis
½ pound strawberries
¼ cup sugar
2 oranges
1 cup vanilla ice cream
1 cup orange ice cream

1. Cut the melon in half and remove the seeds; scoop out balls of pulp.
2. Peel the kiwis and cut into slices. Chop the strawberries. Add the kiwis and strawberries to the melon. Sprinkle with sugar and set aside for 10-15 minutes.
3. Squeeze the oranges. Pour the fruit into 4 goblets and pour over the orange juice. Garnish with scoops of ice cream and serve immediately.

Macedonia all'anguria

FRUIT SALAD WITH WATERMELON (Various regions)

Preparation: about 30 minutes

Ingredients for 4 people:

half a large watermelon
1 small melon
5 ounces kiwis
5 ounces peaches
5 ounces fresh apricots
5 tablespoons powdered sugar
juice of 1 lemon

1. Scoop out balls of watermelon and arrange in a large bowl. Keep the scooped-out watermelon in the refrigerator.
2. Cut the melon in half and eliminate the seeds and stringy fibers. Scoop out balls of pulp and add to the watermelon.
3. Peel the kiwis and peaches and dice; wash and dice the apricots. Place all the fruit in the bowl.
4. Sprinkle with sugar and the lemon juice. Mix well.
5. Scoop out any pulp still in the watermelon shell to make a smooth container.
6. Place all the fruit in the scooped-out watermelon and serve.

Meringhe

MERINGUES (Sicily)

Preparation: 30 minutes
Cooking time: 30 minutes

Ingredients for 6 people:

4 egg whites
1½ cups powdered sugar
a little butter
a little flour

1. Whisk the egg whites with an electric mixer until firm but not dry. Add the sugar a little at a time, mixing gently. Pour this mixture into a pastry bag.
2. Butter and flour a baking sheet. Arrange little heaps of the mixture, leaving some space between each heap. Allow to set for a few minutes.
3. Heat the oven to 200°F. Bake the meringues with the oven closed. Remove the meringues after about 30 minutes; cool and serve.

Insalata di arance
ORANGE SALAD (Sicily)

Preparation: 30 minutes

Ingredients for 4 people:

6 medium oranges
8 dates
12 almonds
2 tablespoons rum
½ cup orange flower essence
1 tablespoon powdered sugar
1 pinch powdered cinnamon

1. Carefully wash one orange and cut into thin slices without peeling. Cover the base of a glass bowl with these slices.
2. Peel and clean the other oranges; cut into quarters. Arrange in the bowl.
3. Pit the dates and cut into slices lengthwise. Split the almonds. Add these to the oranges.
4. Mix the rum, orange flower essence, and sugar. Pour this over the orange mixture. Sprinkle with cinnamon and serve.

Migliaccio alla Napoletana
NEAPOLITAN CAKE (Campania)

Preparation: 1 hour
Cooking time: 30-40 minutes

Ingredients for 6 people:

⅓ cup sugar
5 tablespoons butter
1 pinch of powdered cinnamon
grated rind of half a lemon
salt
10½ ounces (about 1¾ cups)
rough ground yellow corn flour
a little butter
½ cup raisins
½ cup pine nuts
1 ounce diced candied fruit
¼ cup powdered sugar

1. Heat 6 cups of water in a casserole and then add the sugar, butter, cinnamon, the grated lemon rind, and a pinch of salt.
2. When the water comes to a boil, add the flour a little at a time, whipping. Boil for 30 minutes, stirring continually.
3. Grease a medium cake pan with the butter. Heat the oven to 300°F.
4. Take the casserole off the heat and add the raisins, pine nuts, and candied fruit. Mix well and pour into the buttered cake pan.
5. Bake until the top is golden. Cool and sprinkle with powdered sugar.

◀ *Insalata di arance*

Papassinus

DRY FRUIT COOKIES (Sardinia)

Preparation: 30 minutes; 15 minutes resting
Cooking time: 10-15 minutes

Ingredients for 6 people:

¾ cup peeled almonds
¾ cup shelled walnuts
10½ ounces (about 2 cups) flour
½ cup sugar
7 tablespoons butter
2 eggs
grated rind of one lemon
grated rind of one orange
⅔ cup raisins

for the glaze:
3 ounces sugar
1 egg white

1. Chop the almonds and walnuts finely. Heap the flour on a work-top and knead with the sugar, softened butter, eggs, and grated lemon and orange rind.
2. Add the chopped nuts and raisins to the dough and continue kneading until it is thoroughly mixed.
3. Heat the oven to 300°F.
4. Roll out the pastry to about ½ inch in thickness and then cut out lozenge-shaped pieces. Flour a baking sheet and arrange the papassinus on it; bake until golden.
5. In the meantime, prepare the glaze: place the sugar and egg white in a small pan and heat in a double-boiler, stirring well. When the sugar has dissolved, cool for a few minutes.
6. Baste the cookies with the glaze, set aside for 15 minutes, and serve.

Mostaccioli

HONEY COOKIES (Calabria)

Preparation: 30 minutes
Cooking time: 10-15 minutes

Ingredients for 4 people:

9 ounces (about 1¾ cups) flour
3 tablespoons aniseed liqueur
1 cup honey
a little butter

1. Heap the flour on a work-top and mix well with the honey and liqueur into regular, elastic dough.
2. Heat the oven to 300°F.
3. Roll out the pastry to about ½ inch thick and cut out with cookie cutters.
4. Butter a baking sheet, arrange the mostaccioli, and bake until golden. They are still excellent even after a few days.

402

Pastiera Napoletana

NEAPOLITAN CHEESE TART (Campania)

Preparation: 1 hour; 2-3 days soaking
Cooking time: 1½ hours; 45 minutes

Ingredients for 6-8 people:

for the pastry:
10½ ounces (about 2 cups) flour
10 tablespoons butter
⅔ cup sugar
3 egg yolks
1 pinch of salt

for the filling:
10½ ounces durum wheat cereal
2 cups milk
2 lemons
a little powdered cinnamon
1½ cups sugar
salt
14 ounces fresh ricotta cheese
5 ounces diced candied lime
2 tablespoons orange flower
essence
5 eggs, separated
a little butter

1. Place the cereal in a bowl, cover with water, and soak for 2-3 days; change the water every day.
2. Pour the cereal into a casserole and cover with water. Cover and cook over medium heat for about 1 hour.
3. Drain the boiled cereal and return to the empty casserole. Add the milk, the rind of one lemon, a pinch of cinnamon, ¼ cup sugar, and a pinch of salt. Cook over very low heat until the milk is completely absorbed (about 1 hour 30 minutes).
4. In the meantime, heap the flour on a work-top and add the butter, sugar, egg yolks, and salt. Knead to a soft, uniform dough. Let rise for about 30 minutes.
5. Heat the oven to 350°F. Place the cooled cereal mixture in a bowl and mix with the drained ricotta cheese, the remaining sugar, the grated rind of half a lemon, the candied lime, a pinch of cinnamon, and the orange flower essence.
6. Incorporate the five egg yolks one at a time. Whisk four egg whites until stiff but not dry and fold these into to the filling.
7. Butter a high-sided cake dish. Roll out three-quarters of the dough very thinly and place over the base. Pour in the filling and smooth off.
8. Roll up the remaining dough into finger-thick rolls; flatten slightly and arrange in a criss-cross pattern over the cake. Fold over any excess edge pastry inward.
9. Bake until the pastry is golden (about 45 minutes). Cool and serve.

Tarallucci dolci

SMALL DOUGHNUTS (Campania)

Preparation: 30 minutes
Cooking time: frying time

Ingredients for 4 people:

2 eggs
1 tablespoon sugar
1 tablespoon sweet liqueur
1 teaspoon vanilla extract
pinch of powdered cinnamon
flour
plenty of cooking oil for frying

1. Break the eggs into a bowl; add the sugar, liqueur, vanilla, and cinnamon. Work the ingredients together with a fork.
2. Gradually add the flour, stirring continually. When the mixture becomes like bread dough, place on a work-top and knead for at least 5 minutes.
3. Roll out the dough into rolls about 4 inches long; join the ends to form a hoop.
5. Heat the oil in a pan and fry the pastries; then drain. Can be enjoyed hot or cold.

Sebadas

CHEESE AND HONEY FRITTERS (Sardinia)

Preparation: 50 minutes
Cooking time: 10 minutes; frying time

Ingredients for 6 people:

¾ pound sharp cheese
¼ cup sugar
grated rind of half a lemon
16 ounces (about 3 cups) flour
salt
plenty of cooking oil for frying
½ cup sugar
 powdered sugar or honey

1. Place the cheese in a pan with the sugar, ⅔ cup water, the grated lemon rind, and a tablespoon of flour. Mix and cook over low heat until the mixture becomes uniform. Turn off the heat.
2. Heap the flour on a work-top. Add a pinch of salt and, gradually, lukewarm water until a smooth dough is made.
3. Roll out the pastry thinly and then cut out circles or squares.
4. Place a little filling on one half of the circle and then fold over the other half, pressing the edges down well with your fingers.
5. Heat the oil in a pan and, when it is hot, fry the sebadas a few at a time until they are golden.
6. Drain on paper towels. Drizzle with honey or, if you prefer, sprinkle with powdered sugar.

◄ *Tarallucci dolci*

405

Semifreddo alla frutta
FRUIT ICE CREAM (Puglia)

Preparation: about 30 minutes;
3 hours resting

Ingredients for 4 people:

4 bananas
½ lemon
4 oranges
1 cup heavy cream
⅔ cup sugar

1. Peel the bananas, slice, and place in a bowl. Add the lemon juice, so that they do not turn black.
2. Peel 2 oranges, break into quarters, and then dice. Add to the bananas.
3. Squeeze 2 more oranges and pour the juice into a bowl; add the cream and sugar and mix well.
4. Drain the lemon juice from the bananas and oranges. Pour in the cream mixture.
5. Mix well, place in an ice-cream maker and freeze according to manufacturer's instructions.

Torrone al sesamo
TORRONE WITH SESAME SEEDS (Sicily)

Preparation: 5 minutes; cooling time
Cooking time: 10-15 minutes

Ingredients:

1 cup honey
¼ cup sugar
2½ cups sesame seeds
a little cooking oil

1. Place the honey in a casserole and melt over very low heat. Then add the sugar, raise the heat a little, and bring to a boil, stirring continually.
2. Gradually add the sesame seeds and continue stirring until a thick mixture is formed.
3. Grease a marble work-top with a little oil. Place a small amount of the mixture on the marble and cool. The torrone is ready when hard and easily removed from the marble work-top.
4. Now pour the rest of the mixture onto the marble and roll out with an oiled rolling pin to form a long, narrow rectangle about ½-inch thick.
5. Cool and break into pieces for serving. If kept in a sealed container, torrone will keep for about 2 months.

Torta all'arancia
ORANGE PIE (Sicily)

Preparation: 30 minutes
Cooking time: 45 minutes

Ingredients for 6 people:

8 tablespoons butter
½ cup sugar
3 eggs
5 ounces diced candied orange
grated rind of one orange
½ cup brandy
1 cup flour
¾ cup potato starch
1 teaspoon baking powder
a little butter

1. Heat the oven to 375°F.
2. Dice the butter and place in a bowl. Work with a wooden spoon with the sugar to form a soft cream.
3. Add the eggs, one at a time; add the candied fruit, the grated orange rind, and the liqueur. Mix well.
4. Mix together the flour, potato starch, and baking powder, then gradually sift into the mixture to avoid forming lumps.
5. Butter a medium cake pan and pour in the mixture. Bake for about 45 minutes. Cool and serve.

Torta alla panna
CREAM TART (Calabria)

Preparation: 50 minutes
Cooking time: 30 minutes

Ingredients for 6 people:

½ cup sugar
3 eggs
1 cup flour
½ cup potato starch
2 teaspoons baking powder
4 tablespoons butter
some breadcrumbs
2 cups heavy cream
2 ounces candied cherries
1 ounce finely chopped chocolate

1. Heat the oven to 375°F.
2. Place the sugar and eggs in a bowl; work these together well with a wooden spoon.
3. Mix together the flour, potato starch, and baking powder; sift them a little at a time into the sugar and eggs.
4. Melt the butter and mix with the other ingredients.
5. Butter a medium cake pan, sprinkle with breadcrumbs, and then pour in the mixture. Bake for about 30 minutes.
6. When the tart is ready, remove from the oven and cool. Then cut in half horizontally.
7. Whip the cream and spread two-thirds over the bottom half of the cake; cover with the top half.
8. Use a pastry bag fitted with a decorative tip to garnish the top of the tart with cream. Decorate with candied cherries and sprinkle with the chocolate. Keep in the refrigerator until served.

407

Sorbetto al limone
LEMON SORBET (Various regions)

Preparation: 15 minutes; 2 hours chilling
Cooking time: 5 minutes

Ingredients for 6 people:

1 cup sugar
1 tablespoon potato starch
juice of 8 lemons
4 egg whites

1. Place the sugar in a pan and add 1½ cups water. Place on low heat and bring to a boil, stirring continually.
2. Take the pan off the heat and add the starch and lemon juice.
3. Whisk the egg whites into soft peaks and add to the mixture, mixing gently. Pour into a container and leave in the freezer for 2 hours, stirring occasionally so it doesn't form ice.
4. Remove from the freezer a few minutes before serving and pour into goblets.

Torta di ricotta
RICOTTA CHEESECAKE (Sicily)

Preparation: 30 minutes
Cooking time: 30 minutes

Ingredients for 6 people:

⅓ cup raisins
16 ounces ricotta cheese
a scant ½ cup sugar
grated rind of one lemon
4 eggs, separated
½ cup sifted flour
2 ounces diced candied fruit
a little butter
some breadcrumbs

1. Heat the oven to 350°F. Soak the raisins in lukewarm water.
2. Place the cheese in a bowl and work well with the sugar and grated lemon rind.
3. Stirring continually, add the egg yolks one at a time (keep 2 egg whites aside). Then add the sifted flour, the candied fruit, and the raisins.
4. Whisk the 2 egg whites until stiff but not dry, and fold into the mixture.
5. Butter a medium cake pan and sprinkle with breadcrumbs. Pour in the mixture and bake for about 30 minutes. Cool a little and serve.

◄ *Sorbetto al limone*

Index of recipes